Selected Poems

Quest for the One

T0302969

Selected Poems

Quest for the One

Selected by the poet with convenient
end-of-poem notes on theme,
basis for inclusion and setting

Nicholas Hagger

BOOKS

Winchester, UK
Washington, USA

First published by O-Books, 2015
O-Books is an imprint of John Hunt Publishing Ltd., Laurel House, Station Approach,
Alresford, Hants, SO24 9JH, UK
office1@jhpbooks.net
www.johnhuntpublishing.com

For distributor details and how to order please visit the 'Ordering' section on our website.

A CIP catalogue record for this book is available from the British Library.

Design: Stuart Davies

Printed in the USA by Edwards Brothers Malloy

We operate a distinctive and ethical publishing philosophy in all areas of
our business, from our global network of authors to production and
worldwide distribution.

Books published by Nicholas Hagger

The Fire and the Stones
Selected Poems
The Universe and the Light
A White Radiance
A Mystic Way
Awakening to the Light
A Spade Fresh with Mud
The Warlords
Overlord
A Smell of Leaves and Summer
The Tragedy of Prince Tudor
The One and the Many
Wheeling Bats and a Harvest Moon
The Warm Glow of the Monastery Courtyard
The Syndicate
The Secret History of the West
The Light of Civilization
Classical Odes
Overlord, one-volume edition
Collected Poems 1958–2005
Collected Verse Plays
Collected Stories
The Secret Founding of America
The Last Tourist in Iran
The Rise and Fall of Civilizations
The New Philosophy of Universalism
The Libyan Revolution
Armageddon
The World Government
The Secret American Dream
A New Philosophy of Literature
A View of Epping Forest
My Double Life 1: This Dark Wood
My Double Life 2: A Rainbow over the Hills
Selected Stories: Follies and Vices of the Modern Elizabethan Age

A few days later I had a haunting dream which hinted at my poetic identity: a "large face of Orpheus with dozens of green apples in front of it..., as tall as the trees and orchard.... I knew it was Orpheus because of the Thracian hat." The image, received in sleep, of Orpheus among green apples was a powerful one. I assumed that the apples symbolised poems.

Nicholas Hagger,
My Double Life 2: A Rainbow over the Hills, p.368,
from *Diaries*, 26 September 1991

Having combed through *Collected Poems*, I was struck that "my myth is Orpheus: the poet who lost his Eurydice, went down into the Underworld to retrieve her, looked back and lost her again; who was torn apart by Maenads and whose head goes on singing posthumously, as mine will". I noted that I could "call my *Collected Poems* 'Orpheus Singing'". In view of my dream I could have called it 'Orpheus among Green Apples'.

Nicholas Hagger,
My Double Life 2: A Rainbow over the Hills, p.713,
from *Diaries*, 5 November 2005

The front cover shows a Roman mosaic of Orpheus sitting on a rock under a tree, holding a lyre. He is wearing a Phrygian cap and is surrounded by animals, birds and reptiles charmed by the music of his lyre.

*

To my Travelling Companion

Thanks, kind Ann, for being so game
As I quested for truth – not fame –
Before we co-naught in the One
Like two ammonites in split stone.

Nicholas Hagger's poetry and verse plays from
which this selection was made:

Collected Poems 1958–2005 (2006)
- A Well of Truth, 1958–1963
- A Stone Torch-Basket, 1963–1965
- The Early Education and Making of a Mystic, 1965–1966
- The Silence, 1965–1966
- The Wings and the Sword, 1966–1969
- Old Man in a Circle, 1967
- The Gates of Hell, 1969–1972
- The Flight, 1970
- Bulb in Winter, 1972–1974
- A Pilgrim in the Garden, 1973–1974
- The Night-Sea Crossing, 1974
- Visions Near the Gates of Paradise, 1974–1975
- The Four Seasons, 1975
- Lighthouse, 1975
- The Weed-Garden, 1975
- The Labyrinth, 1976
- Whispers from the West, 1976–1979
- Lady of the Lamp, 1979
- The Fire-Flower, 1980
- Beauty and Angelhood, 1981
- The Wind and the Earth, 1981
- A Rainbow in the Spray, 1981–1985
- Question Mark over the West, 1986–1988
- A Sneeze in the Universe, 1989–1992
- A Flirtation with the Muse, 1992–1993
- Sojourns, 1993
- Angel of Vertical Vision, 1993
- A Dandelion Clock, 1994–2004
- Summoned by Truth, 2000–2005
- Sighs of the Muses, 2005

Earlier volumes:
Selected Poems: A Metaphysical's Way of Fire (1991)
Collected Poems: A White Radiance 1958–1993 (1994)

Classical Odes 1994–2005 (2006)
- Book One, A Tudor Knot
- Book Two, In Europe's Ruins
- Book Three, A Global Sway
- Book Four, The Western Universe

Overlord, one-volume edition (2006)
First published in four separate volumes, 1995–1997, as
Overlord: The Triumph of Light 1944–1945
- Overlord, books 1–2 (1995)
- Overlord, books 3–6 (1996)
- Overlord, books 7–9 (1997)
- Overlord, books 10–12 (1997)

Collected Verse Plays (2007)
- The Warlords, Parts 1 and 2 (first published in 1995, abridged version 2000)
- The Tragedy of Prince Tudor (first published in 1999)
- Ovid Banished (1999)
- The Rise of Oliver Cromwell (2000)

Armageddon: The Triumph of Universal Order
An Epic Poem on the War on Terror and of Holy-War Crusaders (2010)

Note to reader

The poems within Part One are by and large arranged in chronological order, as are the poems in Part Two. The two Parts are parallel rather than consecutive, and so the first section in both Parts is numbered 1. For the published works where these poems can be found, *see* pp.vii–viii. Poems taken from the 30 volumes of *Collected Poems* (*see* p.vii) appear under the titles of those volumes. Those taken from *Classical Odes, Overlord* and *Armageddon* appear under the title of those volumes. The extracts from verse plays (*The Warlords, The Tragedy of Prince Tudor, Ovid Banished* and *The Rise of Oliver Cromwell*) are taken from *Collected Verse Plays*. Titles of excerpts in square brackets are helpful descriptions and summaries, not titles of poems.

The poems and extracts in *Collected Poems* and *Classical Odes* are accompanied by notes, which can be found in those volumes. They are not reproduced here, but there are new end-of-poem notes on theme (quest/follies and vices), basis for inclusion and setting.

CONTENTS

Contents

Contents

Contents

Contents

Preface to *Selected Poems*

This selection of my poetic works spans 52 years. It includes poems and extracts from poems taken from my *Collected Poems 1958–2005* (which incorporates my *Selected Poems, A Metaphysical's Way of Fire*, 1991 and *Collected Poems: A White Radiance*, 1994); a few of my odes from *Classical Odes* (2006); and a few extracts from my two poetic epics, *Overlord* (1994–1996, one-volume edition 2006) and *Armageddon* (2010), and from my five verse plays.

The fundamental theme of world literature

In *A New Philosophy of Literature* I identified the fundamental theme of world literature as having metaphysical and secular aspects: the quest for metaphysical Reality (the One), and condemnation of social follies and vices in relation to an implied virtue. This selection presents poems on my quest and growing awareness of the unity of the universe (Part One), and poems exposing the follies and vices of our time (Part Two). The two Parts, 'Quest for the One' and 'Follies and Vices', reverse the titles of the two Parts of my *Selected Stories: Follies and Vices of the Modern Elizabethan Age* (a companion volume to this work), in which 'Follies and Vices' precedes 'Quest for the One'.

The quest for Reality

The quest for Reality (or quest for the One) in literature goes back 4,600 years. It originates in the Mesopotamian *Epic of Gilgamesh*, c.2600BC, and it follows the Mystic Way, which has been found in the literature of every culture and generation since then and is the universal path trodden by Dante, who was lost in a Dark Wood, and more recently by T.S. Eliot. Faced with the seeming finality of death like Gilgamesh, the soul awakens from the social consciousness of the ego; undergoes purgation in a Way of Loss in which things go wrong in the outer world; and turns away from its attachment to the body and the senses. It has its first experience of illumination by the universal Light which is Reality, and basks in visions; and, transformed in the course of a centre-shift from the ego's control, begins to live through a new centre of consciousness that has a growing awareness of the Oneness of the universe. It experiences further illumination and visions, perceives the unity of the universe instinctively and senses the possibility of its own survival.

In my case the centre-shift and first glimpse of illumination happened in 1965, and the experience can be found in extracts from *The Early Education and Making of a Mystic* and 'The Silence'. After a Dark Night my second illumination took place in 1971, and the experience features in poems in *The Gates of Hell* such as 'Visions: Golden Flower, Celestial Curtain', 'More Visions: The Judge' and 'Visions: The Pit and the Moon'. (A few of the poems in *The Gates of Hell* refer to being "seized" or "snatched" by "God", a term used by mystics suggesting the Hound of Heaven. I do not want to undermine the words I used at the time as I struggled to understand the experience, but I would now describe the experience as being opened to the One and the poetic imagination.)

The sensing of unity involves what Coleridge called "the esemplastic power of the imagination" (*Biographia Literaria*, ch.X), "*eis en plattein*" meaning "shape into one". The soul shapes the fragments of the universe it perceives "into one" like an archaeologist piecing together the fragments of an unearthed urn. In contrast, the social ego's reason analyses and dissects, sees distinctions rather than similarities, breaks the One into bits and is separated from the unitive vision. An image can often catch the One more deftly than a statement, and some of my quest poems present images of the One. Others touch on the poets of the literary tradition I draw on to help reflect it, which includes some Roman poets.

In my Preface to my *Collected Poems* I wrote:

It is characteristic of the journey along the Mystic Way that those lost in its "Dark Wood" and experiencing its Dark Night are unaware of the explanation for what is happening to them and what lies ahead; this is only grasped later when, from the serene calm of unitary consciousness, the self can look back and understand the detaching that suffering brought as a gift.

My prose work, *My Double Life 1: This Dark Wood*, throws light on one aspect of what happened to me during this part of my journey. It unveils that – in the footsteps of Marlowe, Defoe, Maugham, Greene and T.E. Lawrence, and probably of Wordsworth (whose name is in the Duke of

Portland's secret book of payments next to the chief British intelligence agent in Hamburg as receiving £92.12s on 13 June 1799) and possibly of Byron (who spent a lot of money that may not have been his own when refitting the Greek fleet and paying the anti-Ottoman freedom-fighting Souliotes as commander-in-chief of the Greek army in Western Greece in 1824) – for four years, from May 1969 to the summer of 1973, I was a British intelligence agent, a role that plunged my personal life into turmoil. For part of this time I was Edward Heath's Top-Secret 'unofficial Ambassador' to the African liberation movements, monitoring the Soviet and Chinese expansion in Europe and Africa during the Cold War. The earlier 'Archangel', which is on Soviet and Chinese Communism, takes on a new significance in view of this secret work. I have included a few poems, such as 'On the Waterfront', 'Mephistopheles' and 'The Code', that have not been fully understood until now because what I was doing at the time was not in the public domain.

Quest themes

Notes at the end of poems and extracts in Part One of *Selected Poems* state their quest themes. They include, in the order in which they appear, the following themes: early yearning for truth; awakening to higher consciousness; the power of Nature; experience of the One; encounter with a future self; transformational centre-shift; the vision of the unity of the universe; the Way of Loss; purgation; illumination; visions of the One; unification of contemplation and action; hindrances of intelligence work; intense moments; glimpses of the One; images of the One; and reconciliation of contradictions within the harmony of the One. All the poems in Part One state different aspects of my Reality.

As a poet, I have found that the myth of Orpheus has spoken powerfully to me: his descent into the Underworld, his loss of Eurydice and of his ego, his discovery of his soul, his charming of all creation with his lyre, his vision of unity, his dismemberment by Maenads and his head continuing to sing after his death.

Condemnation of follies and vices

The secular aspect of the fundamental theme, condemnation of follies and vices, has co-existed with the quest for Reality since early times. It can be found in the classical world and was particularly strong in the 16th-century Renaissance. It can be widely found in the social satire of the Augustan poets: the mock-heroic couplets of Dryden's 'Absalom and Achitophel' and of Pope's 'The Rape of the Lock' and 'The Dunciad' expose vice.

My satire on society can be found in 'The Expatriate', 'The Silence', 'Old Man in a Circle', 'Zeus's Ass', 'Pastoral Ode', 'At Beckingham Palace'; in the two visits to Hell in my poetic epics *Overlord* and *Armageddon*; and in the extracts of dramatic verse from my verse plays. In poems such as 'Attack on America' and *'Shock and Awe'*, in my two poetic epics and in my verse plays I evoke some of the major events of our Age: D-Day, 9/11 and the invasions of Afghanistan and Iraq. Part Two includes evocations – in the case of 'Attack on America' and *'Shock and Awe'*, questionings – of these events and therefore reflects the Age. As readers of my books on contemporary history will know, my version of contemporary events does not always accord with the official version. I am confident that one day my version will come to be seen as being more right than the current official version.

The following follies and vices are exposed and condemned in Part Two of this selection, and are mentioned in the notes that summarise themes at the end of the poems or extracts of Part Two. They are listed below in the order in which they appear in Part Two (numbers in brackets indicating numbers in Part Two where they can be found, F indicating folly, * indicating already mentioned):

self-love (1); genteelness (2); dictatorship (3, 15); brainwashing (3); disharmony (4); discontent (4); destruction (4, 15); escapism (5); lust (5, 7); systemic killing (6, 7, 14, 15); power (6); deviousness (6, 10); ruthlessness (6, 10, 11, 12, 14, 15); cunning (6); ingratitude (6); unscrupulousness (6); ambition (6); pride (7); gluttony (7); greed (7); anger (7); violence (7); sloth (7); executions (7); cruelty (7); tyranny (8); self-importance (8); spin (9, 12); population reduction (9); popularism (9); usurpation (7, 9, 15); vacuousness (9, 12); eccentricity (9); impersonation (9); faking images of institutions (9); delusion (9); frivolity (9); heedlessness (9); rashness (9); naïvety (F, 10); manipulation (10); vindictiveness (10); tyrannical censorship (10); showing-off (10); hypocrisy (10, 11); wrongful banishment (10); shallowness (10, 14);

*usurpation (11); *delusion (11); bribery (11); regicide (11); murder (11); slyness (11); deception (12); mendacity (12); ostentation (13); chaviness (13); blinginess (13); flaunting (13); gullibility (F, 14); credulousness (F, 14); fancifulness (14); mass destruction (14); deceit (14); bombings (15); opulence (15); *murder (15); and blackmail (15).

A comprehensive list of the follies and vices in world literature can be found in the index of *A New Philosophy of Literature*:

abandonment; acquisitiveness; alcoholism; ambition; arrogance; asperity; betrayal; bigotry; blindness; boastfulness; bravado; brutality; bullying; capriciousness; concealment; confidence tricks; corruptibility; corrupting worldly power; corruption; credulousness; cruelty; cynicism; debauchery; deceit; defiance; denial of principles; destructiveness; dictatorial behaviour; discontent; dishonesty; being domineering; drunkenness; duplicity; eagerness to marry; egotism; egotistical sensuality; enmity; envy; excessive mourning; exploitation; fantasies; fortune-hunting; frivolity; greed; hatred; hedonism; hubristic contentment; hypocrisy; idleness; illusions; impudence; inconstancy; infatuation; infidelity; inhumanity; insincerity; interference; jealousy; lack of truthfulness; lust; lust for power; massacres; meanness; mercenary motives; miserliness; misjudgement; mistreatment; money-seeking; moral blindness; murder; naïve beliefs; neglect; nihilism; obstinacy; overreaching; patricide; pedantry; persecution; petulance; pretension; pride; prodigality; rebelliousness; revenge; ruthlessness; seduction; self-centredness; self-conceit; self-deceit; self-interestedness; self-love; shadiness; shrewishness; snobbishness; social climbing; strictness; swindling; thieving/stealing; threatening behaviour; treachery; trickery; troublemaking; tyrannical ruthlessness; tyranny; unscrupulousness; usurpation; vanity; villainy; voluptuousness; war; warmongering; and pursuit of wealth.

All these follies and vices (with the sole exception of 'patricide') can be found in my *Selected Stories: Follies and Vices of the Modern Elizabethan Age*, the companion volume to this work. Its Preface details numbered stories in which each of these follies and vices can be found, and a section at the back lists stories' follies and vices. Readers may like to compare the treatment of follies and vices in the two works.

These same follies and vices can be found in *Selected Poems*. The list below replicates the one above – there is some overlapping with the previous list of follies and vices mentioned in the end-of-poem notes – and each bracketed number indicates the numbered group of poems or extracts in Part Two where each folly or vice can be found (F again indicating folly, * indicating already mentioned):

abandonment (7, 15); acquisitiveness (2, 7, 15); alcoholism (7); *ambition (7, 15); arrogance (7); asperity (7, 15); betrayal (7, 15); bigotry (15); blindness (15) boastfulness (15); bravado (15); brutality (7); bullying (15); capriciousness (7. 15); concealment (7, 12, 15); confidence tricks (7, 15); corruptibility (15); corrupting worldly power (7, 15); corruption (7, 15); credulousness (F, 12); *cruelty (7); cynicism (7, 15); debauchery (7, 15); *deceit (7, 14, 15); defiance (8); denial of principles (7, 15); destructiveness (4, 7, 15); dictatorial behaviour (7, 15); *discontent (7); dishonesty (12); being domineering (7, 15); drunkenness (7, 15); duplicity (7, 15); eagerness to marry (7, 15); egotism (15); egotistical sensuality (7); enmity (7, 15); envy (7); excessive mourning (7, 15); exploitation (7, 15); fantasies (12); fortune-hunting (7, 15); *frivolity (12); *greed (7); hatred (7, 15); hedonism (2); hubristic contentment (12); *hypocrisy (10); idleness (7, 15); illusions (F, 7); impudence (4, 12); inconstancy (15); infatuation (7, 15); infidelity (7, 15); inhumanity (3); insincerity (2); interference (7, 15); jealousy (7, 15); lack of truthfulness (12); *lust (14); lust for power (15); massacres (7); meanness (7, 15); mercenary motives (7, 10, 15); miserliness (7, 15); misjudgement (12); mistreatment (7, 15); money-seeking (7, 15); moral blindness (7, 15); *murder (7); naïve beliefs (F, 13); neglect (14); nihilism (7); obstinacy (7); overreaching (7); pedantry (7, 15); persecution (7); petulance (6); pretension (12); *pride (11, 14); prodigality (7); rebelliousness (7, 15); revenge (15); *ruthlessness (6, 10, 11, 12, 14, 15); seduction (2); self-centredness (7, 15); self-conceit (15); self-deceit (15); self-interestedness (7, 15); *self-love (2); shadiness (7, 15); shrewishness (15); snobbishness (7, 15); social climbing (7, 15); strictness (7, 15); swindling (7, 15); thieving/stealing (7, 15); threatening behaviour (7, 15); treachery (7, 15); trickery (7, 15); troublemaking (7, 15); tyrannical ruthlessness (7, 15); *tyranny (6, 8); *unscrupulousness (7, 15); *usurpation (7, 9, 15); vanity (15); villainy (7, 15); voluptuousness (15); war

(6, 7); warmongering (6, 7); and pursuit of wealth (7, 15).

Additional vices referred to or implied in the poems or extracts of Part Two and not in the previous two lists are, in alphabetical order:

abusiveness (7, 15); adultery (7, 15); attention-seeking (7, 15); avarice (7, 15); cheating (7, 15); excessive materialism (7, 15); false language (9); falsehood (12); fickleness (6); flattery (12); fraud (7, 15); grumpiness (7, 15); impertinence (7, 15); implausibility (10); incontinence (7, 15); lechery (2, 15); misanthropy (7, 15); phoniness (12); preening (12, 15); pretentiousness (7, 15); provocativeness (2); self-harm (7); selfishness (7, 15); sneering (15); superficiality (12); triviality (12); vacuity (12); vandalism (1, 3); *violence (7, 14); and wrath (7, 15).

The following follies and vices (listed in alphabetical order, * indicating already mentioned) are condemned in my *Selected Stories*. They are touched on in *Selected Poems*, if only in the descriptions of Hell:

absent-mindedness (F, 10); aggressiveness (7, 15); *anger (3, 14); bitterness (7); boredom (3); *bribery (7, 11, 15); burglary (7, 15); childishness (7, 15); covetousness (7); *deception (7, 14, 15); desertion (7, 15); egocentricity (7); egoism (7); extortion (7, 15); false jokiness (12); falsely claiming knowledge (12); *gluttony (excessive drinking and drugs) (7, 15); gullibility (F, 12); hero-worship (12); idealisation (12); imperiousness (7); trying to impress (12); injury (7, 15); intolerance (7, 15); know-all superiority (12); lack of good sense (F, 12); long-windedness (15); manipulativeness (6, 12); *mendacity (7, 12, 15); nuns' worldliness (15); overbearingness (6); peremptoriness (6); *phoniness (12); pomposity (12); posing (12); not facing reality (7, 15); rivalry (7, 15); robbery (7, 15); roguery (7, 15); self-deception (F, 12); *self-importance (8); self-righteousness (12); servitude (7, 15); *sloth (14); stinginess (7, 15); suicide (7); terrorism (15); theft (7, 15); and yobbishness (2, 4).

If we do not count the asterisked vices, which are duplicated within the lists, the four lists present 62, 93, 29 and 37 vices; and 10 follies. The total number of vices referred to in all the lists is 221.

Universalist balance of fundamental theme's two aspects
One of the two aspects of the fundamental theme dominates in every age. Now one, now the other has the upper hand. In the English Augustan Age, exposing follies and vices dominated. In the Romantic Age the quest for the One – Reality – was uppermost. The Universalist ideal, which seeks to reconcile opposites and contradictions, seeks to balance the two aspects: the soul's perception of the One and criticism of social vices. Universalist poetry attempts to balance inner quest and outer social harmony. In our present time, the secular social outlook dominates and my allocation of Part One to the quest for the One in these poems goes some way to restoring the balance and preparing for a new metaphysical poetry. This selection deliberately balances the two aspects, a broadly equal number of pages being devoted to each aspect in each Part. The balance is Universalist. The poems within each Part are dated and arranged in chronological order to make the quest and condemnation of social vices truly sequential and easier to follow.

The poet of the One who senses the unity of the universe and captures it in poems is also aware of society and should also be an exposer of social follies and vices. To the poet of quest, the reason for writing poetry is to capture the truth about the universe. Glimpses of the One are 'epiphanies' or revelations. The poet puts himself in readiness to approach and receive the One by restructuring the universe in poems. His poems are models of the One, orderly simplifications of chaotic complexity that bring out the order in the cosmos. In this state of readiness the poet receives a passing glimpse or vision of the One that confirms that the universe is an ordered Whole with meaning and purpose, and not a chaotic mess. Within the Whole, social virtue has a place – hence the necessity of exposing social follies and vices. Man belongs to the universe as much as he participates in society and the two Parts of this selection also balance these differing perspectives of man, which have in the past given rise to differing traditions of poetry.

Basis of selection

Selection has not been easy. There are nearly 1,500 poems in the 30 volumes of *Collected Poems,* and in addition I have written more than 300 classical odes, two poetic epics of 41,000 and 25,000 lines of blank verse respectively, and five verse plays; so there is an enormous amount to choose from. There are poems in every kind of form: lyrics, sonnets, elegies, odes, a quartet, a quintet and longer poems in sonata, fugal and symphonic form. There are poems in every rhyme scheme and metre, including stress metre and blank verse. Because this selection highlights the fundamental theme's two aspects in my work I have necessarily had to omit a number of poems that are jostling for inclusion, including many poems on Nature's *flora* and *fauna*. It would be possible to compile a selection of my Nature poems as long as the present volume. To conform to my two aspects I have distributed excerpts from my pivotal poem 'The Silence' and from other poems between the two Parts, and have reluctantly decided there is no room for excerpts from my longer sonata, fugal and symphonic poems 'The Four Seasons', 'Lighthouse', 'The Weed-Garden' and 'The Labyrinth'.

The two Parts include poems capturing the unity of the universe that could be grouped under five headings: Philosophical, Nature, Spiritual, Historical and Topical. Poems for all these five genres can be found in both Parts of this selection:

- Philosophical poems showing the universe as One include 'A Metaphysical in Marvell's Garden', 'Night Visions in Charlestown', 'Ode: Spider's Web: Our Local Universe in an Infinite Whole', 'The Laughing Philosopher' and 'The One and the Many'.
- Poems seeing the universe as a Oneness that shapes Nature as an energetic force include 'Sea Force', while poems seeing Nature as a vital rather than a mechanistic force imbued with the One include 'A Crocus in the Churchyard', 'Pear-Ripening House' and 'Clouded-Ground Pond'.
- Poems showing the rational, social ego giving way to the mystical life of the soul and spirit as it progresses from awakening to illumination and the unitive vision include 'An Awakening in London', 'Flow: Moon and Sea', 'Visions: Golden Flower, Celestial Curtain',

'More Visions: The Judge', 'Visions: The Pit and the Moon', 'February Budding, Half Term', 'Visions: Raid on the Goldmine', 'Visions: Snatched by God, a Blue Light' and passages towards the end of 'The Silence'. After the experience of illumination the soul can bask in the mystic Light as can be seen in poems such as 'Contemplations by a Sundial', 'Iona: Silence' and 'Sunbathing'.

- Poems seeing history as a unity, and drawing on the cultural tradition of Europe, the West and the world, and of the cultural legacy of Western civilization, include my two poetic epics (represented in extracts) and poems from my *Classical Odes*, which revisit the past at specific geographical places and give history a contemporary relevance. This selection includes 'At Otley: Timber-Framed Tradition' and 'At Catullus's Sirmione'. Many of the classical odes are about visits to the historical and cultural sites of Europe. In a sense each is a localist poem but the combined effect of the classical odes presents the culture of Europe, to which England belongs, and the classical odes must therefore be regarded as Universalist poems. (In a sense all my work is about the relationship between localist and Universalist poetry.)

- Poems on contemporary, topical issues and current affairs include 'Pastoral Ode: Landslide, The End of Great Britain'; my poems about America, Afghanistan and Iraq: 'Attack on America' and '*Shock and Awe*'; and mock-heroic poems after the manner of Dryden and Pope that include 'Zeus's Ass', 'Groans of the Muses' and 'Authorship Question in a Dumbed-Down Time'.

It should be emphasised that poems are cross-disciplinary and can deal with the philosophy of the universe, metaphysical Nature, the mystical, history and the topical in one work as Oneness pervades all levels and layers. This can be seen in such poems as 'Connaught House' and the second 'Epitaph'.

Ted Hughes latched on to my work in 1993. An early letter from him to me can be found in *Letters of Ted Hughes*, selected and edited by Christopher Reid (2007), and he corresponded with me until his death in 1999. He wrote to me about *Overlord*, which originally came out in four parts, and my handling of the history of the Second World War in verse:

"I started reading it with fascination – I rose to it, the omnivorous masterful way you grasp the materials" (20 March 1995); and "I'm admiring the way you bit off and chew up these great chunks of history in your epic. It's good for verse – to become the workhorse for sheer mass of material. Pressure of the actual – the resources to deal with it drawn from elsewhere" (28 January 1996). Later he wrote: "One of the mysteries about you is – when do you get it all done? How many of you are there? Do you never blot a line?" (4 March 1998).

My transformation

The poems present my transformation in the course of five decades in both subject matter and technique. In subject matter they reveal my growing sense of the unity in the universe. There is a progression from my early discontent within Great Britain (as I then thought of the UK) to my metamorphosis in Japan; to my reflection of the Cold War; to the anguished suffering and chaos of my Dark Night; and to a serene consciousness that is outward-looking, unitary, at one with the universe. They also show the transformation of my technique during my exploration of, and experimentation with, technical innovations in the 1960s and 1970s – compressed or abbreviated narrative in a sequence of images, stress metre and sonata, fugal and symphonic form – and in the 1980s and 1990s: the quartet and quintet. I then settle back into more traditional stanzaic forms and metres.

Inspiration from the 17th century

As can be seen from 'A Metaphysical in Marvell's Garden' I derive my inspiration from the Metaphysical poets of the 17th century, in whose works thought and feeling were fused. I make use of the 17th-century love of learning, drawing in a cross-disciplinary way on several disciplines – such as history, philosophy, archaeology, physics, geology and astronomy – within one poem as Donne did. In some of these poems "a combination of dissimilar images" can be found, in which "the most heterogeneous ideas are yoked by violence together". In so far as these yokings carry forward Johnson's description of Metaphysical wit in his 'Life of Cowley', my poems can be seen as carrying forward the 17th-century Metaphysical tradition in which they are rooted. But while the

Metaphysical poets were universalists, Universalist poetry is independent of the 17th century and reconciles the Romantic and Classical perspectives, blending image with statement, organic with structural form and seeing the artist as both apart from society – indeed, isolated from society – and as participating in society by exposing its follies and vices.

Universalist poems

The poems in this selection are Universalist poems: poems about the universe and the shift to the "universal being" which replaces the rational, social ego and perceives the Oneness of the universe. They blend image and statement and reconcile sense and spirit in a neo-Baroque style. They synthesise Romantic and Classical approaches, and implement Universalism's reconciliation of opposites. They present the transformation of the soul on the Mystic Way, its perception of the One and its reflection – and criticisms – of the vices of the Age. They carry forward literary Universalism and continue in our time the 4,600-year-old tradition of the two aspects of world literature's fundamental theme.

I must emphasise that this selection and my *Selected Stories: Follies and Vices of the Modern Elizabethan Age* (also 2015) anthologise my treatment in my poems and stories of the fundamental theme of world literature set out in *A New Philosophy of Literature*. The situations that inspired many of these poems – and many of the stories in my *Selected Stories* – can be found in my two-part autobiography, *My Double Life 1: This Dark Wood* and *My Double Life 2: A Rainbow over the Hills* (2015).

June 2011; 28 August, 11–12, 16 September 2012; 30 April 2014

Part One

Quest for the One

1

from *A Well of Truth* (1958–1963)

Ode to a Prospect from a Window Frame

I sat in wonder at the window edge
And breathless watched the peace of day recline
Over the still green hill. The soft grass sedge
Waved to the fleeing evening beneath the pine,
And oh what glory in that dying light!
My heart leapt clear to streaks of russet cloud,
My mind fell free and walked with unscaled eyes
Down flimsy-paper streets at triple height
And peered through panes. My body was a shroud;
The wilting world wept at my spirit's size.

But then the cooling window froze to night;
There was no noise to disturb the sleeping grass,
No chirp of bird or insect. I had no sight
To glimpse a moonlit movement, for – alas –
Too soon my tingling nerves grew calm and sour;
I saw my hands caress a picture-frame,
A wilderness of art in nature's paint.
My heart was heavy in that shrouded hour,
An artifice that left the feeling lame,
And left the well of knowledge to the saint.

O for a well of Truth that all might see,
A well of clean and lasting Light to soothe
The souls of all who dip their hands, to be
A cure for hearts that are like a soundproof booth.
That picture will soon be in winter's sprawl
And slow Decay will sing the frost of time
And the slow dance that sighs the grave's embrace
For years to come, for aeons past my fall
To a lich bed, beneath the hoar-frost's rime,

Beyond the eternal smile of Beauty's face.

To capture beauty now should be our aim,
Undarkened by the shadow thrown by death
Across the water-lilies breezes tame
And whip to fury with their dying breath.
Who has not stood and looked into the lake,
And seen the dancing pictures flow and fade
Deep in the grey pool's heart? And soon each one
Will dance again. Now sleeping souls awake.
The fleetest shadow might be Beauty's shade.
Behind each shadow reigns a glorious sun.
1961; revised 10 October 2012
Quest theme: early yearning for truth, the Light of the One. The prospect is of
Port Meadow, Oxford.

2

from *A Stone Torch-Basket* (1963–1965)

The Seventeenth-Century Pilgrim

"Wyrd oft nered unfaegne eorl ponne his ellen deah."

Beowulf

Once I complained of many bitter facts,
Of ruins and epitaphs on empty hopes,
That I was born to die despite my acts
Or the futile benedictions of the Popes.
Yet as I watched the seasons ebb and flow
I saw the tides that swirled across my brain
In fickle flood and moon-fall – παντα ρει;
No self of mine felt constant agony.
And I resolved to evolve from pointless pain
(My Hell) and grow a Paradise that I could know.

Since then I have journeyed through rocks and pines,
Have sat by rivers in the summer sun,
Watched timeless dawns flush golden Eastern shrines,
And knelt to my shadow when the day is done.
Now I am still a sequence of moments;
But my abiding eye of strict assent
Nakedly loves the underlying Power
That pulses through existing's every hour.
Don't ask me where I'm bound. It brings dissent
To analyse perfection's senseless sense.

And yet I know from the wild wind's sound
I too will rot to nothing underground.
5 December 1963; revised 2012
Quest theme: awareness of Power. Set in Tokyo, Japan.

3

from *The Early Education and Making of a Mystic* (1965–1966)

Folkestone

All morning we clamoured to go down to the sea,
I chanted "Miss Whitworth's in the ba-ath"
Knowing there would be no ogre to chase me;
At the bedside of the paralysed neighbour
I pulled a face and made the others snigger;
But when, tears in her eyes, she squeezed my hand
I was well-behaved. Being immortal
I found her wrinkles funny, and her silent room
Like an agonised church.
                              On the promenade
The prophet squatted and raked his glowing embers
Of potash, carbon, tugging his mariner's beard
And pointing a scrawny finger at a red-hot omen.
My aunt tried to hurry me past, but I broke away,

Joined the small group, waited for him to speak,
Read the boarded feature from *The Daily Express*:
PROPHET CYCLES BLINDFOLD TO FIND WRISTWATCH.
He spoke in a grating voice through clods of earth,
"Verily, I say unto you, my experiment shows
God died in his bed after a long illness,
God is dead."

So can't God curl down like a genie and spy
Through the window?
"God is dead."
    No one cheered. With uncomfortable smirks
They dispersed. I stayed, aghast.
                  The sea
                      fell
                              away
Into the sky.
"Is God really dead?" I asked my flurried aunt
As she dragged me away.
Quest theme: scepticism, God dead. Set in Folkestone, Kent.

An Awakening in London
(for Colin Wilson)

Digesting Sartre on a Chancery Lane platform
I saw a concave poster, PHILOSOPHY,
And should it not be my free choice for the day?
I memorised the address as the tube rushed in.
In a room off Haymarket, I was reborn;
For two enthralling hours I heard one message:
"Not by reasoning, or words, or learning from books
Is a wise man wise, but by observation,
Awareness of habit, command of experience.
Be more conscious."

On the top of a London bus
I sought enlightenment, in a City suit
I broke the circuit of fragmentary dreams:
First I relaxed, then I commanded 'Stop all thought',
Then, one by one, I observed the senses,
Saw the seat in patterned red and green
And the platinum streak in the middle-aged woman's head,
Heard chesty wheezings under the diesel engine
And inane *non-sequiturs* on foul-smelling breaths,
Felt the weight of my body like a tired machine.
And after, the world was rich in varied detail,
It was as if I had been living in a waking dream,
And I glimpsed a future superconsciousness
Whose shadow crossed the yob in the front seat.

And Amos came up from the country
          and spoke against Baal
                    And town-bred Isaiah listened
                              Before Tiglath-Pileser pushed West;
And modest Jeremiah came up from his village
                    and spoke against Baal
          And cataleptic Ezekiel listened
                    Nineteen years before the fall of Jerusalem.
There was ferment in the Fleet Street coffee-bar,
You could see it in everyone's eyes, the old repudiated,
The new a question; a time of transition,
Few saw we'd settled down into a quiet decline.
When *he* came in we applauded, when he went
We stood in a ring near the empty beer bottles
And, battered with books, we scratched our heads and puzzled
Over his angry message, "Our civilisation
Is in spiritual decay."
                    But I knew,
From the unreal limbo, there is descent downwards,
To the earthy real, and ascent upwards
To self-surpassal in consciousness;

I knew ὁδὸς ἄνω κάτω
The way up and the way down are the same.

And I knew that nothing could ever be the same.
Quest theme: awakening to higher consciousness. Set in London.

The Power by the Lake

No missing breakfast that week. I was down
Early, searched the pigeon-holes daily, until
My father's envelope came. I left the Lodge,
Walked past the Cottages to the College gardens,
Meandered to the lake, sadly detached
From my doom, the entire future pressing
And I observed my feelings, free
Yet foreordained. Could I abandon Law
For Literature? Under the stone arch, alone,
I opened it, swallowed the broken surrender,
"I consent", and some great shadow of authority
Shattered into fragments. Sun-flecked, lawless,
Free, I wept.
              The early morning blazed,
Trees of every green linked earth and blue-white sky
In the lake. Adazzled, a great power filled me.
Purified, I grew, head sun-scorched, feet earth-rooted,
Stomach pulsing water-trees; I towered
Giddy, vast as God, I had always existed,
Earth-trees-sky would die, not I, the life-beat
And order, the permanent sole meaning.
I knew without understanding, as now
Without thinking, I know my own surname.
All creation was me, a pounding power,
And infinitely good.
                    Breakfastless in my room,
I pondered the impure sleep of my lake-like mind

Which, when woken with such purified force,
Could be transformed by such a mystic power.
Quest theme: experience of the One. Set at Worcester College, Oxford.

A Death

This room on the first landing is unfriendly.
Beneath the laboured breathing of the dying man
I can hear the nocturnal ravings of a brother,
The rustle and silence of French *au pairs*,
And my father's quaver from the dark dark corner
As he told me I wouldn't rock my sister any more.
(And I was filled with importance, confided in.)
In the door I wonder whether to disturb him;
Out of the window the stark indifference of lights
In his Council Offices.
                    The last drink,
The ritual Guinness in the pewter tankards
To pledge recission of a lifetime's disagreement.
I raise him, put a pillow under his shoulders,
Then pour slowly to preserve the richness.
(Not too much froth, says his glazed, critical eye.)
He stutters, then his trembling hand reaches;
Disregarding aid, with shaky defiance
He gulps, then splutters. His breathing is convulsed.
He labours. I snatch his tankard. He conquers.
Then disintegrates, crying incoherently in the dark
"I don't want to die"; groping for my hand, gripping
The living, clutching. And I was all and helpless.
"This is the end," he sighed, baffled, angry,
And downstairs the television tube went
And the picture shrank to the size of a postage stamp.

And looking at the moon, he understood:
From one single cell during a gleam of sunlight,

9

Into night and silence, man came and swelled and went.
From the end of priceless existence, he saw through:
An icy cinder, in an endless night.

Later my mother said, "Look there's nothing frightening
About death," drawing back the sheet in that stillness.
I lingered on alone near his grey still face,
Fascinated yet afraid in that awful stillness.
Quest theme: death and the One. Set in Loughton, Essex.

The Splitting of the Dark at the Strawberry Hill Pond

In the late autumn I took my last look
At the pond. By the fallen tree I happened to exist,
In the sunlight I stood bereaved in an inner dark
In the disturbed reflection.

Ah, but the darkness split;
In the late autumn sun I thrilled to the point of the plan,
The pond blazed in an unknowable revelation.
The silver birch caught fire, then I lit up,
The white branches flared up in a living scheme,
Licked and glowed and crackled into flame, burned
Up the blue sky. Mallards and water boatmen
Bobbed, throbbed and sizzled in the roasting orb,
Generation after generation, caught
In a spiralling dance of consciousness,
Whirling round and upwards and up, evolving
To the fire-like power of a higher consciousness.
I thrilled with order, I knew why it all meant,
I turned and left the spreading furnace of my heart
And walked back through the beeches to Robin Hood Lane,
And a deep calm and peace filled my bereaved dark.
Quest theme: experience of the One. Set in Loughton, Essex.

from *Satori*

As I tortured my body
In *satori's* outer form
An amorphous shadow obscured the polished floor
And spoke to my self from a future dawn.
On Tower Bridge, I felt gravity snap,
I fell headlong into space; I was alone
In a vast and indifferent universe, waiting
To die and not-exist for ever, not knowing why:
A smallness in an eternal silence without purpose
While hostesses served drinks and pickled prattle.
And not the lanterns in the gnarled pine trees,
Nor the dark outline of fishermen's boats by the road,
Not the phallic lanterns in swollen Shinto shrines
Nor the bamboo rustling in the breeze could deceive me.
Quest theme: seeking enlightenment. Set in Tokyo and London.

A Vast Palace and a Chiming Clock

In this suburban hall, the dust resettles
On warming pan, on gong and padded stick,
On dumb-bells, on the broken barometer,
On treasure-chest and silver visiting-plate.
Ghosts of aproned maids and side-burned butlers
Glide in the cluttered stillness of neglect.
In the sitting-room window, on a summer evening,
I put on the hands of a clock that will not start,
I am free from historical progression.

Now I am like an improvising actor severed from my plot.
That old man, waiting on the village bench,
Has he taken possession of himself, or does he know only
Fragments of broken moments, fragments of himself?
I said to myself, I must occupy my experience,

For to know one's past is to know one's present,
And unescorted at the exhibition
I could not connect each arbitrary fragment,
Each marble head or faded painting. In no deserted hall
Could I relate myself to a pattern,
Juxtaposition denied the development
On each wall. I said to myself,
I must explore each chamber, for I am like a stranger
In a vastly complex palace of my own construction
Near ivied walls rippling in a distorting mirror.
I ask the wind: a stranger, or a prisoner?
Do I repeat myself according to a pattern?
Who is the agent in my self-creation?
I skulk under the rim of my collar.

Self-discovery is a self-uncovering,
To know one's past is to know one's present,
And the past is a complex image of oneself,
Which is only to be known through experience,
And to know oneself is to cease to be surprised
Both by what one does and what one never
Suspected oneself capable of doing.
To know one's past is to know one's present
And intensify one's everyday consciousness,
And intensification is the beginning of affirmation.
I am the quality of my states of mind,
I am the intensity of my consciousness.

Art leads us back to ourselves: like a hall pendulum.
This sudden chiming of the childhood clock.
Quest theme: seeking pattern. Set in Nobe, Japan.

4

from *The Silence* (1965–1966)
from The Silence

[lines 249–273, Freeman encounters his Shadow]

*1 Said Freeman, "I have rebelled," and arrogantly stood alone,
Opposed to the drifting High Road, parting shoppers like a stone.
But what dream hung over the church, what surpassing image
Like the dream of a fallen seed in a dying season,
What dream like a twilit moon?

                   In a broken life-line
Is a sunset in a library, when, laughter in veins,
What could prevent if one had the belief, what save one's own will?
        To a violin's scales
        I made a renunciation;
        Weeping arpeggios
        I unchose my self for a Law routine.
But now in the electric light each man's shadow spread years before
                    him;
And can they not see, looking through the Hobbies, the motor
                    magazines,
Can they not see that each is awaiting creation,
Awaiting the features of a giant or dwarf?
Do they not know they are sculpting themselves,
This one his drooping jowls, that his sparkling eyes,
Can they not see that every second carves the future idea?
O Shadow, can I not ascend to you? Who are you,
Out there in the future like an inscrutable sage?
        The vision faded like a dream
        Into foggy air;
        An artist's quest began again,
        A Tammuz resumed his despair.

[lines 800–840, death of father]

*2   What is that scream from the summer roses
Like an unbearably beautiful pain?
And what disturbance in the condemned men's ward
As madness raged in a provincial's bleeding brain,
As with terrible logic he proved his tormentors wrong,
What triumphant shriek like a discordant chord
And then silence and the patter of rain?
In a lucid moment, lying in the bottom of a bed,
He groaned, "What have I done, what is the reason?"
And seeing him fall apart into a collage of bones,
I could not shake my head and say, "It is all in vain."

In the lush serenity of a sultry hollow
A distant rumble closed a prayer, and echoed
When will all this suffering reach an end and serenity follow?

In the angry autumn a storm came,
Breaking summer defiance,
Licking down from heaven with a white-hot tongue,
Leaving behind
A blasted bole in the after-calm,
And a charred inside.
Weary, he resigned his pride,
Surrendered a slurred confession to his inquisitors
And heard the twitter of migrating birds
In evening skies.
At nightfall in the unfriendly room,
Baffled by the indifferent lights of a lifetime lost,
He sighed at the yawning nothing round the flimsy moon
"This is the end," and shivered at the early frost.

And looking at the moon, he understood:
On a blind and slumbering retina, one flicker of light
And a universe; was no more:

Man, nothing and all.
He saw through, saw through.
An endless night.

He cried out – panting, labouring, groaning, he cried out –
        groping for my hand, grasping, clutching,
             clutching the living, gripping, gripping
                   under the lamp
And I was all and helpless; while downstairs
The TV picture shrank into a

        postage stamp.

        Night.

        [lines 1045–1064, quest]

*3   And is this the end of the quest, is this all,
        Is there only this uncontainable complex whole,
        This pattern of Becoming, and nothing more?
           This carpet on this floor?

I shall sink to the floor so, and tear out tufts of hair.

Poet of the Self,
You who gave your youth to questioning despair,
Stare in the mirror, and question each greying hair.

In the early spring,
Observing a sea-slug spinning a yellow thread
I transcended my yearning:
XYZ,
It exists; there is no why; it might be dead.

Sunlight on a wrinkled sea.
The jumping of exploding diamonds and the sparkle of crystal,
I flashed jubilation like a white hot mirror:

Might be dead.

Turning in the seasons of my sunlight
I shall continue to seek,
Transcending the indifference of will-less fatalists:
A luminous sapphire-cell expiring on the beach.

[lines 1157–1312, centre-shift]

*4   In the meditation hall
Each breath is unreal;
There on the silence
As the dawn shadows fall
The empty seekers feel
Empty and full existence;
As when the ruffled surface calmed –
Beyond your reflection
You saw the clouded ground
And the towering depths around your rational question.

And when I emptied myself and looked beneath
I was speechless, speechless –
There were no foundations in that darkness,
I understood nothing, confronting that silent ground.
*5 It was all round me, like a cloud of exhaled smoke
And later in the twilit air I knew it would enfold me again,
Rising like a haze from a subterranean furnace, and choke
Me with questions, I knew I must live with it, and live in pain.
Under a scaffolding of rusty girders,
I heard a whisper, as if from a lunch-time stroller,
"Now you will always be two unless you refuse;"
And, queuing for damnation in a mirage of heat and fumes,
And switching off the engine, have you never inquired
"Who is this 'I', intruding on silence?"
And seen your two profiles split in a mirror of cubes?

> red viscera and black
> in impenetrable dark
> could be a Janus-priest
> in a golden wheel
> or, invalid and seer,
> victims of earth and air,
> the chiaroscuro twins,
> red king and black queen
> under a cocktail sun and a lonely moon
>   Through the cracked glass

*6   They were like husband and wife waiting for a train
In a grey and bleeding dawn,
Hands clutched by the androgynous central child,
Divider and reconciler of their scarred disdain.
Watching the white orb boil in a platform puddle
While, adjusting darks, she said, "Isn't it like a moon?"
I knew why, I knew why she completed me, what I had projected
And what, as from a priest or nun, received,
As when, turning the wheel and lowering sunlight,
I drew a shattered reflection from the moon-dark well.
And I knew I must live between, in the child's place,
And, turning to a stranger by the wall,
As to a Reflection who would not abdicate,
I said, "I accept my inner being, I accept it all,"
And saw him slope away, disconsolate.

> I perceive, falsely,
> A Reflection that is *me*;
> To smash it is to be.

*7   Leaving the station, I groped down empty streets
Until, near the stadium, I went down a yawning stair
And lost my way into a hall of Buddhas.
I saw them, my thousand selves in tiers
Like a football crowd at prayer;
Lost in a labyrinth of plaster whores

I panicked, but there,
Beneath the central image, confirming a brawl
I had no fears.
                    The lift went down a well
Into a mine of gleaming diamonds
And golden gods with Egyptian heads were drawn past my closed
                                                        eyelids.
Through falling masonry I rushed up into the shaking street –
And seeing the city crumbled into a thousand ruins,
And the dancing dead, I did not cry out or weep,
Wandering in the girdered rubble of an old personality.

*8   And when i awoke, i was a floor below my thoughts,
Looking out at the dawn as from a tiled bungalow –
And suddenly, nourished by silence
My seed-case burst into a thousand I's
And a central stem broke through the tiled crown of my head.
Hallelujah! in a dazzling universe i had no defence,
round that round white light, life and night were one
and i was afraid, for i did not know
                            if the sun reflected
my reflecting sun

*9   and in that four-sided garden
                      rock and sea and sand
                      mountain and cloud and earth
                      mirrored in an empty mind
                      reveal a refutable truth
                      between stone and stone
                      in an arbitrary frame
                      there is no difference, all is one
                      still or moving, all existence is the same

                      An Eastern sage tempts:
                      "(+A) + (−A) = Nothing,
                      The Absolute is where there is no difference."

18

The Being behind Existence

the stone garden reflects
what you want to see
a mirror of
subjectivity
and on this hill
bristling with monuments to synthesis
gape, earth, and reveal
a thousand insights into the abyss
and, backslider, do you now deny
between system and finality there
is no difference?

11

A blossom of white light
illuminates the cosmic night,
my heart welled out –
a volley, and three men bowed low like acrobats
and under this ghastly sky, the condemned of all nations
are limping and crawling and groaning up the scorched hill,
writhing, screaming, feel their chopped bleeding, be faithful –
Freeman, be faithful to your fellow men;
see – some are ignorant of such matters
but that spurting flesh is yours, you're one of them
and whoever they are, would you abandon one?
between man and man there is no difference.

And when a headlight lit his stump of an arm

In a graveyard of uniform stones, I looked for the stars,
No matter what escaped old bones, I stood by my fellow men.
I thought: 'If just one is damned or dealt extinction,
I will be too, and if all men are a part of One
And all shall be eternal, without exception,
Then without effort all are guaranteed,
And I reject a truth that ends all striving.'

And when I had shaken my head, my mind was calm,
In a long rhythm of shadows, of days and nights
Like the scudding clouds on the unruffled moon-centred pool,
I mirrored the glory,
I was all existence in the silence of that stone garden.

> Darkness within
> Throws a chaotic waste on the empty screen;
> A disc of white-hot will
> Throws an orderly meaning on the sunlit screen;
> And the centre of the universe is in the self
> When only what one is is seen.

> A red-winged ladybird
>> in sunlight,

A meaning of gullwings by the turning tide.
To be
Is to perceive the world
As a stone-like unity.
Therefore, 'percipere est esse',
To perceive truly is to be.

I was all 'I', Becoming,
Before the Journey;
Now I share the sky
I perceive truly
> and feel all Being flow like a surging tide.

I saw them at the break of day,
All my exorcised ghosts, sullenly skulking away.
And from the baked land joyously burst a prepuced palm.

And I was weary, weary – I prayed for rest, knowing
$(+A) + (-A) = $ nothing;
Between red and black, the blaze of azaleas
And the dignified weeping of a dying piano,

In a disintegrating summer I became nothing,
I surpassed myself, on my way to becoming nothing.

And I was at peace.
                    And I had liberated
A great tide of will I did not want to cease.

[lines 1331–1354, on unity]

To outgrow all ideas
Save the important one,
The upward thrust of the sap
To a form of pagan height
And the quiet, stout-timbered shrine,
Or in the fading light,
At one with his fellow man,
The giant Buddha's calm;

to begin in inner silence
behind the outer smile
as empty as the stone garden
between central stem and Shadow
in the mosaic
between child and irrational woman
like the four-faced striking clock
that woke me as a child
and measures an exile.

I heard a cry from the old Professor's darkened room,
"The Age of Analysis is dead!"
Books lined with dust, a buzzing fly....
                              While, naked on the petalled lawn,
A new Baroque age is born.
                              Member, fingers,
Hands, lips, mouth, hair, eyes, nostrils, crown, face – WHOLE.

[lines 1414–1449, ruin and Reality]

*13 "No crumbling forces are unbreakable," Freeman had said.
Grass sprouted from these rotting roofs and walls
But, dictating progress reports, nobody noticed;
And from this Monumental height men are crawling like ants
Hither and thither in a pile of rubble and iron,
Hither and thither without a unifying idea
In a heap of crumbled machinery and falling spires
And, exhausted by aimlessness, drag weaker, falter,
Watch from now smouldering compost in the hard, clear dusk,
As with slow, regular flight,
A steel bird soars towards the crimson sun,
And fall, now burning; and, in a crimson conflagration,

expire.

*14 The angry years, an age like wind and foam.
Let us leave this inner kingdom, let us awaken to that blur.
A skylark twittering above the wheat,
Cows on green fields, primroses in the hedgerow.
Let us dip back into the mind and fly to Trenarren.
Rejoice from this headland, my Shadow, let us rejoice
At this sea pounding these rocks, at these sparkling waves, this tide.
Now let our eyes open to this sparkling, dancing sea,
This watery stone garden, lapping round still rocks.
It images: the starry universe, whose waves
Of cosmic radiation fill the blue sky,
And all Existence enveloped in Being;
The one ocean of manifesting Being;
The Void of unmanifest Non-Being
Behind it; and the One which contains both
For $(+A) + (-A) = $ zero,
Great nothing, the Infinite.

Let us be

The blue meaning of the foaming round the rocks.
Let us be the fourfold sea!

My Shadow sees
With a metaphysical eye.

Let us be the sea!
January 1965–June 1966; revised August 1970, 25–26 July 1974 and later
Quest theme: Freeman's encounter with his Shadow (future self), transformational centre-shift and quest for Reality, the One. Set in Loughton, Essex; and in Tokyo and Nobe, Japan.

The original text has glosses in the margin in the manner of Coleridge's 'The Ancient Mariner'. The positions of fourteen glosses are denoted by numbered asterisks, and the glosses are listed below.

1. Freeman rebels against society and glimpses the form which he believes can bring meaning to his life: a future state of himself as a higher consciousness which perceives meaning.
2. His father has another stroke, and his suffering and death seem meaningless.
3. He cannot reconcile his contradictions. By the sea he falls into despair.
4. In a Zen temple Freeman is confronted with the spiritual world and with the irrational basis of his existence, the metaphysical ground of his being.
5. He feels divided.
6. On a railway platform he accepts the irrational depths of himself. Like a reclaimed Tammuz who understands and accepts Inanna's role, he is about to escape his Underworld,
7. and it seems to him that the power of his Reflection is finally broken.
8. He undergoes a personality shift from his Reflection to the irrational depths of his inner being. He experiences illumination,
9. and perceives the unity of the universe and is face to face with the divine world and with metaphysical Reality.
10. Rationally he resists the prospect of personal immortality, first in terms of death,
11. and secondly in terms of his fellow men.
12. In a graveyard he retreats from the metaphysical, and for the time being

rejects immortality as a privilege he has yet to come to terms with, and immediately stakes all on existence, which he now perceives with meaning. He sees things as they are, objectively, without interference from his sense of 'I'. He perceives Being as opposed to Becoming.

13. Despite a vision of the ruin which is eventually in store for European civilisation,

14. the meditating Freeman glimpses Reality near Trenarren and is able to affirm.

5

from *The Wings and the Sword* (1966–1969)

from Archangel

[lines 1–14, Archangel Cathedral]

Like domes of a cavernous mind
These groined and frescoed vaults
Over pictured pillars and walls
Dream out a recurrent theme
In this Kremlin mausoleum:
Grand Dukes and palaced Tsars
As haloed, Orthodox Saints
Pursue a spiritual quest
In an unequal Christendom
While apart from the rich man's feast
Are rebellions of the starving,
Bread-fisted Leaders and skirmish,
And, as in the nearby palace,
The future tyrants of well-fed Peoples' States.

[lines 249–302, People's Square]

The old men huddled, the woman slunk away;
And, standing at dusk on the crowded People's Square

As on the grey cortex of a great remoulded brain
While, like happy slogans, obedient faces
Wandered painlessly round and round against sterilized museums,
I knew, only in such nightmare cities of ordered streets
And thoughts like lighted windows in Ministry hotels,
Could that cross be a centre, like the Forbidden City –
Like the Archangel Cathedral within the Kremlin wall
The Church must be denied to contain Christ's vision.
Otherwise, established ally of that Welfare board,
In a dwindling parish of tired, habitual aims
And loudmouth individuals whose only quest
Is for a group of skirts near the broken kiosk,
The vicar raffles liquor in the crumbling porch,
And the visionary walks apart in deep forests;
And where, oh where, is that spiritual way of life
That takes for granted icons and sad-eyed Saints,
And could drive all those howling slogans in Trafalgar Square
And shame to shallowness the Red inquisitors
Who, in agonised compassion, wade in blood,
And then, to save the many from their own tormented brains
Degrade them beneath the values of compulsorily happy States?

        Indifferent Tsars and tyrants,
        Compassionate inquisitors;
        Can nothing bring together
        Enslaving Leader and Saint?
        As I stared at the murals' centre
        In this Cathedral-tomb,
        The Archangel became a Shadow
        With a sword and wings outstretched,
        And I saw in the second icon
        The future of the West,
        From the Atlantic to the Urals:
        Into the People's Square,
        From the Cathedral gates,
        File in the morning rush-hour

An *élite* of self-made Saints
Each still on the last hour's quest.
They reach the central banner
In the forum of statues and graves,
The great mazed *mandala*
Under which the supplicants wait;
Decades of contemplation
Show in their white-haired peace
As, trusting to perfect feelings,
They value each equal they greet;
Until, whispering on silence,
They glide to the Leaders' Hall,
Their hearts, with a World-Lord's wholeness,
At the centre of life, of all,
Their hearts where all past and future meet.

An outstretched angel of Paradisal vision,
And a dream of an escapist dreamer in an impossible heat.
11, 20 June–23 July 1966; revised in 1968
Quest theme: rejection of Soviet and Chinese Communism, vision of unity as
coming world government. Lines 1–14 and 272–302 are set in the Archangel
Cathedral, Moscow. The People's Square of lines 249–271 is in Peking (Beijing).

An Inner Home

"The forest which surrounds them is their godhead."
(From a review by Mr. Geoffrey Gorer of *Wayward Servants*,
a book on the Mbuti pygmies in the Ituri rain forest, N.E. Congo.)

I have followed the Waltham stream:
Winding through sunny meadows,
Stilled by lilies and reeds
It seems a long way from
King Harold's rough-hewn bridge
And Edward's two arches,

Till under the Abbey's tower
On either side of stone
Under two modern humped bridges
With a sudden tugging of weed
The stillness overflows
To plunge in a cascade down
And froth into gentle channels
And trickle underground
And I turned away in a panic,
There was weed in my hair and toes.

That child, who, sick from fleeing a baying form,
Lay on the humming Stubbles near the Witches' Copse
Like a sacrificial victim near Stonehenge,
And, seeing a six-spot burnet, suddenly felt secure,
Walled round and alone in a forest enclosure;
That child seemed a long way from that adolescent
Who, sick at having seen the universe
In a string of bubbles blown through a child's wire-ring,
Stood in Loughton Camp among writhing pollards
Like nerve tracts rising to a memory rooted in
The skulls of Boadicea's unconscious dead,
And, under the dark grey cortex, distinctly heard
The silence beneath the distant hum of cars
And knew himself under the patter of falling leaves;
And that young man, who, retching at one last sigh,
Stood where he fished as a child with sewn flour-bags
And skidded to the island on an icy slide
And stared past his reflection in the gravel pit
As if seeking an image in an unconscious mind,
Until his darkness split, and in the autumn sun
The pond blazed in an unknowable revelation,
He said Yes, and, looking back through the blinding leaves,
He longed to be a statue between the two ponds
And gaze for ever on the thrusting of those trees;
Or that poet, who, sick with impending exile,

Having driven round Lippitt's Hill to Tennyson's estate,
Crunched broken glass in the littered Witches' Copse
Alone in the centre of a living *mandala*,
And knew, although before him was approaching stone,
Like a hermit enfolded in a godhead he projects
He would always be enfolded in this Forest,
In this unchangeable image of an inner home.

Like the tree-enfolded face a still stream reflects
Below humped bridges where waving weed is pressed
Before it plunges down and is lost in foam.
13–16 October 1966; revised in 1968 (?)
Quest theme: Forest as image of the One. Set in the town of Waltham Abbey,
Essex and in Epping Forest.

The Conductor
(Or: At The Royal Albert Hall)

Under lights which hang like planets from the dome
A banked society, in tiers to the highest gods,
Is appalled at the orchestra's changing tune:
A diminuendo that chilled a hundred moods
Before it froze our frowning generation's
'Barbarian' breaking down; bar new soloists,
All's finished in the mind on the podium,
On whose fighting gestures every eye is fixed.

Like a demogogue appealing to the pit
In Rome or Athens, he varies old themes,
Then takes his bow, as if for a Cabinet;
Standing in a crisis crowd in Downing Street,
Brooding on Empires and a European Queen,
I wished we had a centre, like these seats',
With a fixed prospect: when he leaves his podium,
Society will be a crowded street.

Like a Saint he has turned his back on the still tiered throng;
But, seeing a drinking orchestra playing parts,
Now simpering, now with a lambasting scorn –
A scowling generation wearing grotesque masks
That have been worn a hundred times before –
I knew he was the Reflection they played to, for applause;
And seeing him as the tyrant who makes false
Should we not cry "Rise up, orchestra, and drive him to the door"?

The orchestra plays false parts but what it plays
Is real; the Artist wears a high priest's mask
And, reciting ritual, rips back the altar-veil,
Makes initiates reel at a hacked-out human heart;
Art, like revolution, bleeds in decay
A dialectic the Red Guards don't know:
If the Artist were the centre of this banked, tiered place,
Only he would wear the Reflection's Leader's robes.

The Leader who waves his arms in a roaring square
Blusters down the deafening Way of Action;
The Saint who stops his ears, retires, and hears
A chord, glides up the Way of Contemplation;
But this Artist does both; see, with screwn-up lids,
He quivers at an unheard crescendo,
And yet, with impatient hands, he acts, to the fingertips –
Without him the orchestra could not play a note.

And I have glimpsed, in mirrors in different rooms,
One not unlike that Flash Harry tyrant
Who directs a hundred reflexes in a stale old tune,
And a Shadow of that masked Artist or Saint
Who summons a hundred memories along
To roll and pluck and screech and clash and blow,
And transcend themselves in a unified ensemble,
And fill with rhythms and phrases this great decaying dome.

18–26 October 1966; revised 2 November 1966

Quest theme: unification of contemplation and action.

6

from *Old Man in a Circle* (1967)

from Old Man in a Circle

[lines 465–514, Shadow over Mount Brocken]

From the mountainside I saw a giant Europe burst into light;
Descending, I walked in the neon-streets of its automated cities:
London, Brussels, Paris, Amsterdam, Berlin,
Rome, Vienna, Prague, Warsaw, Budapest, Bucharest;
They throbbed with a dull pounding, as if from an iron lung,
And, as from a plastic heart, conveyor belts carried things
That were fed into glass tissues by arms and shoots and slides:
The people were calm and gentle, and there was a peace in the air.
Then I came to a City of Images, and I stood in the station
And stopped a passer-by who looked like myself.
"Our time?" he said, recognising me. "Things aren't all that
Much better than in other uniform times, I shouldn't imagine.
Oh yes, there has been progress in the macrocosm – these machines and
    amenities;
There has been amelioration, and everyone is cared for now;
But nothing lasts. Buildings decay, machinery crumbles;
    money gets short, squalor sets in.
Cities sink into the earth. Rise and fall, rise and fall."
I closed my eyes in Whitehall and sighed:
O the Treasury wall, O the broken spires,
Black black black is the skin of this dying city;
O the agony in the body, the sores, the sores
As old John Bull dies away from his greatness like a sick ego,
And, mid dreams of dreadnoughts and distant fires,
Hears remote voices like leaves shaken in the wind;
O the torture as the factories run down for lack of oil,

O the anguish of blasted out city-windows –
O Israel, O Portugal.
O the torment in this dying, before it is understood!
Did not Harold weep when he prayed before the Waltham stone?
O this giant Europe, these nations as federal states.

Time has gone beyond
Winged Kairos with the scales;
On the golden zodiac clock
On Anne Boleyn's rose-web gate;
The black hand with the sun
Has crept up the dark Year,
Like a blood clot that will stun
An old man's unpurified stare.
But, at the first glimmer of dawn,
While the winter sun is low,
Above the windbeaten watchman
On the rocky mountain brow,
High over the East-West border,
On the cloudy skies of Europe, newly born,
Raising his arms like a Conductor
With a cleansed Archangel's scorn,
A lone huntsman hails the future:
The giant Brocken Shadow sounds his horn!

O the giddy hopes as a civilisation gathers its spirit together,
O the grandeur of the new God it throws across the heavens!
O the sadness of the far-seeing huntsman, as undeceived,
He blows the last post for the eventual extinguishing of the Lighthouse
    beacon!
20 December 1966–13 March 1967; revised in 1968
Quest theme: image of the Shadow seen on clouds from Mount Brocken,
Germany during the reunification of declining European cities, including
London.

31

7
from *The Gates of Hell* (1969–1972)

Orpheus Across the Frontier

At five, hens squawked, dogs barked. I was woken by shots.
There were more shots at six, at nine the Tripoli street
Was deserted, the police had gone. Idle knots
Of people on the corners held radios, a discreet
Armoured car dropped soldiers who aimed at
The sky. Then someone said, "There's been a *coup*."
And the shooting.... For a day we crouched in our flat
While the bullets whined, then we were allowed out to
Shop. Army men fired shots in the air every hundred yards,
In the supermarket, soldiers shouted, "No beer."
They wore plimsolls, they crept in, our "freedom's guards".
The skull-capped greengrocer muttered, "King good man here."
So history changes by stealth, and lacking the power or
Will to crush it, the West's frontier contracts a little more.
The Gates of Hell is a Catullan sequence of poems. Quest theme: Way of Loss,
purgation leading to illumination. Set in Tripoli, Libya: Gaddafi's *coup*.

Providence Which Takes

Does will, accident or Providence rule our lives?
I could have gone to Teheran instead of Tripoli.
At our child's school, a mother asked us to a party;
Her act traps me in a chain of events that deprives.
A hot Libyan night under curfew. Black houses, dark sand.
Your birthday. I poured champagne saved from before the *coup*,
Our child danced. We hung our arms round our shoulders, you
Sang, "We're a happy family." She giggled in bed, and
Snake-bitten, you will not be touched.
Poisoned, Eurydice has no warmth at present.
And your friend in her red trouser suit, I could
Have found it as she lay, as on a bed, and clutched

The cliff near the Phoenician ruins... Is there no accident,
But Providence which takes what is not for our good?
Quest theme: Way of Loss. Set in Tripoli, Libya.

Well, Dried Grasses, Dead Butterfly

Now I have begun the next of my descents
Like that foul old Arab down this clogged well.
Here I am, at the end of a decade, of an expell-
-ed regime, thirty, having put up homes like tents
And torn them down, trapped in this turbulence,
The wrong side of the *limes*, in a barbarian citadel.
I want to settle by the spring of life, dwell
There, not roam thirsty in this affluence.
I need to dig out the health in myself, exhume
It, unblock the source of this parched seaside life,
This Mediterranean sloth. It has made you droop.
Today a butterfly flew round our sitting-room,
Settled in my dried grasses and died. Like a wife
It is still lodged there, a painted lady in mid-swoop.
Quest theme: Way of Loss. Set in Tripoli, Libya.

Lump like a Cannon-Stone

Corinna,
Your pomegrantes were red that blue day;
I crept up your drive, your piano warbling,
I tiptoed in, straight back rising you flung –
Teeth gleaming in a Spanish smile – two hands. My
Heart, when you touched my chest, burst into blood.
I was raw, I sang like wind in telegraph wires.
There were no clocks until the bell rang in your ears.
Who squats by you on that red pouffe now? Who should?

Now, under liquid stars, the pye-dogs howl,
Sad army lorries drone.
With a rumble of thunder, curfew comes crashing down,
As it did for me when you spoke of your French class and drove
Off in your blue car this afternoon,
Leaving, in my lungs, a lump like a cannon-stone.
Quest theme: Way of Loss. Corinna was the heroine of Ovid's *Amores*. Set in
Tripoli, Libya.

Two Damnations

After lunch, I drove you down to the sea.
We swam on the Homs Road beach, you lay in the water,
We paddled, then we waded with our daughter.
She dived from my shoulders, like a water baby
In her wings. The beach shimmered with heat waves, we
All lay and roasted in the heat for a quarter
Of an hour. How different from that shorter
Visit, after your sobbing. What heavy
Hearts on the low rocks beyond the American
Base. The waves came in like generations,
We walked among sparkling glass, near sea-lavender,
I bent and picked up two Roman-Libyan
Coins, said, "Like us, green and corroded." Two damnations.
Two pearly tears rolled down your cheeks, so tender.
Quest theme: Way of Loss. Set in Tripoli, Libya.

Wrecked

Now is a time of great sorrow. I patter round
This flat, make my dinner, sit, stare. Nothing, this mess.
She is in love with him. If I show forgiveness,
Ring her, accept her back, will she come? Will she sound
The new Carlotta, or the one who never frowned?

I love her, *but*... I contemplate the bleakness
In a Hell of dreaming of my own creation. I confess
How happy we were last summer, before we drowned,
Without knowing it! Now I feel broken up, I escape
Into wine, valium, the radio, work, anything.
They endure through courage and heroism in Hell.
I know I must encounter the Protean shape
Of my dead self, get to know my heart, my feeling
About her, gouge these limpet eyes, this stopped-up sea-shell.
Quest theme: Way of Loss. Set in Tripoli, Libya.

Cairo

I am in a limbo, between wanting you and know-
-ing it is hopeless. I must not rush, be too swift.
I sit, knowing this wretchedness should be a gift,
And watch ghosts flit through the passages of my bro-
-ken mind. This balcony overlooks the Nile's flow.
Guns thump from Dahshur. Sandbagged bridges. I shift
And watch the curved white sails of the boats drift
Like dorsal fins along the silver-green river. Slow
Eaglets soar overhead. At night the streets make sense:
There is blackout, windows and headlights are painted blue,
Without streetlights this city is a ghostly Hell,
Faces loom and fade in eerie silence.
In this dark tide the permanence of you,
And a damned soul drowning near the Purgatory Hotel.
Quest theme: Way of Loss. Set in Cairo, Egypt.

Way of Loss

I stand in a hotel filled with clutter:
Ceilings, walls, curtains, furniture, tea-
Cups, carpets, music, Scotch, radio, TV,

Luxurious lifts, an at-attention waiter,
Girls, books, newspapers. Outside in the street
There are pavements, restaurants, distractions, cars,
Museums, dance halls to fill in time, and bars –
Where are the sand and stars? I cannot meet
Nature in a city round of social drinking,
Culture and prattle. I live in delusion,
This Western cluttering, endless thinking.
I must go to the desert and strip each illusion
On a Way of purifying Loss, and temple-sleep
Till I see my soul with a head-scarfed Tuareg's timeless peep.
Quest theme: Way of Loss. Set in Alexandria, Egypt.

Ghadames Spring

(Poems like Bubbles)

I drive through the desert, two days of sand
And Czech lorries, till I reach the necropolis
Of Ghadames – a hill of tombs, palms and
Tuareg who live underground in this oasis,
In a Hell of chambered tunnels. Near the Hotel,
Glory! I sit by the spring, on polished stone
Steps: clear water, and green weed; a square well
And bubbles wobbling up in the sun. A lone
Tuareg peeps through his head-scarf's slit, and I know
That at last my hopelessness is over. As old
As the Great Pyramid, this overflow
Fills Roman baths where toga-ed citizens still hold
Court. I have found the forgiving spring in my heart
Whose Divine bubbles pour up into art.
Quest theme: image of the One. Set in Ghadames, Libya, where the spring Ain el
Faras was known c.2600BC.

Eurydice Lost: Expectation and a Tear

Oh hurry, they are at the airport gate,
I run to her, kiss her Malta lips.
Now surely she's come back. A tear
Trickles to her chin, and drips.

Is it a tear of happiness?
In the car I turn and hold her hand,
Peer for her letter behind her dark glasses.
She takes away her hand.

What is up? Now, in my whitewashed room,
Screwn expectation in the grate,
Head bowed she sobs near her tearful womb,
"We must separate."
24 November 1972
Quest theme: Way of Loss. Set in Malta.

A Death of Sorts

I drank bootleg wine late at night in an austere
Villa. The bell rang, a secret policeman said, "I
Want you to come to prison." A large car was parked nearby,
A young Arab in a suit and a cruel sneer
Drove me to a villa like a graveyard, gave me beer,
Then said, "We have had this 'evolution' to cry
Out that Libya is great. You are a spy.
I am in charge of executing journalists here."
And he went for his Luger. To shoot me, he had to choose.
He sat across the table with wild eyes,
Sipping his whisky. Dying, I felt a peace,
I thought, 'He who loveth his life shall lose
It', I stopped clinging to life, serenely realis-
-ing you and our child were safe. Oh, what a release!

Quest theme: Way of Loss. Set in Tripoli, Libya.

On the Waterfront

I walk on the waterfront, after the Libyan *coup*.
Arabs sit in the cafés, the sea splashes.
I walk tensely to this latest rendezvous.
I am a target. If I am shot now, my ashes
Will be "the remains of a Westerner who was rushed,
Who represented a decolonising power
That has been liberal when it would once have crushed".
I am its response. At a dark, secretive hour
I wait for the car, the hand that will give me a wad
So I can go to the supermarket and drop the bright
Notes among tins; enough to buy a squad
Of men for a civilisation that has lost the will to fight.
I am a lost mystic, who should be kneeling in a church,
Not loitering here on the waterfront, on the Devil's research.
Quest theme: hindrance of intelligence work. Set in early-Gaddafi Libya.

Journey's End

So as always I, wounded, seek out Essex,
This green-gated house with its pear tree on the lawn
Under whose eaves I slept, heard tappings that vex,
Strange creaks, cowered from shadows before dawn
As a boy. Now all is October gloom and scorn.
Dusk darkens this dining-room, I sit by the piano
Alone, deaf as this Beethoven to your "No".
I wander out to the garden. And suddenly there
I see myself: a spider hanging in the pear.

Like a spider exuding thread, I wove a web
And wrapped you in a beautiful silk cocoon,

38

I rolled you into a ball and held you, till the ebb
Of autumn blew you free, my mayfly. Too soon
You turned bitter, bitter, and headed for the moon.
I stand on the darkening lawn, and wish that I
Could leave this wretched flesh, and quietly die
Into those roots and twigs and leaves, so that my tears
Could drop each anniversary autumn as ripened pears.

Here I must make up my mind, within this fence,
Among these Michaelmas daisies, under these
Rosy apples, by this wet bark; I must make sense
Of choosing against my will what I dread, to please
You. I feel my trunk and next year's blossom slowly freeze
In the chill night. You were not true – true to yourself
In that – yet I loved you. Like pears on the cellar shelf,
My tears.... But no, these stars the night weeps – for you
My branches shake them down, like drops of morning dew.

Quest theme: Way of Loss. Set in Journey's End, Loughton. (*See also* Pear-Ripening House.)

Weathervane and Wind

A year has passed like mist on grass
With a "Why did it happen? Did she love me?
Did she love like a weathervane
On a misty Essex belfry?"

Questions in the winter wind
With a "When will the weathercock crow?"
I sing the soul of Western man
And a disbelief like snow.

7 December 1972

Quest theme: Way of Loss. Set in Essex.

Orpheus-Prometheus in the Blackweir Region of Hell

We looked in this Blackweir pond at sticklebacks
And minnows with green and silver bellies,
At water beetle, skimming dragonflies –
Looked down through the bars, and then picked blackberries.

As a boy I climbed into the round tunnel,
Crouched underground, under this high-barred grate
Where the pond overflows in a cascade down,
Heard voices echoing up to this dungeon gate.

Now squatting beneath the bars within my mind,
Watching gnats dance from an awful torture cell,
I look up at blue sky from a dark tunnel.
Will there ever be an opening in the Gates of Hell?
18 November 1972
Quest theme: escaping the gates of Hell. Set at Baldwin's Hill pond, near
Blackweir Hill, Loughton, Essex.

Flow: Moon and Sea

I loved you like the tortoise-shell
You loved up on the Downs with me.
The light leaps off your Worthing sea
Like shoals of leaping mackerel.

The sea flows like a bent hawthorn.
Now, up the night, the harvest moon
Floats and sails like a child's balloon
Over this darkly rippled corn.

This glow behind the moon and sea
Affects my way of seeing.
What, oh what is happening to my being?

I thrill to a pebble's flow, and a bumble-bee.
3–4 September 1971; revised 7 December 1972
Quest theme: heightened experience of the One. Set in Worthing, Sussex.

Visions: Golden Flower, Celestial Curtain

That weekend I lay down and breathed at twilight,
Looked into my closed eyes, saw white light flowing
Upwards..., a tree of white fire, flickering.
Then a spring opened in me, for an hour bright
Visions wobbled up like bubbles: from a great height
A centre of light, a gold-white flower, shining
Like a dahlia, the centre and source of my being;
A chrysanthemum; a sun; a fountain of white
Light; strange patterns; old masters I was not certain
I had seen before; old gods. I was refreshed, after this
I fell on my knees in the dark, and breathed "I surrender"
To the white point. It changed into a celestial curtain
Blown in the wind, like the *aurora borealis*.
I feel limp, an afterglow in each moist finger.
10 September 1971
Quest theme: experience of the One. Set in 13 Egerton Gardens, London.

More Visions: The Judge

I buried my eyes in the crook of my arm and saw
A dome of light like a spider's web, an old
Yellow and purple tomb; later a gold
Death-mask, the face of God. I felt shaky, more
Like a child that has taken tottering steps, before
I walked to the Brompton Oratory to hold
A candle lit from the eternal basket, and fold
My hands. Later I saw an egg; a mirror;
Christ on a cross; a flaming devil who trod

Down a haloed saint. Visions poured up: a globe;
A yellow rose; black thorns against a sundial;
A foetal child, and a crowned Eastern god.
Now – o frontal Christ in thorns and a red-brown robe
Gathered with a pin at the chin, help me through this trial!
11 September 1971
Quest theme: visions of the One. Set in 13 Egerton Gardens, London.

Visions: The Pit and the Moon

Frostleaves on glass. Hints of a white flower
And suns and shafts of light. My arms must free
These eyes, black out the dark. A starless, revea-
-ling night, an outline of a rim, a tower
As if I look up from a dungeon-pit, in the power
Of Hell. A point of white light breaks, I see
A long white-hot line, like the trunk of a tree
Down the centre of my being. "I surrender," cower-
-ing, I gasp, and the light swells into a city
Moon. Squatting, I feel a refreshing stimulation,
I feel wobbly at the knees, but now I know
That time is the cutting up of Eternity
Which can be known through this silence. My imagination
Relieves this prison stretch with this mystic glow.
11 September 1971
Quest theme: visions of the One. Set in 13 Egerton Gardens, London.

February Budding, Half Term

The buds are flecks, hawthorn and beech,
A great tit see-saws near its nest,
A squirrel listens from a branch,
Like my daughter, too quiet for speech.

On Strawberry Hill, a sky like smoke
Threatens the suffering, tearless twigs
And looking at this mossy knoll
I know the endurance of a much-gnarled oak.

I feel the rising rhythm thud,
As I scuffle through last year's leaves
The scales unfold around my grief
And burst into joyful bud.
11 November 1972
Quest theme: Way of Loss. Set on Strawberry Hill, Loughton, Essex.

A Stolen Hour

Today I walked through the lost leaves and holly
Of another year. The hawthorn budded green,
The spiked beech showed green thoughts through last year's sharp-
-ness. A great tit see-sawed to the sky, serene

In the Forest where a church with a black rail
Round the wall stands silent. I took the bramble
Path that winds to an oak tree. There I lay
Where four paths meet and made a mental ramble

Through where the silver birches leap to the sky
Like white-hot flames, and the snowdrops glow with heat;
There I stole an hour in scrumptious Eternity
The other side of all tangled defeat.
Quest theme: Way of Loss, time stolen from eternity. Set in Epping Forest near
Church of the Holy Innocents, High Beach, Essex.

Visions: Raid on the Gold Mine

I have been seized by God. I felt the Divine

Presence steal up from the shaft below and fill
My soul, slow my breathing, locking me still
As a fakir. I lay and descended down my spine,
Surrendered the deepest crevices of my gold mine
Of visions – golden furniture, temples with thrill-
-ing columns, a brown head, the celestial curtain – till
I saw a diamond in luminous blue light shine,
The first time I have seen the colour blue
In my secret excavations. Then the Golden Flower,
And an hour of flashing down my inner night
Like a dawn. Slowly the raiding Presence withdrew,
And now I record it in this "newspaper
Of the Eternal"; lifted to a great height.
8 April 1972
Quest theme: visions of the One. *See* p.xxii for "seized by God". Set in 33
Stanhope Gardens, London.

The Furnace

Again I have been rapt. Aglow with Fire
I sat and looked at the lights of Chelsea,
At dusky windows, and felt God enfold me,
I sat rigid, then lay down full of desire.
I murmured, "I have surrendered entire-
-ly. Enter me." I was breathing heavily,
Possessed, in union, till in a sighing glee,
Slipping away, a voice said, "Your loss will inspire
A dark generation, I will give you greatness."
I do not want self-glory. On these fired pots
I paint the mystic truths, as they are revealed
In my vision. Now I know I will have less
Going out. From my window I look down. Among lots
Of plane trees, a white magnolia. I am healed.
17 April 1972
Quest theme: visions of the One. *See* p.xxii for "God enfold". Set in 33 Stanhope

Gardens, London.

Vision: Snatched by God, a Blue Light

I have been snatched by God. Idly looking
Over Chelsea, I felt peace rise, attack
And enfold me. I put down my spoon, pushed slack-
-ly at my chair, sat cross-legged, hands clasped, gazing.
Soon I was breathing deeply and sinking
Into a trance, locked rigid – glory! From that black
Night of closed eyes, a pale blue light shone back,
And became a dazzling white like a diamond shining
In the sun. I sighed out in ecstasy
As if I were throbbing in a pleasure-dance,
Stiffly I rose and lay on my bed an hour
And the Light came and went, only more faintly
This time. Then I came slowly out of my trance,
And the rest of the day have felt full of inner power.
22 April 1972
Quest theme: visions of the One. *See* p.xxii for "snatched by God". Set in 33
Stanhope Gardens, London.

Vision: Love like a Grid

A weekend of sorrow, but the power tonight
Switched itself on. My breathing slowed, my two
Hands locked, I closed my eyes and wandered through
Into my bedroom, got into bed. The white
Light came with blue tints, incredibly bright,
Came near, then went. In an ecstasy I knew
God caught my breath. Suddenly the white light grew
Bigger and brighter. There was a hoop of light,
A round halo before my peeping eyes.

I gasped and fell away, as if making love,
Glassy-eyed, peaceful, happy, not rigid.
Now, with a swelling feeling in my thighs,
I know Love pulses through the sky above
Like a network of wires in an LEB grid.
28 April 1972
Quest theme: visions of the One. *See* p.xxii for "God caught". Set in 33 Stanhope
Gardens, London.

Mephistopheles

You can well blush and look down, so secretive.
Had you not written to me four years ago
Asking me to meet you outside the Bank of North America
We would be living in Tokyo.

I would have paid my three hundred pound debt somehow,
And our meetings on the waterfront
Would not have preyed on her mind, after the *coup* –
Those firing-squad guns, our daily dying grunt.

We were innocent, and you got to know
The secrets behind our privet hedge.
Now, having corrupted, you drop my soul.
You thrive on need, and thirst for knowledge.

You can well blush and look down, Mephistopheles!
21 May 1973
Quest theme: hindrance of intelligence work. Set in London.

Sunbathing

I feel as heavy as a pot-bellied vicar
All flabby in a swimsuit on the beach

As I lie in the gardens and clench my eyes and surrender
And scan for images, and reach, and reach.

An African mask, old temples, thorny briars
And the timid glimmer of a peeping light,
Then dark gold beasts and white, white fires
Flickering in a grate like a winter night.

Three points like midnight stars, then one
That breaks over my basking eyes,
A shaft that shoots from the dawning sun
And fills me with chilly sunrise.

I am leaves, grass, sea, sky, star, girl and boy,
By this brick wall I warm my breathing earth.
I am at blue peace and heave leaves of joy,
I have broken the wall that prisoned my eyes at birth.

Way above the gardens beyond my ruined wall,
Like an August sun, or the skylark's rising flight
I am at one with sky-grass one and all,
Resting, bathing, basking in this dazzling Light.

31 July 1973

Quest theme: image of the One. Set in 33 Stanhope Gardens, London.

The Code

6 of 2	7 of 24
4 of 3	4 of 26
13 of 5	10 of 29
4 of 18	2 of 30
9 of 22	1 of 31
6 of 23	4 of 33
	3 of 49

Contains a simple secret

That explains why you went.
He who cracks my service code
Knows the truth about my torment,

And in four hundred years' time
When the key is on the table
Like the 'Good Friday' manuscript
From Kimbolton Castle's stable

They will say, "Oh, *that* was why,"
As I would like to know
What happened before 'Twicknam Garden',
Whether Donne loved Lucy or no,

And in the next four hundred years,
Let who would summon my ghost
Start chanting from *The Gates of Hell*
At Christmas midnight – almost –

And invoke me by my name,
And I will appear and bring
The Mystic Power to all
Who would triumph over their suffering!
1969; revised 1975

Order of this group of poems reflects order of events. End dates are when poems were written, not when events happened.

Quest theme: hindrance of intelligence work. The cracking of the code requires a full text of *The Gates of Hell*. Set in 13 Egerton Gardens, London.

8
from The Flight (1970)

from The Flight

[lines 1–98]

"Yaren soran soran soran soran soran;
Oki no kamone ni shiodoki kikeba,
Watasha tatsu tori, nami ni kike."

"When asked about the tide, the seagull replied,
'I'm flying away, please ask the waves.'"

(Japanese fishermen's song)

I A Green Country

Apples are green under a fluttering flag,
Green are my daughter's eyes, green is her breath.
Green are the children among brambles and ferns,
"Oi-olly-ocky," they yodle, "I see Liz,"
Stealing on tiptoe like scrumping thieves.
And let us run together now, across the road, down the hill to the
    Forest,
To where the stream trickles from the long arched tunnel,
And, legs astride it, hands on the curved walls, walk bow-legged
And stand under the grating overflow, as if in a Hellish dungeon.
I took you there, and found a Victorian penny.
O this Blackweir pool, where I fished up green frogs in flour-bag nets!
We scuffled up through leaves, leaving the water boatmen and dragon-
    flies,
And at a meeting of green paths plunged right, into beeches,
I held your hand and said, "Look, the banks,"
And we ran on back into blackbirds and sticklebacks and newts,
And there, still under water-lilies, was the pond I had not found for two

decades,
The Lost Pond!

Apples, pears, wasps.
I came from the Essex flats, green fields round beech thickets.
When the daisies were humming with bees, I lay under summer skies.
I see a clearing where I kicked a ball, where my father swung his lame
    leg
And scored with a toe-punt. There I picnicked with two boys from the
    first form.
I ran through the Forest in the summers.
I caught caddice in the ponds, I had a glass aquarium that cracked at the
    top,
And green slime slopped down the sides. Near a fallen apple tree
I grew tall to the trembling of leaves. Upstairs, under green eaves,
I sniffed my death. I said to my brother
"I will live to be a hundred," clicking and reshutting the small black
    cupboard door
Until a voice from downstairs called "Go to sleep."

Brown is the earth of this Clay Country, and hard under frost,
Hard are the fields around Chigwell where we were sent on walks,
Stepping over iced hoof-marks in the frozen mud,
O those glistening stiles and brown dark thorns!
Crisp are the leaves of the heart in winter
When the bonfires smoulder no more. Bright is the air,
Remote the golden suns smashed across the icy pool of the sky.
Fingers are numb, cheeks pink, breath misty, clear.

I and my grandfather walked for tobacco in fog,
He fell and blood streamed from his white hair.
He had a stub of a finger he lost in a Canadian saw-mill.
Later my father took me for a walk. As we left the gate
The siren wailed. We wheeled to a white white flash,
The whole street shook, the windows clattering out.
Five bombs had fallen. Two houses up the road were annihilated

And the cricket field had a hole in it. The war –
I lay in a Morrison shelter and read books, swapped foreign notes,
While in the blue air puffs of smoke ended pilots.
When I moved home, I carried my battleship.

Red bricks and lilacs droop over the wooden shed.
On our rockeries, young hearts have wept and bled.
Ivy, and a garden hose.
A home is a rattling front door,
A broken flowerpot under a scarlet rose.

Green are the clumps of Warren Hill, green and scummy pond,
Green are the Oaklands fields, green round buttercups,
Green are those fields where children squat in camps,
Green is the ride down Nursery Road, purple the thistles,
Green are the Stubbles and the open heath,
Green is Robin Hood Lane, green past Strawberry Hill,
Green and brown are the two gravel pit ponds,
Green is High Beach, green around Turpin's Cave where beechburrs
    cling to hair,
Green round Lippett's Hill and the Owl, green the fields beyond,
Green back through Boadicea's camp, where you climbed the brown
    mud walls,
Brown are the leaves round the hollow tree we climbed,
Green along Staples Hill, where we shuffled through leaves to the
    brown stream,
Green past the Wheatsheaf, green up to Baldwin's Hill
Where we ran down to Monk Wood, and you were remote from me;
Green holly, green beech leaves, green oaks, and only the trunks and
    banks are brown.
Green to the Wake Arms, green to the Epping Bell,
Green down Ivy Chimneys, green up Flux's Lane
Between the poplars and the farmers' fields
Green are the trees round distant Coopersale Hall,
Green are the fields of Abridge and Chigwell,
Green is Roding Valley before hilly Debden,

Green fields, wide open, back into cratered Loughton,
A green country with hosannah-ing pollards, arms raised in jubilation.
And green is that gate, green the lime trees that hide the green porch
    door,
Green is that house of echoes. O how you despised my cradle!
You found the buildings false, the people mean and ugly,
But couldn't you feel the kiss in the swishing wind?

O the medieval churches of rural Essex:
Magdalen Laver, Abbess Roding, Great Canfield
With its 1250 fresco of Mary offering her breast;
A flat country of fields of wheat and rape
And Elizabethan barns and sleepy hamlets,
3 Lavers, 8 Rodings and 2 Easters.
O Essex, I love your green and drowsy haunts!
All this we have known in the green time, and more.
These are the places I return to now, in my heart-sorrow,
These Essex flats. Here I stood, waiting to meet you,
Here I knew you, in a green glade among beechnuts.
Here the city is a boot among yellow lilies, an iron roof that blocks the
    sun.
All this I left for the city, with a young man's impatience;
All this I left, seeking to meet a loyal woman.

I have starlings under my sunflowers.
I love the trunks of these pear-trees, whose ant-bands are sticky.
O these images that haunt me, that I fly to, to which I cling!
August–September 1970
Loss aspect of quest theme. Flight back to memories of Essex.

9
from *A Bulb in Winter* (1972–1974)

The Sun
(Remembrance Day)

This morning's winter sun put out his head
Over the trees of Hereford Square
Like an overalled painter asking the time
Near his dazzling handiwork.
I was out for the Sunday papers, and
All around Gloucester Road Station
People stumbled southwards, their hands in front
Of their eyes like desert look-outs
And wandered smiling northwards, silhouettes
Of twos in a yellow brilliance.
I could not look. I crossed the road to the shade.
But then I had to walk back, stand
Outside the International and watch
The bare trees, the buildings, children,
The men fixing the burglar alarm in
The Post Office – angels splashed in
Golden paint. While the sun shook down his hair
And greeted me with a blinding wink.

11 November 1973

Quest theme: image of the One. Set near Hereford Square, London.

Ode: Spring

Horace, I have been reading about your spring.
What great themes you and Catullus found, what sense,
What skill in hexameters and hendecasyllabics,
What banality occupies today's audience.

Your Bandusian spring I saw one spring afternoon.

I drank its cold water sixteen years ago,
In your Sabine hills. I am limpid, pure, I gush
With refreshing liquor for others to know.

Maecenas gave you your farm. How nice if the wind,
Rearranging, stirring these winter leaves,
Handed me a country spring to make famous.
I have only the gushing of this spring between my sleeves.
20 December 1973
Quest theme: inspiration from the One.

Night: Silence and Sea

I sit in the seafront hotel, a hundred and forty years old.
Silence and brass rails and Victorian red.
Queen Victoria herself stayed here and was
"Sorry to leave". Miss Newton was "much pleased
With the quietude and quite satisfied with the cooking
And attendance." It is in the Visitors' book downstairs –
1875.

It is my honeymoon. I have married again
For peace. My new wife pants with love.
Outside the sea crashes against the promenade
Hiss of shingle, boom and roar
Like a panting of human passions,
The pulsing kicking that will be in my new wife's womb.
A bright star, a lighthouse:
I am in silence. Ninety-nine years
Have leased me above this pounding sea.
22 February 1974
Quest theme: images of the One. Set in Royal Victoria Hotel, Hastings.

Fire and Waterfall

The ivy foams down the lattice wall,
The holly burns up the concrete post,
This prickly fire and waterfall
Leave me feeling dank and lost.

All who've let slip a lifetime, like a jewel,
And seen it swept away by a woman's rage,
Have learned life can cascade and be cruel
To the heart to ignite the soul, and the Age.

On this dining-room mantelpiece
Beethoven listens, white and deaf,
Hearing the cascading fury cease,
Burning to express a vibrant F.

The ivy pours down the lattice wall,
The holly burns up the concrete post.
This prickly fire and waterfall
Leave me like an unquiet ghost.
24, 31 March 1974
Quest theme: intense moments.

10
from *Visions Near the Gates of Paradise* (1974–1975)

Paradise

I sit serene, and read the Sunday papers.
I am at peace, without queries or quibbles.
This is surely Paradise, the state of mind
Man lost with his Fall from the Beatific; and scribbles

From illumined manuscripts, which he lacks knowledge

To return to in our decayed time, and so searches.
The Way is pointed in the writings of the mystics,
Yet these are not taught in schools or in our churches.

Instead we are asked to contribute pence
To social causes, the hungry, the poor, the Hindu –
All in Christ's name. And the Light of the *Bible*
Is allowed to flicker out, save in the hearts of the few.

Paradise. It is a labyrinth we have
To find our way back through. I did not know this
When I sat down before the Gates of Hell,
Waiting for them to open to this maze, this bliss.
Quest theme: image of the One.

De-Frosting

I open the fridge door: great slabs of ice
Bulge round the top compartment, where the three
Ice-trays are. I unplug the switch and pour
A scalding kettle on the chunks near me,

Then hack and gouge with a knife. They crash below.
One slithers across the floor. I am like this fridge.
I keep, deep-frozen, in a separate compartment
Images that freeze into blocks of language.

They solidify by themselves. They fill the sink.
The fridge is clear. I switch on, and indulge
In a peep. A frost has begun. So it is with me.
Each minute I ice up moments, until they bulge.
2 March 1975
Quest theme: images of the One.

A Vision Near the Gates of Paradise

Hell is a dungeon like Wandsworth prison,
With a portcullis and gate clock. How many know
Paradise is a Cathedral a sun shines on?
We are admitted through studded doors, below
Statues of saints, to the sunshaft under a rose-
Window, where God sits in the centre. Bright
Planets surround Him, great saints. The blue that glows
In the petals of that Kingdom of azure light
Is Eternity's air. Here stand, Heaven streaming
Down on the bare floor. Paradise is a fire in the eyes.
Peep in this afternoon quiet, see the guarding
Angels dance and cavort like butterflies
Round the portal, welcoming each peaceful heart, flit-
-ting round new souls' petals, sipping each nectared spirit.
Quest theme: images of the One.

11
from *Whispers from the West* (1976–1979)

A Shower of Pussy Willow and Hazel Catkins

We park and walk along the gravel track
Between oaks to the silver birches beyond
Which lick upwards like flickering white flames,
And the crackling gorse, to see if, in the pond,

There is any frogspawn like glarney marbles, or
Are there tadpoles round sticks like thorns? By the flags
The brown water has lily leaves, newt weed,
There are children with jamjars, water in plastic bags –

Sticklebacks, minnows, bullheads, but no frogspawn.
We are too early, Easter is not yet here.

So I look at pussy willow, hazel catkins.
I am clay and sky, I am Nature, at this shower of the year.
Quest theme: unity of the universe. Set near Strawberry Hill Pond, Epping
Forest.

Words like Ditches

In this Forest, the silver birches writhe,
Gorse flames and crackles as the dry bush burns.
I stand between silver and golden fire
And feel existence lick and curl in turns.

I have to perceive the world in terms of lang-
-uage to understand it, I do not know my experiences
Until I have seen them in words. A painter fix-
-es his scene in paint, I in nouns and tenses.

Words are like ditches for these streams of image
And thought. They are the stones over which streams have swirled,
The walls of the mud-banks. They channel and carr-
-y this spring of perception from the forests of the world.
Quest theme: catching the One. Set in Epping Forest.

Heaven: Glass like the Windows of a Soul

We enter Chartres Cathedral under cloud.
The blues of the stained glass stand out. We walk about
And linger in shadow, stare up at three rose
Windows, each with a centre and petals spreading out.

As we watch the sun comes out, and the dark blue
Changes to red and yellow, and pale azure,
And the window over the Royal Door is a vision –
So beautiful in its organised details! Sure-

-ly, here is Heaven in a pictorial form!
Yet how impermanent for the artist who painted
It on glass! Did he not fear cannonballs? Or did he
Think it was high enough to be protected?

How wonderful to paint Heaven, and set
It here in this Cathedral, so the sunlight
Can change its tones, and when dull, make it dull;
When bright, illuminate it with this pale blue bright-

-ness! An Englishman lectures twice a day
On the pictures, and the meaning of each one;
Has he seen that this Cathedral is a soul
Whose windows let in Light as shafts from a sun?
Quest theme: image of the One. Set in Chartres Cathedral.

12

from *The Fire-Flower* (1980)

A Metaphysical in Marvell's Garden

The House is hidden down lanes of the mind,
It stands "Strictly Private" amid green fields,
Over the redbrick front, a weathercock.
Behind, sunny lawns. Shaped evergreen shields
A huge cedar. And here a long green pond
Winds past the stone arch of a nun's chapel.
A Roman tomb ponders the October,
The ragged roses remember Marvell.

Here shed body like a sheepskin jacket,
Discard all thought as in a mystery school.
By this nun's grave sit and be the moment,
A oneness gazing on the heart's green pool.
A universe unfolds between two stone columns

And takes a leafy shape on clouded ground.
The sun-lily floats. Question its waters,
It will trickle through your fingers and be drowned.

The South Front sundial says in coloured glass
"*Qui Est Non Hodie*". I am a bowl.
In the North Hall the piano-tuner
Ping ping pings and trembles through my soul.
Who would not live in this delicious quiet,
Walk among columns, lie on the grass and wait?
Who would not teach a Fairfax daughter here,
Escape all bills, be free to contemplate

A flowered soul rooted like a climbing rose,
Metaphysical swoon of gold moments
Whose images curl down through thorns and leaves
(Wit and wordplay), spirit and satin sense;
Petalled layers and folds of whorled meaning
In whose dew-perfumed bowls a divine breeze blows;
Or like the prickly flame of the firethorn
Which crackles where purgation merely glows?

With drowsed eyes glance at solid grass and be
In whirlpools of energy like a sea.
Breaths heave the light, and answering currents pour
Through spongy stones and stars, or seaweed tree.
Now see with eye of mind into swelled form,
Imagine sap wash, oak wave in acorn.
Knowers are one with known, and are soaked by tides
That foam and billow through an ebbing lawn.

Gaze down on galaxies in a stone bowl
Like curved rose petals (small tip, large end),
Bent, cracked to holes. Travel faster than light
Through wisdom to where many curled worlds bend,
See nightmare multiplicity, then go

Where the bud of each universe is found,
The great Rose-tree of light where grown Ideas
Drift into form as petals fall to ground.

The vision has now passed. Condemned to crowds,
Town seers must teach hordes and leave halls' green waters
To lords who never peep for secret flowers
Or climb their souls up walls; and to their daughters,
And now a cloud flits through a fairy ring
And I glimpse for an instant my little "T.C."
And feel a dreadful shudder across my calm,
A "May it not come yet, but wait for me".

Wall-high climbers, whose many blooms reflect
Glimpses of the rose on the great Rose-tree
Which forms all souls in Time from one rose-hip,
Whose past growth glows gold moments they still see,
Are, in the present, one essential rose;
Which novices may see as a watery
Dark's shimmer and glimmer of the timeless
Dew-filled bowl of one gold water-lily.

Nymph everywhere, for whom men sacrifice
Paradise for a mortgaged, salaried mask
To keep you where Tennyson longed for Maud
Or where you board, we town climbers only ask
That, eyes closed, you grow a golden lily
And be a bowl for it, and simply start
To wimple in your wanting. May you be
A rose-sun-leaf-ground-cloudy fire-gold heart.
24, 28–29 October 1973; revised 4, 16–17 February 1980
Quest theme: glimpse of the One. Set in Nun Appleton, Yorkshire.

A Crocus in the Churchyard

Hoofs clop clop clop between the silver birch
That hide the arrowed spire and this Forest church.
Come through the lych-gate, down steps by the yew:
Where the bracken tangles, wood-pigeons coo.
On this green carpet, pause: a nightingale
Sings through eternity by a black rail.
A crocus blooms where every heart believes
That unknown faces mean more than autumn leaves.

The aisle is quiet, tiptoe to the chancel.
Altar, pulpit, stained glass, lectern eagle,
Hammerbeam roof, a tiled Victorian floor,
The font and cattle brands, organ by the door.
Here on the wall two marble tablets state
The Ten Commandments, and how to contemplate.
Red and black, a life like scullery tiles;
Where a robin hops, a wife is wreathed in smiles.

"No graven images", "no gods but me",
No murder or covetous adultery.
A time when no host wanted, it would seem,
And manna was not yet a juicy dream.
A city smile is like a warm pillow,
Here girls are like a shower of pussy willow.
A rooted life, like the evergreen yew:
No glass or redbrick spoils each woodland pew.

The church is faithful to its hillocked dead.
Whether poet, agent, or Department Head,
Their deeds, like bluebells on a mound of moss,
Attest a Britain like a marble cross.
They, like bent gardeners in their commonwealth,
Cut bellbind and preserved their belief's health,
Conserved the diamond lead window standards

From the stones of revolutionary vanguards.

Silver birch, bracken and folk who seldom sinned
Now feed the silence under this March wind.
Shh! Rest in the eternal; hear a snail
Dragging beneath the warbling nightingale.
Here rustling moments are time's muffled thieves;
Faces under hillocks, unlike old leaves,
Are compost so a crocus can proclaim:
To glimpse a Golden Flower is man's true aim.

Under this hillock, a decaying heart
Feeds the roots of a crocus and takes part
In the lost blowings of time from a windless
Ecstasy's silence and brimming stillness,
And, filled with dews, can, like an art-work, hold
A mirror down to Nature and still gold
Sunshine so posthumous meaning can wave
From fields of silver light beyond the grave.

Under the spire that towers from the slate roof
With arrowhead and vane like rational proof,
Look up at a high tripod which can view
White clouds that scud across the darkening blue,
And startle God at His theodolite,
As, measuring the angles of clouds and night,
He takes a reading of time's speed and flow
And calculates the centuries still to go.

Death has its beauty. A hearse, a squirrel's tail,
And your coffin is lowered by this black rail,
Between laurel and holly. For companions,
Unknown Belshams, Cookes, and rhododendrons.
A crocus under buds, now blink and brim
At dew-dipping finches, a tinkling hymn,
Snug in grass, safe from brambles; and in fine rain,

Gaze at the still arrow on the windless weathervane.
24 March 1974; revised 17 February 1980
Quest theme: glimpse of the One. Set at the church of the Holy Innocents, High
Beach, Essex.

Fire-Void
(A Rubbish Dump at Nobe, Japan:
An Investigation of Nature and History, Pattern and Meaning)

A seaside village, thatched fishermen's huts,
Paddy fields, pines, threshers, and a light that cuts.
I stare at the rubbish dump under this hill:
A heap of litter by a dusty track, still
Boxes, rusty petrol cans, panniers below
Old timber, paper; red cannae, a mallow,
A purple flower that blooms only at sundown;
Pine-bristles, wire-bars; a mess that makes me frown.

Cicadas, like a sawmill, go fee-fee-fee-fee-feeee.
Ants crawl up and down a bamboo cross. See,
This dump is in proportion to the hill,
It balances two sweeping curves that thrill.
Pattern is relation, of lines to whole:
Spring, fall; skull, scroll; shape the inverted bowl
Of Nature and history. Birth and decay
Are contours that are redesigned each day.

The pattern of sunrise and set, and soul,
Holds green and white in a harmonious whole.
Opposing seasons and ages are a part
Of a hidden order known to the heart.
Meaning relates pattern to what it's for,
Yet ask priests "Why is man?" and be shown the door!
The artefacts of the Great Architect
Are not grasped by reason, but the intellect.

Meaning is a perspective eyes cannot see.
Artists' squints say: hills do not mean, but *be*.
"*Dieu*" means; without the enlightenment of French
It is a four-lettered pattern on a schoolbench.
"Nature" has no meaning to surface eyes,
There is patterned "isness" only: sunset, sunrise.
Like "history", Nature springs and falls and is gone,
Like a mallow in a field, or a Napoleon.

But seen with contemplation's X-ray gaze,
Nature is a dark fire, a void ablaze
With latent shadows that crackle and spit
Brief sparks, hot seeds and years, each opposite,
Glowing, decaying things that never still.
There is a smouldering in dump and hill.
To those who see in negative one power
Flames through Nature and history and mind every hour.

Its leaping forms take shape, fade, leap, proclaim:
Our universe is the dance of one flame.
The fiery Idea which ferments all forms
Heats them with light and then cools them with storms,
Dissolves old shapes into their formlessness,
Empyrean's spiralling whirlpool of "mess".
A dump, a hill flicker with the same light
Which alchemises souls and cleanses sight.

Like fire and irons, Nature and man candesce
Into one stuff in history's huge furnace.
Angels descend to try their souls, which burn
And, when softened, tempered by fire, return.
Earth's hills are fire by which dull souls are shaped.
Banked up, sea-blown, storm-bellowed, and stone-scraped,
They turn base minds to gold until, destroyed,
Like a burnt dump they sink back to the void.

The most important question of philosophy,
"The meaning of life", has been defined as "me"
By men who say their search for truth *is* truth,
That "meaning" is in the jaw, like a bad wisdom tooth.
But fire transmutes the pattern of hill and heap
To a meaning that transforms an angel's sleep
And hatches golden fire-birds beyond death.
Hills lighten souls, hence angels put on breath.
17 July 1967; revised 10–15 November 1979; 20–22 February, 5 April 1980
Quest theme: glimpse of the One. Set in Nobe, near Kurihama, Japan.

Pear-Ripening House

A gable behind lime trees, a green gate
Which says "Journey's End". In the porch we wait
By the grained door, then go by pebbledash
Garage and shed which have seen small boys bash
Centuries before lunch against Australia,
Past roses (at square leg), a dahlia,
And a splurge of storm-beaten daisies, for
The old pear tree tumbles by the back door.

Now in this room peep – under four black beams,
Sloping ceilings – for the mirror where gleams
The yearning of a reaching out to moons,
Where flit the ghosts of a thousand afternoons.
This, and the black Victorian clock that cowers
Between two prancing horses, measured the hours
Of falling generations, crops of pears,
The sunsets and winters up and down the stairs.

Here floats a battleship on a lino sea;
The day war ended, this was ARP.
Here slides the ghost of a brooding schoolboy,
A fire-warmed clerk reading in lonely joy.

Here flits a brief affair, a wedding eve,
Here steals a separation. The shadows grieve.
Families, funerals.... A Parthenon,
This house is permanent, we are the gone.

Now thirty years are less than the straggly twines
That were honeysuckle. And still the sun shines!
Dressing for church is the green of last spring's
Lilac; young ambitions and hankerings
Are now the floatings of a dandelion clock.
What meaning had they? Is Time just the block
And blackened stump of a hewn sweet chestnut?
Cascading ivy that drowned a summerhut?

Young wants and hankerings have a meaning
To the hard-skinned ego's slow mellowing.
The journey through maturing hours and years
Ends in wrinkling pith and pitying tears.
Cores fill with heavy juices from one flow
Whose sap softens to soul the hard ego.
All life ripens to drowse back to the One:
Fruit and old men fall earthward from the sun.

Ripe pears return pips to the ground, and sow
A next life's genes, patterned on this one. Know
That soul inherits genes from its last spring now
To gush a vision of buds upon a bough.
Leafy lives fill with the sap of all that's green
And are God's mind, whose code is in each gene,
And grow centuries of purpose into fruit
And show: soul ripens so new seeds can shoot.

We journey through a house and garden, shore
Up, improve, order and pass on the law
Of growth and fruit. The long way gives ample
If we soften to the universal

Sun. We journey, pick pears and paint old wood,
Teach sons. Seed is the end of parenthood:
The hard, small pear on the tree on the lawn,
And a ripe pip sprouting in a distant dawn.
4 August 1974; revised 23 March, mid-April, 26 May 1980
Quest theme: glimpse of the One. Set in Loughton, Essex. (*See also* Journey's
End.)

Clouded-Ground Pond

On Strawberry Hill, a break in forest trees.
We park on mud and cross the road in breeze:
A brown pond, yellow lilies. It is cool.
We could stay all day here at the Horseman's Pool,
But it is near the road. We take the track
Past logs and stones in clay, turn into brack-
en, hawthorn, beech. And now, beyond holly,
A pond amid gorse and birch, and a fallen tree.

It has seen the agonies of the seasons:
How fathers died in autumn; the reasons
Young men married, were exiled, lived alone,
And their returns. This pond has also known
The stealings-up through sawing grasshoppers,
And secret comings far from eavesdroppers.
It has sensed small girls crouch in these gnarled roots,
And dreamt of the netting of speckled newts.

A touch of sadness taints the autumn tint.
Like a daughter leaving till spring, a hint
Of absence skips round the deep gravel pit.
Across its quiet eternal stillness flit
The changing shadows of dragonfly time,
Newt and lily months. Sticklebacks stir slime.
This gravel is honey, this cloud is cherry

And the heather and gorse smell of strawberry.

Now time disturbs the eternal with raindrops,
Voices. Ducks clack, dogs splash, a robin hops,
Frogs watch and plop in mud, a rustle rolls
Through the silver birch near where, in spring, tadpoles
Cluster like thorns round submerged sticks. At noon
The shimmering mirror, teeming with June,
Can blaze into nothing, while two hearts bound
As a face drowns in clouds to gasp on: ground.

Four worlds make contact in beauty, and when
The ground reflects a leafy, clouded sky, then
All four dance in the mirror of a pond.
Through layered leaves, the groundless soul beyond
Reflects clouds of spirit, and, in high moments,
The sun's divine air, blinding experience
Of the first source when all say yes and see
The One that shines within layered complexity.

Sadness and joy are one to this still *Tao*
Whose horn of plenty, like a watery bough,
Gushes buds, leaves, petals, and pours faces
From warm clouds into each self and all places.
Six months are one ripple that smoothes away
All sad twigs till the dancing, wintry day
Restores a universe like a green shower:
The *Tao*-self renews the earth, stroking the hour.

As old genes teem new lives, *Tao*'s hidden sun,
Which joined the heights and depths and fused into one
The clouded ground, is now this lily, it
Gushes from clouds, is blown with pure sunlit
Wind, and rooted in mud, yet still, pours All.
The lily on-in water is a call
For Essex men to leave their cars and say "Yes"

To grounded roots in cloud-bordered stillness.
4 August 1974; revised 23 March 1980
Quest theme: glimpse of the One. Set at Strawberry Hill pond, Loughton, Essex.

Two Variations on One Theme

1. Time and Eternity
I held her hand at this Omega gate,
She wanted to paint the yew,
And now the moment has blown away
Like dandelion fluff on blue.

Now, on the High Beach forest church
The passing clouds and years
Are like pattering footsteps in the porch
Or the silence under bedsit tears.

In the city I am scattered like poplar fluff
Blown on the wind of echo,
But here I breathe, with the quiet of stone,
The white light these dead men know.

Oh bury me behind this grave,
At the low black rail,
That all who have suffered and been brave
May pass the yew and wail
For all whom golden hair enslaves,
Till the past is a squirrel's tail;
Then, like the boom in childhood caves,
Oh hear beneath the breeze
The mystery that flows through stars and seas,
Where the autumn bracken waves.

2. The Bride of Time

I

Time held a dandelion that day,
Blew the clock by this yew;
Now the moment has blown away
Like fluff across the blue.

To the porch of this forest church
The passing clouds are years;
Pattering feet feed silver birch
And silence under tears.

In the city men are scattered
Like poplar fluff, and waste;
Moss enfolds all who are shattered:
An embrace that is chaste.

All who are broken and are blown
On the wind of echo
Here breathe in the quiet of stone
The light these dead men know.

Eternity connives at pains
Which mould spirits that sinned,
But trembles when tears ooze from veins,
Consoles like whispering wind.

II

Listen beneath each gentle gust,
Hear the meaning of life;
The silence of the after-dust
Taunts like a flirting wife.

Seek her, she hides yet will be found,
Cooing from leafy den;
This nothingness empty of sound

Pregnantly woos all men.

Nothingness round an empty tree
Is full of rustling love.
A something woos men passionately
Like a cooing ring-dove.

A black-hole womb sucks in dead things
And then thrusts out new grass,
But waves of light and angels' wings
Swirl down where ebbed fins pass.

This black-hole void preserves all souls
Like fish in tides of love.
Expanded souls are like a sea
Sucked out from a foxglove.

Eternity lets all men know
She loves stillness not haste,
Yet preserves tides fish-spirits flow
Before their bodies waste.

III

Eternity blows in the breeze,
Yearning for years and graves.
I Iear her soul pant through stars and seas
Where sighing bracken waves.

O carve two verses on a grave
Before this low black rail,
That all who suffer and are brave
May pass the yew and wail

For all whom golden Time enslaves
Till Time's a squirrel's tail;
That, like a pshsh in childhood caves,

Trembling a leafy veil,

The wind may whisper through these trees
With a soothing shsh of "still",
Drop to a hush, reveal and freeze
A hidden Void of will:

"Eternity blows like a bride,
Billowing springs and graves.
Her meaning foams through star and tide,
Teases where each leaf waves.

Seek her secret beneath the breeze,
Leap this three-stone-stepped stile:
Hear silence surge though years and seas,
Know her mystery, then smile!"
14 November 1972; revised 21–22 June 1980
Quest theme of variations: glimpse of the One. Set at the church of the Holy
Innocents, High Beach, Essex.

13
from *The Wind and the Earth* (1981)

Reddening Leaves

The October leaves have reddened better this year.
You felt unwell as if you had a cold,
As you felt before your last heart attack here.
An evening turn. Gasping for breath, pale, bold,
You sit on a chair, dial, say as if giving birth
"Can you come now," then sit and wait patiently,
Your chest tightening with a weight like earth.
I see my brother lie you on the settee,
An Asian locum comes and prescribes rest
And I want to say "Don't you know she might be dead?"

Next morning your doctor's face tells she has guessed
As she rings a hospital which has a bed.
The call came to leave this life and these eaves
With all the beauty of reddening leaves.
Autumn 1981; revised 1 November 1993

Rosy Cheeks, Blurred Eyes

O sad as I drive through glass and stone
To the hospital where your body lies
Propped up in "Resus", and find you
Somewhere behind red cheeks, blurred eyes.

O sad is the doctor with the moustache,
Loudly you say "This is my son."
And I shake hands with a stranger
And sit and wait while your X-ray is done.

O sad as I ask my 'friend', "How long?"
And he says "A heart attack, two weeks";
O sad as you return with hope,
I see the dark round your rosy cheeks.

Sad as you dictate how I must ring
Violin pupils, bring files that are red.
When three doctors come, I kiss you,
Not knowing you are on your deathbed.
Autumn 1981; revised 1 November 1993

Turnip Lanterns

This sunny day is an ordinary day. You
Seem well, sitting in the window, out of bed,
Writing letters, looking at the great view,

Not realising you will soon be dead;
And I knowing my sister will have been
And posted your letters, drive to the sparkling sea.
And return at nightfall, on Hallowe'en.
My boys light turnip-face lanterns with glee
And carry them down the road. Two Indians stare,
Park outside and ask me to help them change a wheel.
I stand with them on an ordinary day and hear
The telephone ring and the hospital sister appeal,
"You'd better come. There has been irreversible damage."
A turnip grins like a demon in a cage.
Autumn 1981; revised 28 October 1993

Chill Fingers

A sobbing in my heart as I drive through the night.
Will you wait for me, will you still be there? Further east
Dark roads and streetlamps hurtle through my sight.
"Her lungs have filled with water, kidneys ceased."
A thousand memories well up in tears.
"Her heart's worn out like a run-down clock." I am stone.
I tiptoe down the corridor of the years,
And there you lie, eyes closed, in a room of your own,
Oxygen mask on, wired up to a drip, I am awed.
"She surfaced ten minutes ago. She's being brave."
I sit and take her hand strapped to a board
As if I could warm her back from the grave.
Her heart-rate zigzags on the screen, in my hold
Her fingers have the chill of an early cold.
Autumn 1981; revised 28 October 1993

A Shaken Head

Out of a sleep as deep as any grave

You raise your head and the board at your wrist and frown,
And in slow motion as if under water, wave
To tear off your oxygen mask and drown.
I press down her arm, steady her pulse so we be,
Keep watch till the next distress and nurse's call.
With laboured breathing, her chest heaves like the sea,
Each breath echoes like a distant baby's waul.
She opens her eyes. "It's me," I say. She smiles.
"Is there anything I can do?" She shakes her head
Slowly, three times, as if to say "I am miles
Beyond help", and boxes the air, wanting to be dead,
To tear off her oxygen with a limp fist,
Wishing we'd let her sink into the mist.
Autumn 1981; revised 28 October 1993

Moaning Wind

Midnight, all dark and quiet in the hospital room.
I sit and hold her pulse. She whimpers and sighs.
I strain to listen. "Hot," she whispers from gloom.
I feel her frozen hand and arm, then rise.
And go to the window: the lights of Essex, the free.
I slide the double glazing like a veil.
The wind moans like Hallowe'en spirits flee-
-ing before All Hallows souls, rises to a wail,
Then drops. I sit and she gasps "So tired" and pants,
And as the eerie moaning rises and falls
And she throws up a hand and it flops with insouciance,
As something tender sinks, oblivion appals
And I wonder what is life, what death? What made
A mother of this near-lifeless corpse, to fade?
Autumn 1981; revised 28 October 1993

Crack in the Earth

The room is calm, her breath is still, she knows.
All quiet save for the hissing of oxygen.
Nurse listens with her stethoscope, then goes.
Windows are closed, we whisper on quiet again.
Across her we brothers recall seaside holidays,
Inviting her to listen and share, but not to speak.
And now "Oh dear" she moans and as I gaze
Two nurses sit her up and feel her cheek,
Puff up her pillows, change her water-bag,
Remake her bed, say "Would you like a drink?"
Standing at the end of the bed my hand like a gag,
As she sips water I can see as I blink
The crack in the earth through which I crawled, to cry.
O why do we live in order to die?
Autumn 1981; revised 23 August 1993

Heart like a Stopped Clock

A fitful sleep, the phone goes by my bed:
"Mother went just after seven" – like a sting;
A numbness chills my heart. "She woke and said,
'Pills' or 'white powder', and once just 'tired'." I ring
And hear, "I went down the corridor for a drink;
The student was fiddling, when I came back in,
With the oxygen mask. She said, 'I think
You'd better get the staff nurse.' I went. Within
Two minutes she'd gone. She was too tired to fight.
Her heart couldn't stand any more, somehow
It stopped like a clock, she went out like a light."
Again I sit and stare. Where are you now?
Are you in the air? Blank exhaustion, and faint
Relief. All Saints Day, God has a new saint.
Autumn 1981; revised 31 October 1993

A Flickering Candle

A room with two candles, an altar – and you
Lying in your coffin, a veil over your white face.
I stoop and reluctantly force myself to kiss your too
Cold brow, eyes closed, mouth tight, slight frown at space
Over hooked nose, but at peace; white cheeks, white hair.
The blue satin stirs – can it be your breath?
I whisper "It's me, you are dead though in the air,
O God please guide your latest angel through death."
As if answering one candleflame flickered and split.
Was it a wind from the high up window-cage
Which did not flutter the candle nearer it?
Or your spirit rushing out to its next stage,
Having realised you were dead? How sad as I
Kiss your cold forehead through the veil goodbye.
Autumn 1981; revised 31 October 1993

Wind-Chaser

Wind howls around your empty house, earth groans –
All your recitals, like a fallen pine.
Aghast, Beethoven scowls. Your violin moans
Arpeggios down the years, fades with a whine.
No log burns in your hearth now, and the chair
You slumped on is bare, devastated wood.
Seventy years you weathered home despair –
Six children lost, disease and widowhood –
And taught children and pupils to aspire
To what Beethoven heard in a storm-sky,
You chased the wind yet hugged the leaping fire
And turned to ashes with a fearless sigh:
"Death's not the end." Now, numb, I reach for one
Warm ember from beyond, but there is none.
2 January 1982

Beethoven

I sit on the settee you made into your last bed.
I gaze at your violin and blankly stare.
It seems inconceivable that you are dead.
Your room, lacking your lovely smile, is bare.
Beethoven deeply frowns and scowls and groans
Pacing his room with a vibrant, beating hand;
With flowing tails, Beethoven deafly moans,
Listening intently near your music-stand.
The wind howls like inspiration, disciplined
Like a dog whose mistress has gone away;
You taught us to rise to Beethoven, catch the wind;
You went into the earth with a fearless yea.
I strain to catch what Beethoven heard. Now, numb,
I want to echo a chord, and I am dumb.

Autumn 1981; revised 7 November 1993

Earth

I know that I must follow you. I chose
The place where my body will lie under High Beach air
And as I slowly move towards my close,
My appointment with the hooded skeleton there
Among birch trees, I give my life a hid-
-den symmetry and proportion, a straight
And linear beauty. This is not morbid.
It is not the laboured breathing I anticipate,
Lungs filling with water, an echo on each gasp
As life sinks and wind ebbs in a quiet distress,
But rather my rendezvous with the earth, which will clasp
Me, open to me, gape like a foreign mistress.
Thinking about her dark embrace fills me with slime
And a current of energy to make use of time.

Autumn 1981; revised 8 November 1993

79

Violin Sighs

Christmas. We all sit round after our lunch,
Christmas tree lights shine in the lead windows,
Paper chains drape the lights, in hats we munch,
And from the stereo comes your repose,
You playing the violin to Somervell
Thirty years ago. The slow chords float from beyond
From an evening we spent with a baby-sitter (I thrill),
Miss Willis who drowned herself in a Forest pond;
And I see the serious expression in your eyes
As you play for the audience, all now dead,
Like Mrs. Gould, who hosted your breathless sighs,
Knocked down near our school, by a car which crushed her head.
And you live again through your notes, which might have been lost
As I live now through these words, though under frost.
1 November 1993
Quest theme of sequence: death and the One. Set in 54 High Road, Loughton and
Princess Alexandra Hospital, Harlow, Essex.

14
from *A Rainbow in the Spray* (1981–1985)

Cambridge Ode: Against Materialism
(Or: Newton's Enlightenment)

I. Strophe: 300 Years of Darkness
We walk through King's past Fellows' rooms and brood
On one who has died, go out to the lawn which slopes
To the river Cam where punts glide in sad mood,
Survey from the Chapel the academic hopes
Of minds cloistered from Nature in dark rooms.
What is this rational mind, this doubting eye
That probes for alphas, pokes in dusty tombs?
Is it just a squelching brain, waiting to die?

I think of atheists who cooled their heels
Here, of one who walked with Wittgenstein and saw
All mind as how someone behaves or feels,
A reduction to be laid at Forster's door;
Of a red-haired militant who took aim and blew
All art to signs and ciphers, and would attack
The moral meanings that the poets knew
For social dark and Marx, till he got the sack.

Such clever men deny God and contend
Reason, feelings and mind are merely brain;
Bleak Humanists who claim "Death is the end"
And derive all values from material pain.
Materialism! Cambridge has been a shrine
For three centuries of dark Enlightenment,
Divided peering-out in spiritual decline
That makes a culture squint, its belief spent.

Materialists know a world of "massy stones"
In which minds are "reduced to material things" –
Electrons, brain cells – and, solid as bones,
Thoughts and sensations are "brain-functionings",
Observations are trustworthy, "like bald pates",
Images, perceptions, emotions are
"Mere brain-processes" or mere "body-states".
But is the still engine the speeding car?

I go to Trinity where in three green
Years Newton read Descartes' "*cogito*", saw
Mind separate from Nature's "inert machine",
Discovered light, gravity, calculus, and more,
But then turned to Hermetic alchemy,
And matter in mechanistic motion round
The sun, sought to balance contracting gravity
With an expanding force in light – which he never found!

Young minds squint through dark telescopes which block
The expansive force in the sun, measure and frown
The universe to a mechanistic clock
With a spring, coil and winder that will run down.
To seek Enlightenment through a telescope,
What folly of the Age of Analysis! Which knows
Cause and effect, not the start of the chain, not Hope,
The First Cause, which all miss – the Mystic Rose!

And see an Observator measure clock time
Which differs from star time throughout the year;
In the Wren Octagon see Flamsteed climb
A laddered sextant telescope, and peer
And with his mural arc measure the height
Of stars as they pass the meridian
And chart three thousand to raise Newton's spite,
And miss eternity, though a clergyman!

II. Antistrophe: The Reaction Against Materialism
O all who ask, having seen a loved one die,
"Is there a soul, a something more?" – you know
The immaterial spirit has survi-
-ved three centuries of darkness in a candleglow
Which incarnates a rose of Light that blows –
The 'I' behind all leafy thoughts – in a breeze
That lifts a veil to what's beyond, and knows
It is not unlike the wind that blows the trees.

See the brick hearth Wordsworth sat by and pined
For living lakes and peaks where weather seethes,
Or in King's Chapel read "the eternal mind"
Of Brooke the soldier, who knew Nature breathes,
Or go to Orchard House, which now serves teas,
Where Brooke was snapped at breakfast with a sideways glance,
And at one with the pink-white blossom of apple trees
Dream of Newton's apple where the petals dance.

Where Brooke revelled, where the green waters float,
Look over the Vicarage fence, smell the lilac hour,
Then walk back to Mill House, where Whitehead wrote,
For whom Nature was "organism", a power,
A "process" in which we find ourselves, no stone
Which "bifurcates" daylight so the mind's apart.
Green fields, cows, apple blossom all make known
The blossoming of minds and the summer heart.

But now see what an Einstein's science gave:
Green fields billow with a subatomic tide
As matter converts to energy or wave,
One force foams all to a goal Darwin denied
And we now live in a sea of consciousness.
A Counter-Renaissance floods the West's crisis
Where ebbing spirit left a seaweed mess –
Did not Blake, Yeats and Eliot foresee this?

Now the mind is part of this tide of "growth", this white
Blossom that swells and pours from the One through the crown
Into apple trees, with expanding Light –
Not contracting gravity that draws apples down;
Thoughts grow like segments of a thorny rose,
A mind is like a rose whose petals fall
As books, whose perfumed 'I' remains through all that flows
Within the living One that buds and ripens all.

Now the mind that sees is part of what is seen,
One sea of mind-and-matter that shatters where
An observer crests, for though part of the green
Ocean of being, like a wave he looks out at a sphere;
No more can a poet sit and regard the world
As if from outside the sphere, as if a babe
Had drawn the stars on a flat surface, unfurled
The heavens on a planospheric astrolabe.

True mind awakes from measurements and peeps
Where Imagination sits like a fire-bird.
Mind feels the sap rise in the leaves and leaps,
Flies into it, at one with the power that stirred.
Did young Newton dive with a meteorite shower,
Ascend the rainbow bridge up the black sky, or
Climb the World-Tree in one evening hour,
Fly like a falcon through the sun's trap-door?

III. Epode: Newton's Expanding Force of Light
I drive home and ponder, what is the mind?
Are mind and matter dual (Plato, Descartes)?
Do they interact so consciousness is entwined
Between mind and flower? Or are they one mind-star?
Is mind immaterial, is matter its frozen form
As water freezes to ice (like atoms and bones)?
So am I conscious "matter-mind", cold-warm,
Like a Zen stone garden, where mind's a sea of stones?

The moon is up, shift the perspective now
And float through space like an Angel-naut, then stand
On the moon and see our earth hang near the Plough,
Your home and loved ones hidden behind your hand –
A tennis-ball of seas, mountains and cloud;
See it recede with all its human kind,
Then leap in ecstasy, bound, shout out loud
For where's the contracting force that freezes mind?

I recall Newton's search for the expanding force,
The single fermental "levity" that creates,
That would balance gravity, change science's course,
Attract and repel wherever light radiates:
Four-sided rays of light pierce bodies, shoot
Through them, ferment them with growth in each limb and lung –
A harmonising system that would refute
The nightmare he created when he was young.

Working in his Temple Molecular,
Studying alchemy for thirty years, he held
(Or guessed) this creative force was in ether,
"The body of light" where "the spirit is entangled",
That the universe is filled with ether-eal Light
Which, caught like a sperm, ferments and creates
Spirits as well as minds and bodies from night,
Manifests through four worlds into matter's gates.

Ether – Divine Light, Holy Spirit – rapes
Souls, CBR-like *prana* pervades our earth
Through which divine Imagination shapes
All things, brings all matter and mind to birth,
Flows into our *chakra*s, shivers up the spine,
Lights the spirit like a bright candle-flame –
"*Samadhi*" – and makes immortal all who shine,
Divine Enlightenment whence our soul came.

The moon is high, the first stars out, and I
Look at the human who sits by me, alive,
And am not now sick for seeing a loved one die
For I know she is more than matter, and will survive.
I can return to the warmth of the human night
And dream of my Garden where I can see in the sun
How each acorn and oak swells in from Light
In an expanding Nature, in which mind and matter are one.

I have a Pythagoras' Garden in a mystery school
Where I grow qualities my destiny needs,
Contact the hawthorn forces, by whose rule
Being expands the universe among flowers and seeds,
And between two fields railed-in with iron, I stare
At gates in the hedge, where thought and shade are green,
Swing back their rust, and in one field declare
Against Materialism! by my hedgerow screen.
11–12 August 1982; revised 20–21 April 1985

85

Quest theme: image of the One. Set in Cambridge, Grantchester and Oaklands School, Loughton, Essex.

Night Visions in Charlestown
(An Ode)

I. Dark Night
I sit on the harbour wall in dark Charlestown
And gaze up at a trillion budding stars
That flutter as a breeze blows gently down
From the sparkling Plough through Cassiopeia, Mars,
And I ask again "What is space? What is night?
What lives beyond death?" and hear my own echo.
This void which scientists cross with a satellite
Has a branchy fullness behind each glow.

In blackest dark I clasp the granite wall,
The sea laps calmly on a shingle beach.
A soft light dances where boats rise and fall,
The wooded cliffs are dark, and out of reach.
Here I can crane my neck and stretch into the tree
Whose blossoms glow, and there a firefly darts
For it is meteorite time. Here my soul can be
A hawk and fly to its higher, leafy parts.

Galileo, Descartes, Newton, Darwin, Freud
Emptied the air of all intelligence,
Made the cosmos a dark, mechanistic void,
Split body and mind, our species and conscious sense.
But now Einstein, Hubble and Penzias stand
For a cosmos full of atomic waves that sprang
From two hundred billion galaxies that expand
With background radiation from the Big Bang.

Our subatomic physics have destroyed

The Materialist paradigm of common sense.
Now Bohm, our Newton, grapples with the Void
Which unfolds fields that come into form, whence
Order unfolds, like Plato's Idea.
So matter comes from nothing, and so do we,
Implicate Oneness budding into air,
Flecking with petals this speculative Tree.

Our Darwin in morphogenetic fields
Makes Nature live again; a Sheldrake heaves,
The organicist triumphs, the mechanist yields,
One nothing somewhere burgeons into leaves.
Whitehead and Jung affirm, like Einstein and Bohm,
The cosmos is full of waves and infinitely wide.
How can one empty the sea and leave the foam?
Explain the sea-horse yet ignore the tide?

The new philosophy casts all in doubt.
The metaphysical proudly proclaims
That Humanists and Materialists merely shout
Sceptical faiths and lazy, rational claims.
So now I sit like Donne at the dark start
Of a new Baroque Age, when once again
We reach for stars, scrump meanings beyond the heart
Which the fresh soul knows are One, like a daisy-chain.

II. Flight of the Soul to the Coming Age
Now shift perspective. From space our globe's at one,
As the mounting soul floats near the Milky Way;
And whirling round its galaxy, our sun
Is no more a centre than is Christmas Day.
The universe is as vast as the dark round one soul,
Which can travel faster than light to future heights.
Now the dark earth below turns rose-red round one pole
As an Age of global union dawns its delights.

Like old Baroque, I see its sun shine through
Appearance and illusion, the ego's mask,
Dye red the social carnival's ballyhoo
(All dress for parts as on a stage) – its task
To reveal the truth its sunrise mirrors, Light,
And wake souls to a sensual-spiritual face,
To pastoral peace and the bliss of celestial flight
Up this shaman's Tree to a canopy of space.

A Universal Age – Baroque in sunny art!
I think of one who paints peaceful landscapes,
Spanish Teresa's smile, the ecstatic heart,
And as I soar a prophetic vision gapes:
The Baroque started as a Catholic rose –
I see a waving Pope regenerate
All Christendom to rose-blooms, and oppose
New Eastern hordes again at Europe's gate.

I see the nationalistic darkness strewn,
That fragmented, separate time of nightmare toil
Whose reason conquered atoms and the moon,
But lost authority, empire and oil,
Whose states near-perished in an angry shout
As liberal causes broke like a golden bowl,
An Age that reached a dead-end, and cried out
For a replacement vision – for its lost soul.

I see Europeans bring to Charles's town
A sunshine *zeitgeist*, an Age with a new still –
Their dynamic universe and a lit crown
Like a kestrel hovering on a wind of will.
A new Dark Age is as near as a gust of air
As Islamic terror threatens Europe's gate,
But I see their union overcome despair
As they seek an Age of Hope that they'll create.

I see it blow across the sunlit sea,
A Resurgence of the spirit which will unite
Occupied Christendom's soul with its body
As the Communist darkness fractures into Light!
I see Hungarians, Czechs and Poles declare
For Europe's sun! Though intellect wants proof,
Let the mind seize in beauty a grand Idea,
Let starlight trickle through its rational roof!

I see a space telescope, and the first Voyager,
Now map two hundred billion galaxies
And a lumpy universe in which dark matter
Pulls curving sheets to clumps; and show it is
Like Dyson's and will expand forever, a bowl
Less dense than three atoms per cubic metre – or
It would collapse and vanish into a black hole
In twenty billion years, space-time no more.

I see a quantum Void, Non-Being kinked
Beneath the four tidal forces which bind
All that is into one; quantum particles, once linked,
Behave as one, join vacuum, matter and mind.
This sea-like Void contains all that exists
And consciousness – those ripples Being craves –
And God, who enfolds what is like morning mists,
Is immanent in the sea that supports all waves.

I see man who evolved from stardust know
A fifth expanding force behind the known four,
And the solar wind, dust blown by our sun, and go
To where the heliosphere ends at the heliopau-
-se so that when the sun runs out of hydrogen,
Becomes a red giant, swallows the earth
In five billion years' time, shrinks to a white dwarf, then
On a safer star man will hail mankind's new birth.

Now I see men who think they're matter, their minds mere brain,
Who are imprisoned in five senses' skin,
Whose earth is a flightless Hell, endured in vain.
But the highest vision of an Age brings in
The next Age; great art does not reflect the 'id'
Of this dark Age, but creates a Sun-Bird's style,
And when the organs of perception have atrophied,
Few can see an Angel peep through an artist's ecstatic smile.

III. The Soul Aglow
I glow on the harbour wall back in dark Charlestown
Like the light on the mast of the fishing smack at sea,
I glow from a visionary power which has folded down
From an implicate nothing-and-One to what buds in me.
Away from all towns I sit in the dark and bask
As if in the church by the sea on Gunwalloe's shore,
I rediscover ancient powers, and ask
To know the tides that lap at my well-lit door.

So hail the Universal Age of Light!
Whose waves flow in from every time of quest,
New rising of Baroque in its own right,
New sunrise for the Holy Roman West!
I look down from the Age with which I glow
And see that after all our questioning breath
Men will see our search as a Way of Fire and know
The Tree-hung star-rose souls that light dark death.
6 August 1983; revised 17–18 April, 20 May 1990
Quest theme: image of the One. Set in Charlestown, Cornwall.

Crab-Fishing on a Boundless Deep

Go out in a boat in early morning mist
As fishermen put up sail, with a hose thaw bait,
Slice slabs of ray whose smear spreads through the fist,

Leave the Mount for six miles out, where gulls wait,
Where the bay is sheltered from the east-west tides,
Where crabs do not bury themselves in sandy spots –
In this autumn equinox each crustacean hides –
And winch up the first string of dripping crabpots.

In the first pot, put down an arm and throw
Good crabs into a tea-chest; into the sea lots
With soft bellies, or crabs too small – no
Meat: dash and smash diseased shells with black spots,
Bait the trap with fresh ray, pile pots at the back,
When the string is done throw them in; with a knife, and Frank,
Nick each crab between each claw, and hear the crack!
Then drop it, powerless to nip, in the water-tank.

This sea which is so calm can blow up rough
If the wind comes from the south-east and whips
Water to waves, and this calm can be tough
In winter storms that keel and roll big ships:
The waves wash onto deck from the windward side
And fishermen need sea-legs to see-saw
High, stomach above the horizon, then slide
Down into a trough, as the boom becomes an oar.

This sea encompasses each horizon's tide
And we are alone on a dipping, lapping bowl.
This sea, which yields such crabs, on every side
Is an irreducible, inseparable whole,
Ebbing from east to west, pulled by the moon
Till it floods back from the west as the moon goes by.
Its tides make currents from which crabs hide in a dune,
This boundless water is ruled by a ball in the sky.

As so it is on land, that misty cloud.
Trees, earth, stones, rocks, clouds, water, air and fire
Are seen as different as each wave, as proud-

-ly separate, yet all are part of an ocean of mire
As indivisible as the inseparable sea
Whose waves rise, dip, and then return to the One.
I see currents of Existence pulled inexorably,
Till crops flood back again, by the moon and the ripening sun.

Both sea and land first came from air – from night.
As an unseen sun made Being's atmosphere
To unfold a world of currents pulled by Light
So our sun whirled a collapsed cloud to air –
The dust and gas which cooled into planets –
Whose cold froze molten rock, then melted seas
From ice whose water clouds raise as droplets
To fall as rain on hills, so that rivers please.

And now I see this vast expanse of sea
Is like the unconscious mind on which 'I' stand,
Which came from Being's air and sun – psyche.
And 'I' am this boat, my reason, ego and
Identity on a mind both vast and deep,
As wide as the world, as deep as the deepest seam
Of rock, pulled by a moon that is asleep
Which sets blind currents swirling through its dream.

Bait pots with the smear of time and let them slip
In this boundless, endless sea, then have a snack,
Then winch them up. Images claw and drip.
Take out the good ones, throw the soft ones back
And the small ones, smash diseased shells, then seize
Each one that will bite its own legs off with its claws
And nick it so it's lost its nip. Then sneeze
And toss it in a tank of crowded metaphors.

Then you can sell them to be devoured, this haul
Of Being's dripping symbols. Such small works
Epitomise the vast and boundless deep, so trawl

Where thirty fathoms down great beauty lurks,
Hiding in sand when the currents swirl and free
To emerge in slack-water between the tides,
And I'll pray that the Being that made this sea
Can yield its plenty up these dripping sides.
11 August 1983; revised 19–20 April 1985
Quest theme: image of the One. Set in Mount's Bay, Cornwall.

Copped Hall

Turn off the Epping road well before dark.
A clearing leads to ornate gates, there park
And walk through pines past many a bluebell,
Over a hill till the great large-chimneyed shell
Of the third Copped Hall looms up, all overgrown.
Boarded up with corrugated iron and stone.
See the eighteenth-century pediments, as the light fades
Go to the tangled garden, and sunken balustrades.

The first Fitzauchers' hall passed to the Waltham abbots;
Then the King so Mary Tudor took Mass on this spot;
Then to Heneage (a present from his guest, the Queen),
Who rebuilt it and married the mother – hence the *Dream* scene –
Of Shakespeare's WH; to Suckling; Sackville;
Till Conyers built this shell that survived till
It was destroyed when a hair-clip used as fusewire
As the household dressed for church, lit the final fire.

O Edwardian glory – four-columned pediment,
Italian gardens where walled terraces went,
Stairways, iron gates, fountains, figures of stone,
Parterres, summerhouses where caryatids moan,
Conservatory and ballroom, no clop of hoofs,
A grandeur of pavilions and domed roofs –
But now decay, a roofless shell again,

And desolation in moonlight, or this fine rain.

Alas for great halls, like this ancient seat
That stood against time and then crumbled to defeat,
Alas for past grandeurs like this stone shell
In which a style challenged the dark, then fell.
Salute the vision and energy of its prime
Which kept an estate going in a ruinous time.
As civilisation lost dignity, it saw
A way of life perish, now home for the jackdaw.

Now see the ruined foundations of Heneage's hall;
Elizabeth stood with Shakespeare by this wall,
And saw his *Dream* performed in the Long Gallery
At the wedding of his Theseus to Countess Mary.
How overgrown the yew walk now, climb through
To a ruined tower, headless marble statue.
Time, like a clump of nettles, winds about
Past glories and stings the hand that reaches out.

There are two forces – order and chaos.
Out of the forest: a fine house, gain from loss
Yew walks, stone steps, square gardens and statues,
And candles blaze against twilight's night blues
And a play is acted, all are in good cheer,
Then the ground moves and gigantic cracks appear,
The house is abandoned or razed, the people go –
Or else burnt down by fire, and the nettles grow.

But its scenes are retained for ever in these walls,
The voices that laughed linger as history falls,
Those images are present to our mind now,
We see a queen, a wedding, a frown, a bow,
And for all eternity each triumph matures
This Hall copped it from time, but its art endures.
Like Greek – or Roman stone, or art of Copt –

This ruin embodies events, as if time had stopped.
30 May 1984; revised 19 September 1993
Quest theme: image of the One. Set at Copped Hall, Epping, Essex.

Oaklands: Oak Tree

I look out of my study window at
Green trees in chestnut flower, with candles that
Snuggle round a corner of green field, in the sun
On which blackbirds hop and two squirrels run,
Iron railings, where magpies and jays flit,
Where a woodpecker and a bullfinch sit.
Closer, two goldcrests swing near nuts, like thieves
And buttercups tint yellow between green leaves.

A Paradise, this field, where all aglow
I lay a childhood through a life ago,
Near the shady oak puffed at an acorn pipe,
And watched bees hum in clover when all was ripe.
A log, a pond, a horse, and everywhere,
Nature dances in the flower-filled air,
And among butterflies it is easy to see
A human gathers pollen like a bee.

A Paradise of sunlight and skipping feet
As swallows skim and swoop in the summer heat,
As a robin pecks in grass near children's speech,
The green only broken by the copper beech.
Here birds and flowers and insects perch and run,
And humans grow like berries in the ripening sun.
And tiny heads grow large like bud from stalk,
Like the spring bluebells fluttering round the Nature Walk.

It teaches that man is part of Nature's care,
That a boy can become a man without moving from here,

As a bud becomes the fruit of this apple tree,
Or this downy chick the nesting blue tit's glee,
As a grub hatches from pond slime into dragonfly;
This field is full of transformation's cry,
Of bees and birds and boys and girls and showers,
Observe your true nature among these flowers.

See the great oak like a druid tree – divine,
Filling with acorns that will make a *soma* wine,
And give the sight of the gods to all bound by sense,
Who see merely social faces across the fence.
Your true essential nature must include
This Tree of Life that pours spirit as food
Into the world, like acorns into leaves, and feeds
A horn of plenty that pours out souls like seeds.

30 May 1984; revised 14 September 1993

Quest theme: image of the One. Set in the grounds of Oaklands School,
Loughton, Essex.

Greenfield

Greenfield has mountains all round it,
And trees and hills where whitethroats flit
Beyond a bridge, where black-faced sheep
Baa in bracken, and brown cows sleep;
On its green slopes town men can graze
Till social eyes see with soul's gaze
And feel with trodden celandine
Or swoop with swifts, rejoice with pine
Where eagles fly, and midges swarm,
Or fish for trout (wince with hooked worm);
Town men can share country delights
During the days or the light nights,
And climb Ben Nevis when it's clear
Or drive and sample Highland beer

Near where the rose-bay willow-herb
Pinks every wayside's floral kerb,
Visit castles if days are full
Or disappear to Skye or Mull,
Or see glass blown, or flower-press,
Or look for monsters in Loch Ness,
Or draw water from Garry Loch
When burns have dried to bouldered rock;
In Laddie Wood, under Ben See
Deer dart across a path, then flee.
Near mountains wrapped in mist or clouds
Far from all noisy coach-tour crowds –
Green days in sun, red faces glow,
Log fires that blaze when night chills blow;
Bees hum in harebells, and men fill
Quiet, tranquil hours in a deep still.
3, 10 August 1984

Quest theme: image of the One. Set in the Scottish Highlands, near Inverness.

Iona: Silence

By ferry cross blue sea to green cliffs where
The grey Abbey stands out. Once ruined, it
Is now restored. Dolls' houses, we grate on the pier.
I walk from white sands to where whitethroats flit,
Look back at the deep blue of each northern wave,
Then glide on grass through the roofless nunnery
And a pilgrim now, feel where nuns who gave
Up mainland charms went to their church in glee.

The path winds on to St Oran's chapel. There
I sit in twelfth-century quiet – two pews
Under a light, and a carved hearth – then peer
At kings' tombs in the Street of the Dead, and choose
St Columba's shrine, which two wheelhead crosses face.

I sit where his tomb once was in a still like sleep
And feel the energies of this ancient place
And sink into silence on which baa sheep.

Here I am at home, apart from the outside day
And noisy children – or a singing choir;
Here I can sink into deep quiet and pray
Where Christendom began in Columban fire,
Go back to the roots in silence of our free
West. Here in Nature's beauty I feel the hour
A culture put down roots like a growing tree
That feeds our leafy consciousness with still-living power.

I find the grassy site of Columba's cell,
A doorkeeper's small door in Paradise.
By the Abbey altar where Columba fell
I sit, feet chilled on ancient stones to ice,
And feel the earth's power surge up through each limb.
I stand again before St Columba's shrine;
The cross that has a druid's sun as a rim
Throws its shadow through the door in the sunshine.

The shadow of the ringed cross is on my back,
Feet on the earth, there's a tingle up my spine,
I lift my target-ringed heart so I soar till – crack!
Light breaks, prickling my scalp, flooding my shadow line.
The Light is in me, I am in a trance inside,
I surge and feel the heart's love burst in heat,
Full of the Light's orgasmic power, I glide
On a silence that has seen heathen hordes retreat.

Where else in Britain can one know in shrines
Religion is contemplation, not hymns in a church,
The truth Zen masters know in mountain pines?
I know Columba, who killed in his saintly search
Three thousand men (sense and spirit indeed!),

Who sailed thin coracles in a whipping breeze
And stamped a hermit's gaze on the pagan creed
And loved the beauty of these northern seas.
7 August 1984; revised 18 April 1985

Quest theme: experience of the One. Set in Iona, island in the Inner Hebrides, Scotland.

Staffa: Wind

We sit in a small boat which dips in a high
Sea against the tide and, the sun behind, flips wet.
All huddle under oilskins to keep dry
But I, salt on my cheeks, ignore each jet
And think of how I breast a tide each day
And sometimes glimpse a vision as I go.
I look and see a rainbow in the spray,
An arch in the flicking foam of a glimpsed rainbow!

We go to where Fingal lived, hermit of hypes!
Iona's last abbot. We pass the cave
Of basalt rock, it looks like organ-pipes.
The boat stops by rocks, we jump into a wave,
Squelch up island cliffs, tread the green top, edge
Down on black hexagonal columns, so
We reach the great cave, and inch along the ledge
Deep within where the sea waps just below.

Above the boom of the sea as it roars round
I stand where Mendelssohn once stood, and hear
The strange, clear piping of a woodwind sound –
But there is no pipe, it is only the wind and the ear.
The wind I cannot hear plays reed-like round
The ghostly crevices in the rock's rough seas.
I listen for the flow that makes this sound
And think of the quiet wind that makes my lungs wheeze.

My body is, I am rock, cave and deed
And through me blows a wind that makes me pipe
For joy a sound like *"Om"* on a woodwind reed,
That flicks froth that gives my third eye a wipe.
And I am a boat, and at me blows the green-
Filled foam in which I see this windy day
A rainbow that unites seen and unseen,
A rainbow of the mind in corporeal spray.

On my night-sea boatings I can sometimes see
The wind-whipped visions in the water-spray
And then plunge into a deep cave and be
The piping of the wind that sounds all day.
O wonderful wind that gives such sights, please heave –
O wind I cannot see, but can surmise
Through your deeds in my hair and flapping sleeve,
Cleanse my lungs and blow joys to my ears and eyes!

Now I have opened to a diviner wind
Of which the Staffa sound is an echo
And heard a symphony blast, all sound unthinned,
Twelve seconds of swelling *fortissimo*
With a clash of cymbals, awesome roll of drums,
And I have heard the majestic Angels cheer,
But I still think of the Hebridean wind that numbs,
That echoes in rocky pipes the divine Idea.
August 1984; revised 19 April 1985
Quest theme: image of the One. Set in Staffa, island of the Inner Hebrides,
Scotland.

Sea Force

Sea surges onto craggy Cornish cliffs,
Wave after boiling wave pours round the cove;
Flinging up spray on a dozen rocks, it biffs

And dashes where I sit like Olympian Jove.
What energy keeps its breakers rolling in,
Splashing with surf, thundering from the curl?
Scientists say "It is the moon", and grin,
But I know it's a force, a power, a swirl
That crashes in from calm and froths to shore
And rolls each wave that fumes where the foam droops,
And as the wind blows in the low-bent gorse
I know it is itself, a thudding law,
An elemental power where the gull swoops,
The endless boom and roar of life's tidal force.
18 August 1984
Quest theme: image of the One. Set in Gunwalloe Cove, near Porthleven,
Cornwall.

Hauling up Nets in Mount's Bay: Divine Plan

Dawn at six, gulls scream behind every chimneystack.
In June or July, if it's clear they scream all night.
I drive to the quay in a yellow fish van's back
And chug out of harbour in early light
With two Cornish fishermen, to haul nets "well".
St Michael's Mount hangs above mist and clings
As a south-east wind whips up a choppy swell.
A gannet flies by, long neck, beating wings.

We sail towards the glancing sunlight and raise
A five-hundred-yard net, the boat at rest:
Turbot, monkfish – jaws wide, angler-rod – gaze
And are held by the eyes and thrown into a chest;
Crayfish with antennae and flipper tail,
A blue lobster, ray with undermouth plead,
Camouflaged with false eyes, or a pebbled veil;
Crabs, starfish, coral, scallops and seaweed.

The nets burn hands and tear fingers. I tug my
Float side. Fisherman tugs leaded weights and knots
And removes sea-slugs, which squirt a yellow dye,
And huss, which will be bait for tomorrow's pots,
Plaice with orange spots and squinting eyes flay.
Cutting begins: monk are cut in half on
Deck, head and stomach bag thrown, like guts of ray,
Black-backed gulls bark and swoosh for carrion.

And now the nets, piled up, are returned to the sea
And the lead weights wap on the back wood and rail,
Till the last rope is held taut so that the empty
Net is with the tide (across, next haul may fail).
Next week the tide is high "at the moon's will";
Neap, equinox and Michaelmas tides are high
There is more cutting, and fish innards swill
On the deck and send up a nauseous stench as they dry.

There are three more nets like this, and life is cheap.
Crabs have legs pulled off them and shells are cracked.
I stare at the smooth sea thirty fathoms deep
And the life below which is slaughtered, attacked
So men can make a living here down west,
And I look at the mist and cloudy sky and then
Wonder at this brute survival of the fittest.
Did God create creatures to be caught by men?

Says Kingsley: "Everything is intricately
Created. Half an hour from birth a calf can stand.
Bantams an hour old eat obediently,
Their mother grunts 'Yes'/'No' to food, it's planned.
Break a crab's leg here, it will discard the rest.
This monk angles fish in and then snaps its jaw,
Camouflaged like the sea-bed so it can kill and digest.
Everything knows what to do, and follows a law."

So there is a divine plan in which each has a need
And purpose is related to another's locale.
Naked necessity! This lives so that can feed,
And the scavenging black-backed gull devours offal.
Everything exists for its own sake and for the plan;
We, too, can live or be useful fodder.
O wonderful, cruel Creation that gives man
And every creature a hold over another!
23 August 1984; revised 16 January 1994
Quest theme: image of the One. Set in Mount's Bay, Cornwall.

Orpheus
(A Dramatic Monologue)

"Knowledge enormous makes a God of me."
Keats, 'Hyperion', book III, line 113

I, who can sing and play my poetic lyre
So that kestrels lie at my feet and oak-trees dance –
I, with my celebration of the rising sun,
Am condemned to walk among the Maenad hordes
Who scream and rush about among the groves
And look at me askance when my trance comes
And I know they will tear me limb from limb
And swallow me for my power. I serve the soul,
Not their bodies and their erotic touch.
Time was when I was enslaved to one of them,
Till she ran with them and died with a ghastly look.
I followed her down to the underworld
And sang my numbers and she followed me back.
I felt she was not behind. "Do not look back,"
I was told, but turned and looked and she was gone.
And so I still have use for Maenad flesh;
As I stand on the mountain top to greet the sun,
A priest of Apollo, not of Dionysus –

Spirit and sense at one, I watch from my groves,
They taunt me as they run with their wobbling breasts.
I lost my love in Hell, but found my soul,
I was reborn in the death of physical desire,
And am now glad I turned and opened my head
To this other mind which pours words into mine,
But still consort with Maenads for company.
Until my fans tear my head from my trunk
I, Orpheus, am a shaman without a people,
I sing to a crowd that does not understand.
I have knowledge beyond the powers of man
And know I must pay for it with dismemberment
By adoring hordes who think it is what they seek.
13 September 1984 (?); revised 4 October 1993
Quest theme: Way of Loss, finding the soul.

At Porthleven: All One

At Porthleven I walk out on the pier
Whose rail makes it resemble a submarine
The red flag flaps as great waves curl and crash
At the starboard end, splash and wash our deck clean.

Out in the waves, despite the flapping flag
A surfer in a wet suit rides as if in sleet
And goes head first as a great curl crashes down –
I see the board tied to his flying feet.

Up in the sky a plane breaks low, circling
A glider on a thermal above the town
Rises, riding currents like an air-surfer
As the steepling clouds threaten to crash down.

Wind flaps the flag, whips spray and cloud, and I
Feel my heart leap for joy, and in triumph glide

For all is one on land and sea and sky,
And breasts an invisible wind that flows like a tide.
19 August 1985; revised 14 September 1993
Quest theme: image of the One. Set in Porthleven, Cornwall.

15
from *Question Mark over the West* (1986–1988)

Question Mark over the West

After Fernhurst we turn up a wooded lane
And drive across Lord Cowdray's estate till
A three-gabled stable cottage and urbane
Line of chestnut trees, facing a wooded hill,
With honeysuckle over the front door.
I stand near a French drain with my cousin and gaze
Across sheep wire and mounded mole-hills for
Wild life, and potter in the house and praise
The white-wooded windows and life of a squire,
Then sit in one wing at the birch-log fire.

And now at night a deep peace in the dark.
We stroll under a brilliance of stars and swoon –
W of Cassiopeia, Plough like a question mark
Or sickle in the sky – and gaze at the moon,
A cusp on its back above a line of firs
And I smell the sweet smell of the earth, digest
The moisture of woods, this idyllic quiet that spurs,
Wonder at the question mark hanging over the West
Like a sickle set to recapture lost ground
And scythe all Western gains without a sound.

The rabbits have eaten the growing shoots,
A fox escaped the hunt up hill somewhere,
An owl sits on the fence-posts and hoots,

The baaing of new lambs fills the evening air;
A green-topped pheasant sits in the green field,
I hear a gun's report, a squirrel runs
A hare lopes among hedgehogs; may the gun yield
To the bird by the chestnut fencing. The Englishman's
Country life is as old as Chaucer's day,
The sweet smell of the earth has its own way.

Who would think here of a threat to democracy?
This remote lane through a lord's estate, these woods
Keep at bay the bad news on the TV,
The darkness round our sickle moon, our "coulds".
We who threw up computers and man's quest
Through NASA saucers and voyaged through a comet's trail,
We masters of chips and reason master our West
By carrying homes on our backs as we work, like a snail.
I see the Plough fall in a shiver of stars
And a question mark scythe the fir-trees to stubbed bars.

Before the fire and flintlock guns, we recall
Our roots in our grandmother's garden,
The shed we scooted to, where Percy stood
Over the grinding wheel, sharpening knives,
A fir and frogs in a cellar, the sunlit grass,
"Shut this gate" wood with primroses to each knee,
A bomb blast at the gate and shattering glass;
We made the best of forties austerity
Like the arcade minstrel doll with a hand held out
Who popped a coin in his mouth, we never went without.

This Sunday country air at six hundred feet,
Is heady like wine; we walk past suckling lambs
Up the wooded hill to Northpark Copse and greet
A crack down the blue sky to where a feller jams
Felled chestnut trunks as fencing poles in the ground.
I look between the Downs over the Weald

Towards Black Down and the Pilgrim's Way, which wound
From Winchester to Canterbury across field,
And then we plunge down to Verdley Edge and the chime-
-less clock in the woods that measures a timeless time.

The air is scented with spruce and pine tree,
We cross the road, climb to Henley through beech
Where a stream splashes and pours down the hill, and see
Ears of bud, crocus and snowdrops gush and reach,
Sip draught cider at the Duke of Cumberland
By wisteria, wheel and posthorn, gaze and doze
And watch dark trout dart, turn and dash, get canned
By the pool that collects the spring and overflows
To trickle and splash and gush down the road
With a freedom that our land has always showed.

Over cheese and chutney sandwiches we talk
Of how you settled here – but not how, looking at Mars
That first spring day after a five-mile walk
I saw the night fall in a shower of stars;
Of the peace of a family inside their fence,
Each individual free in the scented air
To think and talk and be, without interference –
And to open their hearts to the One in each easy chair,
So that pinpricks of light pierce from on high
Into this one ball, the mind and inner eye.

Lunch is finished. At four a wet mist sweeps
Up the valley, the horse edges towards the poles
On the leaping flames in the farm as the dark creeps.
In this peaceful country life men find their souls
And live in the shadow of the moon-like One
And go to town to work the West's machines
And then return to enjoy the quiet, the sun,
Or go to the ancient Norman church, grow beans,
Graze sheep under the crooked crozier of the Plough,

The shepherd's crook that hangs in the night sky now.

16 March 1986; revised 23–24 October 1993

Quest theme: image of the One. Set in Burchhill Copse and Henley Common, near Haslemere, Surrey.

At Gunwalloe: The Tao

A blue sky, green turf on cliffs, a calm day,
But as I sit on this rocky promontory,
Hair tugging in the wind, feet splashed with spray,
I am the surging of the mighty sea.
Waves curl and hang and dip and explode and boil
And foam on this once molten rocky tower;
A haze hangs over the tranquil bay, I coil,
Am taut with frothing white and swirling power.
The winds, the sea, the earth have motions that
We take for granted till we wake in shock
And gaze at the headlong dash and boom-thud, at
The conflicting stillness of this glistening rock.
Two opposites are reconciled in spray
In the haze on the still blue sky of this surging Cornish day.

16 August 1986

Quest theme: image of the One. Set in Gunwalloe Cove, near Porthleven, Cornwall.

Out on the Alone, or, The Mystery of Being

Up before four, I drive to Newlyn quay
And put out in a boat in a dawnless dark;
The black water's calm, town lights receded as we
Leave social man for the Alone in an ark;
One says, "Twinkling lights in clear air, there be rain."
And now I am timeless on sea, in sky.
Moon, stars, and land-thoughts shrink and fade. Again

I see with a perspective that asks why.

We head for an old wreck and eat below
While dawn breaks. The Lizard is in our wake.
We winch up the first net, a dripping glow
Of pollack, cod with pointed beard, and hake.
The tides flow east and west every six hours,
"We can't fish each other week, there's a spring tide."
Fish drawn from fifty fathoms down – strange powers! –
Get bends and flop on deck, their gills blown wide.

The sun is high, the crew knife out the guts.
One puts a heart in my palm, it still beats,
A little tickling jumping that rebuts
The death that befell a cod in a Lost Land's watery streets.
Now we are over the wreck of a troopship.
The nets have torn. A spur dog gasps for breath,
Gills open and close like shutters at each sip.
A huss has slit eyes that blink up in death.

"The gills take oxygen from water – it's droll,
You can drown a fish if you hold it by his throat."
Inside a hake is another, swallowed whole,
"It's eat or be eaten under this boat."
Two spines on the spur dog can cause a stir:
"They inject poison that can swell an arm;
The only antidote is its liver."
Nature gives and takes the power to harm.

I glimpse a cod's swollen phallus and peep
At a female hole, a slit to a roe-store,
And I marvel at the order of the deep
As far as the eye can see to the line of shore.
The mystery that it is amazes me,
Each creature is unique, in perfect breeds,
Each "Amness" or "Isness" that roams the sea

In mindless tides that give it all it needs.

Existence fills me with a sense of its "Ownness";
All that has Existence differs like all fish
From unified Being, which moves like waves that press
But have no heart to love a mate or wish;
Human beings and creatures perceive the sun,
Being is manifestation of what has sight,
Has form, lives in or shares its inseparable One
That permeates tides of mind, the sea of Light.

Being is the sea in which all Existence breeds,
In which all particular weed and fish subsist;
Being is the universal tide that feeds
All states of manifestation which exist.
Like outer space Non-Being contains all
Non-manifestation as Void, before the Big Bang
From which Being unfolded. The Infinite One Fireball
Flames through Being and Non-Being from which all galaxies sprang.

Embark on the Negative Way and we understand:
Awake from the social dream of the blind ego
And leave Existence like a stretch of sand,
Glimpse Being in the freedom of this tidal flow,
See the Void in negative bob, as from a space-buoy,
Let the Infinite One pour in like infused sun,
And the Way of Fire is now one of detached joy
And its serene gifts make our suffering seem well done.

We return through sea mist, and now fine rain.
People stand on the harbour wall, some old;
I climb a steep ladder, back in time again,
I have returned to the social blindfold
Which shuts out what is real and the Black Head's haze,
Heedless of boats on the Alone of sea and sky
Or men who now see with the Shadow's Fire-won gaze

Who glimpse meaning as Being that does not die.
18 August 1987; revised April 1990
Quest theme: image of the One. Set in Mount's Bay, off Newlyn, Cornwall.

16
from *A Sneeze in the Universe* (1989–1992)

Ben Nevis: Cloud of Unknowing

Ben Nevis's low slopes are hidden in cloud.
Climb from the glen, leave the crowded world below,
Ascend and be wrapped in a thin white shroud,
A mist that seems a cloud unless you know;
Now grope in a fog which obscures every view
Save haversack and rocks, flip-flops on feet,
Till wisps roll clear, and a high ridge shows through,
Awesome where mountains and a pale sun meet.

There are glimpses along the mystic way;
Ascend into a cloud that separates
You from the deep ravine, the towering day,
And in detachment from all loves and hates
Hear rushing water through a lifetime's smoke;
The trembling veil lifts on a rugged scene
But still the peak is obscured. Who can invoke
A summit that remains behind a screen?

Discard illusions, how you thought or dreamed;
People see from the level they are at.
The peak must now be higher than it seemed;
Others toil past on a mountain that seems flat.
Mist lifts on flowering grass above a tarn
And at the turn of the bouldered path, now see
Like a close-up spider on a distant barn:
Fort William, dewy heather, and a honey bee.

111

There is a height of mind like barren rock.
Be mindless now beneath the upper cloud.
Now mop your brow, now pant for breath, take stock
Of a rugged landscape, a wilderness's crowd
Of granite boulders, shingle, screed or shale.
All you with furred-up lungs from city air,
Seek out these snow-stretched heights where all can fail,
Climb pure Ben Nevis and surmount despair!

On the last long haul up to the grey summit
The sun breaks through the all-enfolding haze.
At the top trig point, the cairn, small whitethroats flit,
Now flop and recover your breath and, mindless, gaze
Down a clear precipitous drop to a green glen
Four thousand feet below, and at north-face snow;
Look down upon the awesome ridge again,
Now insignificant and very low.

Each man has his own private mountain slope
Which corresponds to Nevis's winding way;
Having ascended, he understands pure hope,
Having taken on trust the divine ray;
Knows warm air, rising, cools and is condensed
To cloud, which he must bravely go within,
That purges what his wordly self has sensed;
Knowing what he now knows, would he now begin?

Now struggle back down to the world of ills;
Legs wobble three hours down; longing to sit,
Pass dozens bent double, trudging up hills,
Believing the next ridge is the summit.
Now pause and loll at a turf spring and drink
The cool, sweet mountain water that is so clear,
And, stiff as Keats in back leg muscles, think
Of the achievement of rising to sunlit air.
25–26 July 1989

Quest theme: image of the One. Set on Ben Nevis, Scotland.

The Church of Storms

I sit on rocks at Gunwalloe. All's well;
The Church of Storms nestles to the cliff across the bay.
Blue sky; only the sea birds on the swell
Are within reach of me, and this flung-up spray.
The sea's sparkle and rolling in calm;
Barnacles, limpets, mussels and boiling surf.
Another year has curled by under the charm
Of a sunlight-and-stone vision. Near green cliff turf
We squat on timeless rocks and perceive the All
And on a cloudless day, open to a heal-
-ing self-luminous Being that sparkles our brief stay
As phenomenal months roll on to our nightfall,
And know we are immortal in what is Real,
Warm beams melting white foam that measures out our day.
18 August 1989
Quest theme: image of the One. Set in Gunwalloe Cove, near Porthleven, Cornwall.

At Gunwalloe: Light

I sit in the Church of Storms near the beach
In sixth-century peace, I don't pray.
It is deserted, I sit in a pew
Under the red light this hot day.

Outside it is sunny, in here cool.
The door is from a wrecked ship. I respond
To wooden roof beams, quatrefoil squint,
I am back in the Middle Ages and beyond.

I ask the Light for its knowledge.
I feel the surge come into me,
I quiver, and soak up what is given.
I am full this hot day, and can be.
18 August 1989; revised 21 December 1993
Quest theme: image of the One. Set in Gunwalloe Cove, near Porthleven,
Cornwall.

Candleflame Storm

A power cut throughout the village, the darkness shocks
The wind howls, rain lashes the windows,
White surf tears in and foams on the dark rocks.
I huddle without heat where the candle glows,
A roar in the empty chimney, blow on my hand
And sit among the shadows like the Georgian poor
When this cottage was built. The wind that has banned
The TV's noise now rattles the front door
And all is stillness beneath the wind and rain
This December night, and I am still within
And hear the silence beneath the furious storm.
How good that still Eternity should strain
To make us gaze at the candleflame in our skin,
So that we who cower in dark can know Its form.
19 December 1989
Quest theme: image of the One. Set in Charlestown, near St Austell, Cornwall.

A Man of Winds and Tides

A Cornish sea captain with a grizzled beard,
And weather lines round his elemental gaze.
From the cliff he gazes at where the horizon's cleared
And slowly says, "There be rain later, and haze."
He knows the weathers and can steer by stars:

"Orion's three-starred belt, there: his top knee's Rigel.
His bottom shoulder's Betelgeuse – not Mars.
See the triangle down to bright Sirius – he's well –
And up to Procyon. See Regulus, and Pollux too.
Up to Aldebaran, Algol and Capella.
To the Pleiades, and Cassiopeia's 'W',
And the Plough's two pointers to Polaris, the Pole Star."
He lives among winds and tides and does not know
Quick town-men envy his being, which is slow.
20 December 1989

Quest theme: image of the One. Set in Charlestown, near St Austell, Cornwall.

Being as a Ripple or Two

Green hills, an exploding sea and veiling of spume
Which hangs like mist across the sunlit bay.
As the energy froths, a perpetual roar and boom;
Foam leaps halfway up the cliffs. I turn away
And enter the small stone church, stepping over a snail,
And linger under arches from another Age,
And on the silence, like a distant gale
I can hear the roaring where seas boil and rage.
And now, sitting in the graveyard, quite alone
I watch black petrels wheel and mew and soar
And gaze on rocks as old as time. From the stone
Wall a wren hops and pecks near the church door,
And I look out on Being as the dead must do
And see its fountaining energy as a ripple or two.
15 February 1990

Quest theme: image of the One. Set in Gunwalloe Cove, near Porthleven,
Cornwall.

Skylark and Foam

As that skylark soars twittering towards the sun,
I, in this church on a curved foam-touched shore,
Soar sunwards. I sit between pillar and steps, shun
The world in a seat under the oak roof, withdraw,
Still body and mind till my spirit sees image-
-s break in my soul below like the foam in the bay:
Strange architectural sights from a bygone Age.
The waves break gently, throwing up Being's spray
On many different rocks outside. I correspond:
My soul is under a tide of Light within;
This sea of Being which comes in from the beyond
Like cosmic radiation, penetrates my skin.
Where shore meets sea, there I am washed, and swoon,
Till the skylark plummets down into a dune.
12 April 1990
Quest theme: image of the One. Set in Gunwalloe Cove, near Porthleven,
Cornwall.

Ode: Spider's Web: Our Local Universe in an Infinite Whole

"Does aught befall you? It is good.
For it is part of the great web of all creation"
Marcus Aurelius

I. The Vastness of the Universe
I walk on the dark stones of the harbour wall
And gaze at the choppy foam round two dark rocks
(Gull Island and crag) and the swirling sea recall-
-s the stone swirls where an infinite Zen truth shocks.
The bobbing boats, the harbour lamps that dip
And land are reflected in the endless deep;
The last clouds blow inland, stars wink and drip
And soon the universe will awake from sleep.

The universe is like a spider's web from here
And stars tremble like drops of suspended dew
On invisible threads that engulf the black hemisphere
And hang like globules under the spider's view.
I gaze at the spiral that holds all in place
And marvel at God the Spider who spans its thread,
At the millions of stars that throb and drip down space,
As the web vibrates with a breath beyond the dead.

There are more stars than grains of sand in this bay.
The most luminous object emits energy an Immense
Thirty thousand times as powerful as the Milky Way,
Is sixteen thousand million light years hence;
And can be a young or proto-galaxy, just
Eighty-three per cent back to the Big Bang, or can be
A bright quasar embedded in a cloud of dust –
The most luminous star is too dim for us to see.

I think of Bohm who knew Einstein, who knows
The vastness of the visible universe
From equations, who greeted me, then close-
-d his eyes, then said with Einstein's mildness, terse-
-ly: "You can't have a vision of the Whole, it's infinite;
Our universe is a local event, a wave
In a sea of cosmic energy that's implicate.
There's something cosmic behind how atoms behave.

"The universe emerged from the vacuum,
The quantum void which is infinite in space.
Our vision's finite, a view from a room;
You can't measure the immaterial from our time and place.
The Big Bang is limited in importance, as is
Cosmic background radiation, its residue;
I see no unification of the four forces,
There are no prospects for such an optimistic view."

The unified sea foams round two rocks, the earth.
I think of bearded Gunzig with curly hair
Who told how an unstable vacuum must give birth
To a stable universe with an atmosphere:
A quantum vacuum expels pairs of flee-
-ting virtual particles, which return without trace;
Some are transformed into real ones by energy
From the geometric background of the curvature of space.

"A vacuum is unstable and Nature prefers to give
A stable state to a vibrating trembling, so
The energy linked to curvature is negative gravitational
And combines with positive mass to give zero.
It costs no energy to make a universe. But then
The price is entropy, or running down."
So something comes from nothing. Is there anything hidden
Behind physics? "It is not my field," he says with a frown.

I recall the view of a bald Dutch Professor.
As I sat in All Souls he said, "We are born to die.
Between, humans make society. An 'I' before
Birth? After death? Fantastical! How? Why?"
The Void's Fire is received in human consciousness
And passed to society; not created by mind.
The human mind that lives in this vast web's "mess",
Did it create these millions of stars that are blind?

II. The Oneness between the Firelit Soul and the Universe
The mind is the measure of each blind star.
I recall Winchester Cathedral, and the bones
Of seven kings in mortuary chests, and going afar
In the Venerable Chapel, feet on ancient stones,
I said to the Fire, "If you are there, inspire
What Hawking and Gunzig claim is the air,
Come into me," and a terrific surge of Fire
Poured into me, nearly knocking me off my chair.

If the infinite Whole manifests from Fire
Which we receive in our finite brains and see
Then there is within us that which is infinite desire,
Takes part in it, is of the infinite Whole and free.
And as in a hologram the whole's in the part
So in our galaxy the infinite whole can be found,
So in my mind roll the infinite wastes of the heart
Of a bright, eternal vastness that has no ground.

To some there are thirteen signs in the zodiac sky,
One each full moon, for each twenty-eight days,
And Arachne is between Taurus and Gemini,
The spider who spins a thread into a web and sways.
Go within your mind and ascend the universe
And climb the spider's web within the soul,
Look down on the star Arachne, and traverse
And bathe in its translucent glow, and see the Whole!

The spider that creates also destroys,
Weaving a web from nothing, killing its prey.
This spiral net of stars that traps hangs joys,
A web of beauty across the phenomenal day.
The spiral universe converges at the Pole
Where lurks the transcendent creator Godhead.
Each life is entrammelled in the web of the Whole,
A different shape caught up in the same thread.

Look down and see earth like a round baseball,
The size of a fist held at arm's length, so sublime,
So fragile and finite. Look down and fall
Towards dry, cold Mars. Now travel back in time.
From here the web looks like a ripe fruit tree.
As in a car wash, globes on a windscreen band
When driven by air, then rush apart, now see
The Big Bang's blast, our corner of the universe expand.

Now forward, see Mars' colonisers toil
To give the Red Planet breathable air,
With orbiting mirrors heat the red soil
Till water flows and vegetables grow there,
As the ice melts plant life and forests grow;
And see the pink sky turn a brilliant blue.
The cold planet now has farms, and towns. Oh,
I see a New World for Voyagers with derring-do!

This vast universe, does our consciousness
Fit in or is it just an accident?
Two hundred billion galaxies, each with no less
Than two hundred billion stars – if any less extent
Then the Whole would not have existed a long enough span
For man to exist. The Anthropic Principle!
Astronomy, physics, biology, all centre man
In the planets, electrons, double helix of the web's spiral.

III. The Oneness between Soul and Universe and the
    Soul's Vision of the Infinite Whole
All is interrelated, corresponds perfectly.
Can consciousness be the exception? Is all a mess?
We are the outcome of the universe's symmetry.
Within one law: matter, body, consciousness.
The Fire behind Nature and history shines
Into and through all things, and holds for evermore
Galaxies, matter, bodies, minds, and entwines
Everything in the universe within one whole web-like law.

Like God, the poet sits in a spider's web
As large as the universe, spun from his head,
Waiting for images to float on the winds from the ebb-
-ing beyond and tremble his hung silk thread,
Making him scamper to his winged catch, run round
It, roll it up in a ball, wind it and climb.
He knows a poem is an image caught and bound

In a twisted net of fibrous words that rhyme.

And, hung in the night among stars that drift and flit,
He sees the earth fly into his webbed sunrise
And winds it round with silk and fixes it
In a great web of being, hung with other flies.
And now from the centre of this galaxy,
Woven in light from deepest space, like some
Marble, he holds the earth – white cloud, blue sea –
The earth between his forefinger and thumb!

Gaze at the outward burst of web-hung things
And sense the infinite Fire which moves beyond
And manifests into subatomic strings
And, inseparable from the whole, swirls round this "pond"
's two rocks in this local corner of England,
And with my ego and my infinite soul (and Bohm)
I see the dark whole and local froth, and
Symbolise the infinite in Gull Island's foam.

And I who can see the oneness of sea and sky,
Who can see the Being behind this phenomenal earth,
See also, with X-ray vision, the dark Void, high
Up where atoms unfold from nothing in an endless birth,
Where infinity swells to finite form, like the sun,
Where eternity enters time like a moving sea.
And as I close my eyes and gaze at the One
I hear the wash on rocks of cosmic energy.

A vision of the whole can be a partial one,
A symbol's fragment of wholeness in a place,
And it can be an inner glimpse of a sun,
Of a Fire like moonlight in infinite timeless space.
So I sit on the wall near dark Charlestown and ga-
-ze on a loving mind that is fifty fathoms deep
And stretches far beyond the Milky Way

And spy with a finite eye on the infinite whole asleep.
2 April–July, 16 August 1991; revised 27 May 1992
Quest theme: image of the One. Set in Charlestown, near St Austell, Cornwall.

At Polruan Blockhouse: Soul and Body

Like a guard in this ruined blockhouse,
Looking out across the Renaissance bay,
Winching up a chain to stop all boats
And collect their tribute, and their pay –

Like a guard in these ruined stones,
Wandering from window to hearth,
Which he shares with the keen west wind
And the honeysuckle up the path,

I, my soul, in this ruined flesh
Like this butterfly, this herring gull,
Beating in these ruined bones and walls
Flutter in my imprisoning skull.

O flying soul, you are happiest
Out near this calm wide, sparkling sea
And long to escape this prison and know
The oneness known by a bumble-bee.
20 July 1991
Quest theme: soul knowing the One. Set in Polruan, near Fowey, Cornwall.

The One and the Many

"The One remains, the many change and pass....
Life, like a dome of many coloured glass
Stains the white radiance of Eternity."
Shelley

A late night walk. The moon is full
Beside the cliff with a sloping side
That joins the dark sea and curves back
Where its black shadows lap with the tide.

Transfixed on the pier, I stare, I stare
As the moon-like One manifests through space
Into the Being of a silhouette
And its reflection in existing place.

Transfixed on the pier, I gaze, I gaze
At a moonlit void where – mystery! – lurks
A sloping Being and its shadow,
I gaze at how the universe works.

A late night walk, and a spring in my step
As I tread the granite back to my home
And sit agog that the One has shone
Into sloping things that have stained it with foam.

9 August 1992

Quest theme: image of the One. Set in Charlestown, near St Austell, Cornwall.

17

from *Sojourns* (1993)

The Laughing Philosopher

I

Walk up a tree-lined avenue to a gate
And an orange Quattrocento fortress with great
Curved walls and barred windows and a high walk
Where sentries and lookouts stood in idle talk,
Go into an open orange courtyard
Whose arches echo with birdsong and the voice of a guard,
And the summer villa of Cosimo Medici,

Patron to the arts and philosophy.

Here Cosimo held court, limping with gout
Into a long upper room with a ruler's pout
And received the Platonist scholar Ficino
And his Academy, when they all ro-
-de through heat and dust from his small house on a near hill
To report on translations done at the Prince's will.
It is now a nuns' hospital, but the past chimes:
Stand in this place and feel those ancient times.

Here perhaps the Greek Gemistos came the May
He inspired the Pope's banker to revive Pla-
-to's Academy when his doctor's son was six
And had not left medicine for Greek and candlewicks.
Scholars say the Renaissance began to show
When the Ottomans sacked Byzantium's libraries so
Greek books came west, but in fact it was born, we find,
When Ficino became a doctor of the mind.

Here severe Ficino stood and read and ate
As proud Medici sat in pomp and state
Like a Maecenas filled with a divine desire,
And passionately spoke of Plato, Christ and Fire
As like Clement of Alexandria he reconciled
Pagan and Christian teachings, and never smiled
As he brought about a shift in the Christian west,
Brought in a New People with a new quest.

From here he taught Botticelli to transmute
Carnal, erotic love to its divine root:
Sad Venus and the Humanist ideal
Not as mournful shadowy form, but Platonic real.
From here he replaced the halo with a bloom
And expressed Platonic beauty in a womb
And, religious Humanist who believed in Fire,

Secularized the virtuous human with desire.

From here he became a priest and challenged this feat.
Sometimes Cosimo left him to go on retreat
To the Dominican monastery of San Marco
And walk near his cell and watch Angelico.
The Renaissance birth of Venus dethroned Mary.
Now I see Cosimo die in this Villa Careggi.
Ficino reads Plato as he lies sublime
And sighs, "Ah, I have wasted so much time."

II

Philosopher and physician, astrologer, priest,
First and last of the unified men, creased
Ficino saw learning as an aspect of one,
Of incorporeal light behind the sun
Which spread from God, the angelic world, to soul,
Nature and earthly matter, and, being whole,
Paganised the Church for a universal grace –
In Maria Novella, look at his crumpled face.

Downstairs I hear how Gemistos presuppose-
-d the Fire of Heracleitus, under old frescoes –
Temples, swans, gardens, villas and ships, one wrecked –
The Renaissance round my head, and now reflect:
Today a new Renaissance is in the air
As we recover the unity of being where
The mystics and Ficino lived, and see
The universe and soul as one energy.

Last week I sat in my Academy's gloom,
A dozen philosophers in an Uxbridge room,
And spoke to a modern group about the Fire,
To philosophers who know the real and aspire
To change the *zeitgeist* back to the unified One
That warms each virtuous soul like a sun,

Not back to the atoms of Democritus –
One graceful reality licking down to us.

Alchemists see changes souls undergo:
Blackening (Dark Night) in an underworld of No;
Whitening, *coniunctio* of mind and soul in Light;
Yellowing, ripening of imagination's insight;
And reddening, *unus mundus* of body and soul
And cosmic consciousness, oneness of the whole.
Ficino and I both died from the world and 'me'
To be reborn in our souls and unity.

III

Now in this garden look back at the walls that tease,
The mauve wisteria, small bowled orange trees
Where images hang, touch a Greek goddess, then prowl
To where two boys ride a tortoise and an owl,
And the fountain pool where red fish rise and blow,
Listen to birds, pick and taste leaves and glow
With the smell of scents, all senses like a choir –
See pink chestnut candles like a mind on Fire!

In our Universalist time, when the Fire and
Incorporeal Light blaze across our land,
My books echo Ficino and reconcile
Western and Eastern Fires in a new style.
I must not be a preacher in a church
Or lecture on the Fire as a pentecostal search
As my six works show the universe's law
In an interlocking picture, like a child's jigsaw.

In a picture in Milan by Bramante
Two philosophers stand by a globe, one sad, one gay.
Democritus knew atoms before Rutherford's ball,
He laughs because men believe transience is all.
Heracleitus weeps as all believe "everything flows"

And no one sees the Fire – which he himself knows,
And so should smile. Sad Ficino, laugh and inspire:
For all is flux, but underneath – the Fire!
1–12 May 1993
Quest theme: image of the One beyond transience. Set in Villa Medicea or Villa
Careggi, Florence, Italy.

18
from *Classical Odes* (1994–2005)

By the Arno, Pisa

I take a bus to the brown wide Arno
And walk along the waterfront to where
Shelley lived near the large *ponte* and wrote
'Adonais' about Keats, in despair.
I wander via the tiny Templar church
Across the river to the other side,
See where Byron lived in Toscanelli
And see them meeting after poor Keats died.

Shelley suffered in Italy. He brought
Allegra to Byron's Venetian home.
Byron gave him and Mary a villa
Where their baby girl Clara died. In Rome
William died as at Caracalla's Baths
Shelley wrote part of *Prometheus Unbound*.
They returned here with a new son, Percy –
Allegra died and then Shelley was drowned.

I stare at a Roman wall, sense the ghosts
Of Shelley and Byron, and think of Pound
Who wrote *Pisan Cantos* while detained here,
Welcomed me at his mountain home I'd found
In Rapallo twenty-three years ago,

Urged me to make a start on my epic
Which I'd outlined to him: "If you can see
It, you can do it. Seeing it's the trick,

It's half the battle. It is like making
A table. It does not matter which leg
You start with so long as the table holds
Up. T. E. Hulme said to me" (one leg's peg)
"'All that a writer has to say will go
On half a side of a postcard; the rest
Is application, elaboration.'
Have you got that application – and zest?"

I gaze at the Arno. Red and orange
Houses shimmer in the water at me
In the warm afternoon. A high feeling
Elevates me, I sense my destiny –
To write an epic like Virgil's, Dante's,
Homer's and Pound's. Like Virgil I have shirked
A huge task for twenty years: to pattern
The war in verse, dark Hitler's fall reworked.

I must begin by the Arno's mirror
Which Dante knew in Florence, and Pound knew.
I must bring together the Fire, history,
Cosmology, science in a new view,
All disciplines patterned in one verse work
With the novel eye of Galileo,
Who had a new view of the universe
Here in Pisa by this same brown Arno.

I shudder for my achievements so far
Are but preludes to this impending task,
A clearing of my head for what's to come.
I must portray, wearing a tragic mask,
Universalist world history in verse,

The height of goodness and depth of evil,
The struggle between Christ's and Lucifer's
New World Orders; vision, heroic will.

Elevated pure feeling wells up, wets
My eyes. I tremble with intensity
At the enormity of the huge task,
At what I have to do to embody
All Western civilization's culture
In one twelve-book poem. I quiver in
The exalted vision of perfection
And my inadequacy to begin.

I sit in a bar on the Lung'Arno
Mediceo, near where Byron lived two years,
Sipping a glass of tea, for ten minutes
On and off my eyes mist over with tears
Which I blink back, now knowing deep within
The next phase in my work. I've had, I grasp,
The equivalent of when Dante saw
Beatrice by the Arno, felt his task's clasp.

I sit by the Arno and sense a call,
Know with awed certainty what I must do,
And after my epic I see I must
Make the Italian and Greek pasts run through
My verse, as Shelley and Byron once did.
I take a taxi to my luggage, lurk,
Sit on a fountainside waiting to go
Back to England, knowing my future work.

O Pisa, besides the Arno's mirror
That reflects coloured houses that shimmer
I've found a spring of creative feeling,
Imagination wide as a river
That can reflect the world and universe,

And I know the roots of our Europe grew
In the Greek-Roman and Renaissance worlds
With certainty Shelley, Byron, Pound knew.
Conceived 3 May 1993; written 21 August 2001; revised 20–21 July 2002
Quest theme: image of the One. Set in Pisa, Italy.

19

from *Overlord* (1994–1996)

[book 2, lines 2187–2241, the two forces in the universe]

The universe is governed by two laws
Which are opposing forces held at one:
The expanding Fire and speed Hubble found
That counteracts gravity as Newton
Thought, and spits out galaxies like bonfire
Sparks; and the contracting Darkness and wreck
Of decaying Dark Matter and black holes,
Destruction and evil – like the black hole
V404 Cygni six thousand light
Years away which is swallowing a star
Nearly as large as our sun, whose weight it
Exceeds twelve times, and is so massive that
Nothing, not even light, can escape from
Its gravitational pull, and devours
Any thing that comes close enough to it,
And leaves no trace of what it has eaten.
Each force has its own law, and each one has
Its time. Look at expansion, and the age
Of the universe is sixteen billion
Years; (and the most distant galaxy known
As 8C 1435 + 63
Is fifteen billion light years away, and
Contains stars that were old when their light set
Out); look at decomposition – the stars –

And the age is eight to twelve billion years.
Time is many sequences of events.
Out of white holes (one near this earth) pours stuff,
As from a Roman *cornucopia*;
Into black holes like drains stuff disappears.
Both forces are in balance, birth and death,
New and old, light and dark, plus and minus.
God the zero Fire holds all opposites:
Zero equals plus A plus minus A
$(0 = (+A) + (-A))$,
The universe both expands and contracts
And thrives on the tension between forces,
The balance Newton sought and Einstein found
(The cosmological constant), and then
Doubted, the tension that balanced Hitler
And brave Stauffenberg, who was cheered in Heaven;
Nazi tyranny and brave Eisenhower
Despairing at Montgomery's slowness,
Moving his headquarters to Normandy.
God is Cosmic Christ plus Cosmic Satan.
God, Fire, contains what reason separates,
Making one two, truth into illusion,
Reducing the whole to conflicting parts,
Laws, forces, Heaven, Hell, Christ and Satan,
The sea to eddying currents and tides,
A multiplicity of opposites
Which intuition restores to a whole,
Seeing all division is of the One.
God, Fire, shows difference is deception
And unites and blends the Darkness and Light.
God, Fire, includes the Darkness and the Light.
Quest theme: image of the one universe.

[book 5, lines 3489–3511, why did God allow Auschwitz?]

God, Fire, from which all forms at first emerged,

131

Transcendent One and immanent Light, is
Like both the silence in a timeless cave,
Eternal stillness in whose sea we are
Like white wave-crests, with which we are at one,
As in Capri's Blue Grotto's blue-white light,
And the loving tide in which we all live,
With crabs and shrimps, starfish and all creatures;
The current that carries us through our time,
Gently pushing us to warmer waters,
Sad that some men are predators who hunt
And devour their brothers in great numbers
As sharks kill shoals whose souls dwell with the Light,
But, ever moving history forwards, glad
That men as brave as Dorebus resist,
Fight back for universal peace and right.
"Why did God allow Auschwitz?" you ask. So
Evil energy could be neutralised
And souls made pure by suffering could crowd
Into Heaven's tiered amphitheatre and,
Released from the fierce gladiator's sword,
By their endurance chord Europe's discord,
Express hidden harmony in one choir.
Quest theme: agonies of Auschwitz reconciled within harmony of the One.

[book 6, lines 1–56, 117–136, invocation to Homer: Ithaca and Troy]

O Homer, you who, though blind, wrote the first
Western literature about your hero
Odysseus, King of Ithaca, who won
The ten-year long Trojan War by a trick
And who then journeyed home for ten more years
And killed the usurpers in his palace,
So many places claim your birth – besides
Ithaca, Smyrna (now Izmir), Chios,
Colophon, Pylos, Argos and Athens,
Salamina in Cyprus, Rhodes, Kymi –

From 800 to 550 BC,
And learned men assert that you were just
An oral tradition, not a person.
Yet I intuitively sense that you
Grew up here in Ithaca in the eighth
Century and absorbed your local legend,
Odysseus, and detailed geography
Of the island you first knew as a boy:
The Cave of the Nymphs with a round hole in
Its roof for nymphs and gods to enter, and
Just a slit for mortals, where Odysseus
Hid Alcinous' treasure; and the Hill
Of Hermes, Pitikali, where his great
Palace was, from which three seas can be seen –
The Ionian, Tyrrhenian and Gulf
Of Patras – by an ancient round stone church,
And, across Polis Bay, Asteris isle,
Daskalio, where the suitors sought to lure
Telemachos. I feel you visited
Troy for local detail and sat where I
Sit now on this hot July afternoon,
Wind in my hair from the Scamander plain
Where Achilles once camped and heroes fought,
By the altar of Alexander's late
Temple of Athena, and looked back as
I do at the east gate where the Greek Horse
Was brought to the approach and dragged inside,
Barely big enough for a few men to
Hide in, then up the steps to the royal
Palace where it stood as a wheeled trophy;
And, before you went blind, while you could see,
Gazed as I do now back at house VI E,
Paris's well-walled house ten yards down steps,
Where Helen lived, the prize for whom all fought.
From this vantage point, then a stone terrace,
Where I sit now, your Helen sat and watched –

Content with Paris, flattered and troubled
Just ten yards up the steps from her front door –
A thousand ships gathering to rescue
Their kidnapped queen and take her back to Greece.
You too wanted to show war is absurd,
That thousands died so Helen could go home,
A war that Zeus wanted so he could curb
The overpopulation of the earth;
You admired their exploits and bravery,
Not the futility of ten years' war....

O Homer, you who were so wise on war
And understood its folly, how brute force
By one side is matched by its opponents,
Whose stance was neutral between Greece and Troy,
And who understood how deviousness
Wins wars, as I sit on a stone and gaze
Across the plain to the distant blue sea,
My tongue parched at the end of a hot day,
July sun warm on my left cheek, the wind
Whipping from the sea and drying my sweat,
Sparrows chirping, cicadas sh-sh-ing,
A tractor cutting an early harvest,
And wonder how the Greeks found wood from dry
Olive trees and made a Trojan Horse on
That dusty plain, and see your Troy VI and
VII A, blanking out the rest, and dream –
Help me now that I tell of Hitler's trick,
How he deviously hid an attack
Behind a feigned defensive *"Wacht am Rhein"*
To stun the Allies into surrender.

Quest theme: image of oneness of history, influence of Homer. Set in Ithaca,
Greece and Troy, Hisarlik, Turkey.

[book 12, lines 4544–4571, poet as shaman who catches the One]

The true poet is a shaman, who leaves
His unspiritual environment, his
Sick society, and in solitude
And darkness in his cave, in a deep trance,
A quester into unknown powers within,
Contacts and channels an unconscious force,
Spirits of ancestors and animals,
Strange images that fill with fear and awe,
And a Light that bestows a new knowledge,
Truth that now flows through him, a Muse's spring,
And returns to his fellows estranged like
A hermit with healing powers, and stands on
A stage before a curious audience
And speaks from holy power in images
That catch the One, and cures his fragmented
Culture and civilisation, his sick
Materialistic, compartmentalised
Society, with gleams from the beyond,
Gives understanding of complexity,
Brings order to the chaos of modern
Life, Spirit to everyday pettiness,
Meaning and pattern to what seemed obscure,
And then, avoiding contamination
From impure, social minds, he retreats back
To his solitude and again sits by
The spring of Truth that runs through his green soul.
A poet heals society with Truth,
With Spirit that washes through unclean minds.
Quest theme: images of the One.

[book 12, lines 4843–4854, the One balances opposites]

God saw no dualism, just the One
Whose positive and negative forces,

Plus and minus charges, both Light and Dark,
Like day and night, and life and death, both form
A Unity comprising contraries,
Extreme white-black ends of a grey spectrum,
Pairs that fire through necessary conflict,
Apparent opposites which complement
The One Whole that God is, and God was pleased
That contradictions were back in balance,
Reconciled within the cosmic design,
With Light just uppermost as it should be.
Quest theme: image of the One.

20

from *Classical Odes* (1994–2005)

At Troy VI

I enter by the east tower and am by
Troy VI, which Turkish archaeologists say
Was Priam's city: yellow blocks. I walk
Past the east wall and reach the east gateway
Where hung the Dardanian Gates no Trojan
Returned to when Achilles stalked; explore
The small rooms of Troy VIIA where US
Archaeologists find the Trojan War.

I pass the Troy VI *megaron* houses
And look at the north-east tower and cistern;
And Temple of Athena – victors' god –
Where Xerxes slaughtered a thousand oxen
Before his invasion of Greece; Troy I's
City gate and wall; the ramp of Troy II
Where Schliemann found Helen's treasure and thought
It was the city where Achilles slew.

I pass the VIM building, perhaps once
The royal palace in view of its sprawl;
And a sacred precinct to Cybele;
And walk back along Troy VI's block wall
To the Great Tower, look through the Scaean Gates,
See their sewage channel; house 630;
The pillared house; where old men sat and watched
Helen stroll along the rampart deftly.

I return full circle to the east gate
Where the Trojan Horse was left and wheeled in;
It's narrow so the Horse was long, not wide –
Held six to open the doors from within.
This gate was nearest to Scamander's plain,
Had no sewage channel to catch Horse wheels.
The Greeks would have left the Horse on this sand.
I see them tug with ropes, lean, dig in heels.

I reach VIC and VIE, the houses
Of Paris and Helen, perhaps. I climb
Ten steps and sit on Athena's altar,
Peer for distant blue sea, Greek sails – springtime!
Round here was surely Helen's high terrace
From where she saw the Greek army arrive,
The thousand ships anchor, men disembark
And cross the dusty Scamander, and drive.

I sit in the hot sun, pad on my knee,
Scribble my impressions – while my neck burns.
The cooling wind across the plain tempers
The heat, dries my sweat. My shadeless heart yearns,
I am drawn to this place and brave the sun.
My tongue's parched at the end of a hot day.
I peer for the Achaeans' harbour where
They beached their ships in Cape Sigeum's bay.

I see the wood Horse dragged through the east gate
And up the ramped steps to the walled beauty
Of the fifty-bedroomed royal palace
Where it is set up as a wheeled trophy,
And think, as I look back to house VIE,
Zeus wanted the Trojan War to prevent
The overpopulation of the earth;
A goal our Bilderbergers implement.

This is where it all happened: the *Iliad*,
The departure of Odysseus, the course
Of Agamemnon, the flight of Aeneas
Which led to Rome's founding. This was the source
Of Greek drama and verse, it feeds my soul
Which feels its warmth as my neck feels the sun.
This ruin bore and haunts our literature.
The literary West was here just One.

The war? I see Trojans as Luvians who
Spoke different languages, Homer avers.
I see the Greeks come in twelve hundred ships,
Each with a hundred and twenty warriors.
The Trojans had one tenth of the Greek force.
An unequal contest dragged on ten years
Till the Greeks sacked this place, pulled down its walls,
Began Western expansion, Eastern fears.
Conceived 15 July 1995; written 25 August 2001; revised 30–31 July 2002
Quest theme: image of oneness of history, influence of Homer. Set in Troy,
Hisarlik, Turkey.

In Byron's Ithaca

From the ferry I probe wild Ithaca,
The rugged sights that blind Homer once saw:
The Korax rock or Ravens' Crag, the Cave

Of Eumaeus the swineherd who lived raw,
Watered his pigs at the spring or Fountain
Of Arethusa; and as we enter
Vathi harbour, look for the Nymphs' Cave where
Odysseus hid the Phaeacians' treasure.

We dock and I wander out from the quay
Immersed in Homer – the pigs swilled acorns
And black water, bees hived in the stone jars
In the naiads' cave; rosy-fingered dawns!
I pass under, no! – Byron's bust in stone!
I'm shocked, then grasp: the British ruled this bright
Ithaca from 1809 before
He went off to Messolonghi to fight.

I bargain with a driver, set off round
The island – the Cave of the Nymphs, a pit
Four kilometres off up a steep track,
Through loud cicadas. I squeeze through a slit
On the north side, descend steps to the floor,
See the smoke-hole in the roof where gods could
Enter. Here Odysseus hid the gifts from
Alcinous. I stand where Homer stood.

We drive past Phorkys cove, where Odysseus
Landed, to Mount Aetos (one site for his
Castle), across Agros, Laertes' fields,
Up a steep slope, then skirt Odysseus's
Birthplace on Mount Neritos (in a cave)
To Polis Bay, alternative landing
Spot, where Tennyson's Ulysses set sail
In his old age for western stars, yearning.

I see the island of Asteris where
The suitors tried to lure Telemachos,
Go to Stavros and Pelikata's Hall

Of Hermes, seat of Odysseus' palace
Which has a view of three seas as Homer
Describes, and the museum's Mycenaean
Pots, and Odysseus' "drinking cup" with ringed
Stem for fingers – grip – found in a broken

Cave I visit in Polis Bay, collapsed
By earthquake. I stand near the sunken mole
Where Tennyson's Ulysses would have stood,
Then pass near Melandros spring's gushing hole
And Homer's seat, where he taught his pupils,
And then go back to Phorkys where Odysseus
Landed to be away from the suitors,
Disguised as a castaway, and thanked Zeus.

I swim from sharp stones in clear cool water,
My clothes piled by an olive trunk in heat
Where sailors laid Alcinous' treasure,
Then lie where Odysseus lay in a sheet
Of linen, and muse on the poet who
Brought me, blind Homer of the wine-dark sea,
And again see Byron's face, am haunted
As much by him as by the *Odyssey*.

Like T.E. Lawrence, a British agent
Who led the Arab revolt against Turks,
Byron supported the Greek freedom-fight
Against Turkey and *lived* while writing works.
He came to Kefalonia as agent
To represent the committee in Greece,
Spent six weeks in Argostoli, then moved
To a healthier, prettier place, for peace.

I think of the house in Metaxata
Where Byron spent the last four months before
Leaving for Messolonghi, with its view

Of the plain, castle and Mount Aenos, saw
The ivy that's survived the house's wreck
And the rock he sat on in Lakithra
Near Mycenaean tombs and, inspired, wrote
Unaware he'd soon die of a fever.

I used to think Byron an egotist,
An Augustan, not a true Romantic,
But now fondly recall polished stanzas,
Wit, turn of phrase and easy rhetoric,
Models for my own verse, and, philhellene,
The love of Greece and Italy I share,
And reckless urge to fight tyranny, be
A British agent for freedom and dare.

O Byron, rediscovering you here
In Vathi, your alertness to the hour,
I bow before your bust and to your heart,
To racy narrative and pulling-power,
To you as a British secret agent
Resisting the imperial power with thrills
And sitting on rocks and scribbling lines
That will be as immortal as the hills.

And despite your rational, Augustan thought
Your material's acutely Romantic.
I honour you for your dashing panache,
Stanzas dazzlingly accomplished yet strict.
Through your philhellenism I bear fruit
On the much-gnarled Romantic olive tree,
Rooted in the classical and Nature:
Ruined stones and the sparkling Phorkys sea.

Conceived 22 July 1995; written 22 February 2001; revised 28–29 March, 31 May 2001
Quest theme: image of classical oneness, influence of Homer and Byron (who
may not have funded the refitting of the Greek fleet and the anti-Ottoman
freedom-fighting Souliotes from his own money). Set in Ithaca, Greece.

At Virgil's Tomb

I take a taxi from Naples and reach
The Porta Puteolana, pay – I wave –
Under Santa Maria's railway bridge,
Through the bay grove past Leopardi's grave
Climb to a Cumae-like sandstone cliff-face,
Cross the top, jacaranda in blue bloom,
Of Agrippa's tunnel, descend steps and see:
Virgil's reputed reticular tomb.

It once stood by the road, but's now high up.
It seems a family *columbarium*
With weeds round the roof's two holes. I enter.
It does not seem one man's mausoleum:
Ten empty sunlit niches for ash-urns,
A long window, three air vents and a door,
A metal water stoup. "*Hic Vergilius*,"
I read, "*Tumulus Est.*" A sandy floor.

Taken ill in Megara, Virgil died
In Brindisi, where his ashed bones had been
Raked from the pyre and brought (Donatus says)
To Naples and placed in a tomb "between
The first and second milestones of the *Via*
Puteolana" near land he had bought or
Inherited from Siro, where a white
Temple to Virgil was built, that I saw.

Was this the place? Where did the *Via* start?
I muse on words a friend (Horace maybe)
Inscribed here, Virgil's last dying distich:
"Mantua bore me, Calabria snatched me,
Naples holds me. I sang pastures, fields, kings."
Statius, Silius Italicus enjoyed
This place, as did Petrach and Boccaccio.

It fell into ruin and was destroyed

In the time of Robert of Anjou, who,
Holding that the fourth *Eclogue* prophesied
The birth of Christ, not of Antony's child,
Ordered that Virgil's ashes should reside
In a wooden casket in a chapel
In Castel dell' Ovo where the Siren
Parthenope landed, causewayed island,
So he could be Christianized, brought to Heaven.

A train hoots, the traffic roar is distant.
I sit in glorious silence, quite alone,
And ponder the soul of Virgil, who knew
Octavian, on whom Aeneas was grown,
Celebrated peace and guided Dante;
Gaze at the arch and the steep grove outside,
A place fit for Aeneas's creator.
Someone's left laurels that have shrivelled, died.

I trace my origins as a poet
Back to this place – many of my school hours
Were spent translating bucolic *Eclogues*,
Rural *Georgics*, *Aeneid*'s herbaceous flowers,
Whose scents, entering my soul, later inspired
Me to create my own epic garden.
As much as any he was my mentor
And guided my pastoral and martial pen.

I leave and walk back down through the bay grove.
The shock of traffic thunders through the arch,
Choking with fumes; the modern world returns
With a roar that assaults me as I march.
But I am still lost in that peaceful tomb
And muse on Virgil's burned bones and the verse
That outlived Augustus's world Empire,

Will last as long as gold coins in his purse.

O Virgil, you lived through civil unrest
And saw at close quarters Augustan peace,
The ideal life of shepherds and farmers
And soldiers who return to ploughs and geese
That I now see in arable Essex
And Suffolk and, too, catch pastoral and war;
You caught the *Pax Augusta* Caesar dreamed
In fine sculpted verse that fills me with awe.
Conceived 18 October 1995; written 19 August 2001; revised 22–23 July 2002
Quest theme: image of classical oneness, influence of Virgil. Set near the Porta
Puteolana, near Naples, Italy.

At Horace's Sabine Farm

Near Licenza I take a dusty track.
We park, get out and I see, deserted,
Low walls below green foothills with small trees:
Horace's Sabine farm, villa gifted
Him by Maecenas. I wander through twelve
Rooms grouped round an open courtyard with square
Water, above gardens and swimming-pool.
It is serene: grass, wild orchids, clear air.

Some of the low walls enclose mosaics:
The bedroom floors. I stand on one labelled
"Horace's bedroom". Was this the room full
Of mirrors so he could, with desire swelled,
See his sex acts from all angles? I note
The net walls and see lead piping that awes.
It channelled water from the square court pool
Under neighbouring rooms' mosaic floors.

Here Horace turned his back on busy court,

Ran his estate with a foreman, eight slaves;
Wrote *Epodes* and *Odes* modelled on Pindar
In Sapphics and Alcaics, Greek *enclaves*
Learned as a student in Athens. He'd fought
At Philippi, and met Maecenas through
Virgil. A girl brings a Visitors Book.
I leaf; one a day mostly, some days two.

I wander up to the Bandusian spring.
The cool brook gushes down by the track's twist.
I dip a hand in, scoop and taste limpid
Water "clearer than crystal". On my wrist
I have a leech, flick it off and recall
How thirty-nine years ago I came here
And drank at this Muse's spring and became
A poet. That day clings like a leech, near.

I recall clearly standing with schoolfriends
And Peter Croft, Latin master long dead,
Young with hooked nose, bleary eyes, stick-out ears.
"The water's pure, you can drink it," he said,
And so we did. I wander up with ghosts –
Green hills all round, bamboo, crab apples, twee
Farming – to the rocky fountain Ninfeo,
Fifteenth-century, built by the Orsini.

And now I sit at school two weeks before
The end of term – Croft then the party's purse –
On a seat on Lower Field in March sun,
Reading *The Faber Book of Modern Verse*:
'The Wreck of the Deutschland'. Suddenly I
Knew that despite my classical background
I was to be a poet, had been stirred
To a life-long vocation I'd just found.

That perception which led me to read Keats

145

And Shelley that cricketing summer, blank
And turn away from Law and read English,
Was ritualized, chalice-like, when I drank
From this spring, which seemed to flow underground
From the Muses. I'd communed, drunk romance,
Immortal liquid, and now part of me –
My soul – needed immortal sustenance

From the poets of Rome's Augustan Age.
I walk down to the villa's swimming-pool –
Clearly outlined in grass – and see Horace,
Maecenas, Virgil dip and play the fool
Though under pressure to hand in good verse,
Reflect I've followed Virgil most, yet see
My works reflect bits of Virgil, Horace
And Ovid; all go back to the Big Three.

O Horace, friend of Augustus, you filled
Your works with lovers he excused (to see
Latin lyrics that rivalled Greek lyrics
Though he'd campaigned against adultery).
Were you really dissolute, or were they
Make-believe lovers in literary forms?
He chose you to write the 'Secular Hymn'
And so, as his laureate, to convey norms.

Your Greek sophisticated sadness mixed
With your Italian vigour, rhetoric
(Like my Englishness and Europeanness).
You did not look back to the Republic,
Saw religion as a social practice,
Content to be Augustus's laureate,
Balance love, friendship and enjoyment; death,
Bloodshed and duty – the private with State.

Conceived 24 September 1996; written 18 August 2001; revised 24 July 2002
Quest theme: image of classical oneness, influence of Horace. Set in Licenza, Italy.

At Otley: Timber-Framed Tradition

Flailed hedges bud, corn shoots are a lush green;
The Suffolk countryside has burst with spring.
As I drive up Hall Lane the brown woods screen
The four tall double chimneys and nuzzling
Gables of this studded red brick and white
Moated Tudor Hall. A willow weeps where
Ducks splash in green. The high hedge is alight
With the last sunshine in the languid air.

I peer through an arch at the rose-garden,
Cloven Pan, croquet lawn, budding chestnut.
Beyond the vegetable garden I then
Peep into the high cage where peacocks strut.
One fans his tail: false eyes like works of art.
The nuttery is dark but lilies glow
From H-shaped fishponds (or stews) where rudd dart
Down to the viewing mound and barn below.

I turn the ring on the studded front door
And stand in the mullioned Great Hall and gaze
At the ancient brick screened cross-passage floor.
Adam de Otteley in Crusade days,
The Cresseners and then the Gosnolds sat
On a raised dais in an earlier hall
And fed guests. John Gosnold the Second, at
Henry the Seventh's reign's start, beamed the far wall.

Robert the First rebuilt and carved "RG"
Round the now walled-up ancient entrance and
Added "RA" on beam brackets when he
Wed Agnes in 1506. His grand
Linenfold parlour wall-panels predate
The "hung linen" of Lavenham Guildhall
Built by his cousin. Heir to "R's" estate,

An old Robert the Third stares from his wall.

Upstairs in the Banquet Room "R" built, my
Bedroom, Robert the Third aged twenty-four,
Fair-haired, and his bride Ursula, sit high,
Naked, columned, between the arms they bore,
Gosnold and Naunton escutcheons, beside
A Green Man who blesses their flowered union
In 1559, mark of "R's" pride –
They moved in when he died some twelve years on.

I descend the stairs that are scratched and scored
By spurs Colonel Robert the Sixth wore at
The siege of Carlisle, where, Royalist, bored,
He survived nine months eating dog and rat.
He fought on the wrong side and was then fined
By Cromwell's men, who filled parts of the moat.
I gaze at the deed Robert the Seventh signed,
Which sold the lands. The Hall went like a coat.

No more bowls and cock-fighting, cheer and shout,
In the "Plahouse" under the Banquet Room.
For two centuries the Rebows let it out
To farmers who barely wielded a broom.
And so, miracle! Much is still intact
And this Hall is a living monument
To a family who were at court, backed
It as JPs and had a landed bent.

Here Bartholomew's voyages were planned.
In 1602, funded by the Earl
Of Southampton, he reached Virginia and
Named Martha's Vineyard after his small girl,
And perhaps sat at this hearth with Shakespeare –
Who based Prospero's isle on his new world tale
Of springs, sassafras logs and Indians there:

Caliban knew the Vineyard Indians' trail?

Five years later he returned and founded
The first English-speaking settlement in
The US at Jamestown, which he then led
Until his death of swamp fever. A thin
Stockade had then colonised the US
Thirteen years before the *Mayflower*, a base
From which to chart America's progress.
The USA began round this fireplace.

And now I am custodian of these beams,
Part of our manorial heritage at
One of Britain's top twenty (so it seems)
Historical houses, I am glad that,
Instead of sailing abstractly across
An unseen past of submerged homes and art,
I have found actual ancient rooms to toss
And anchor in as I voyage the heart.

The mind is larger than uncharted seas
And I have always been a voyager.
History is vaster than five continents' trees;
We grow in woods and make a Hall's timber.
The literary night flits with ghosts that
Loom and retreat, and I am glad the days
Have brought me to a room where de Vere sat
With Southampton to plot empires – and plays?

Night. I leave my gabled chimneys and grasp
Timber-framed Tradition shuts out a crowd
Of brilliant stars. I look upwards and gasp
For this year's comet, Hale-Bopp, trails a cloud
Of bright gas that might cool to fragments, bump
And cluster in galaxies. One pace, mark,
And Tradition's chimneys obscure its clump

With age-old warmth and shelter from the dark.
8–9 April 1997
Quest theme: image of the One. Set at Otley Hall, Suffolk.

Contemplations by a Sundial

I sit by a sundial's stone pedestal
And watch a shadow creep from its *gnomon*
Round Roman numerals and a central
Compass with eight points, aligned to the sun.
One end is empty, older dials are so;
And on the plate, among the tossing flowers,
A rustic Elizabethan motto
Proclaims: "Amyddst ye fflowres I tell ye houres."

How simple, to tell the hour of the day
By a sun's shadow on a flat surface
Marked with a diagram of hours which splay.
The length of days varies as seasons chase
And so hours varied in length with each change
And were known as "temporary hours", in length.
The Greeks and Romans used such time till strange
Arabs introduced "equal hours", with strength.

As many times as the eight winds have been:
Apparent solar time of sundials; shocks –
Dynamical, sidereal (true, mean);
Mean solar time of seventeenth century clocks
Local to prime meridian's time zones;
Daylight-saving; co-ordinated chime
Of universal time; atomic tones.
With so many times what, I ask, is Time?

Time cannot be seen. Only its effects –
As ripples on a pool or tossing trees

Suggest a wind – wrinkle what glass reflects,
Turn the air chilly with a cooling breeze,
Corrode metal, cause buildings to decay,
Thickets to turn to jungles, flowers to droop.
Time is the passing of each blue-skied day,
And slow ticking of waddle into stoop.

Time is a succession of events. Ten
Thousand million million million have bred
Each second since the moving One knew when.
Past events are not obliterated
But added to by all present events.
The past always persists in the present.
Space is the order of co-existence,
Time of succession, of events now spent.

I contemplate by my sundial, and gaze.
In medieval times a dial was grass,
A human body its *gnomon* to laze
And cast a shadow on its maze, and pass.
Now I sit with the sun upon my back,
My head a stick with contemplative eye,
And show time as my shadow moves in black
To the course of the sun across the sky.

I tell the hours by how my shadow creeps
As, wrapped in contemplation, I reflect
On the sun which created Time and peeps
At its universe, cause at its effect.
I sit with the Light behind me and feel
Its warmth rise up my spine, cast a shadow,
My silhouette, on the earth's surface, steal
With dark outline, hint at the One's bright glow.

I am a sundial in a sun as bright
As ever did shine on these rustic flowers.

I am a *gnomon* who receives sunlight
And shadows it so all can see its hours.
I am not measured by my sunlit side
But by the shadow I throw from the One.
I tell hours and proclaim, eternal guide:
"Behind each shadow reigns a glorious sun."
30 July–4 August 1997
Quest theme: image of the One. Set at Otley Hall, Suffolk.

In Dante's Verona

I

I walk streets of Verona with a guide
After the worst of the heat, and hear how
The Veronese were Ghibellines, who'd been
With the German Hohenstaufens, and now
In Dante's time banned the Guelfs who were with
The Pope (who could not enforce domicile).
Dante visited the Ghibellines here
Three times after his disgrace and exile.

As a White Guelf he had opposed the Pope's
Ambition to rule the Holy Roman
Empire and expand Papal territory
And, sent to San Gimignano to plan,
Solidified the Guelf League for its war.
When Charles of Valois arrived at Florence
(The Black Guelfs' HQ), Dante was chosen
Ambassador to make the Pope see sense.

While Dante was in Rome, Charles had entered
Florence, allied with Blacks. Whites, though absent,
Including Dante, were accused and fined
For Ghibellinism, embezzlement,
Opposition to the Pope and Charles –

Payment in three days. He could not return
From Rome to pay in time, and in default
He and fourteen Whites were condemned to burn.

Now in exile, Dante contacted most
Pro-Ghibelline families and came here
To the della Scala, planned his return.
I stand by the Scaligeri's palace where
He stayed with Bartolomeo Scala
(Now a police station) in 1303
And see the stone staircase where he first saw
The ruler's brother, the young Cangrande.

His great-great-grandfather Cacciaguida,
Speaking as shade in 1300 (in
Canto 17 of *Paradiso*),
Had foretold the first refuge he would win:
At the court of the "mighty Lombard" who
On a ladder bears an eagle. He'd see
A youth with him who would become famous,
In whom he could place his trust: Cangrande.

Now he urged Albert the First, German King,
Habsburg Emperor, to come to Italy,
Regarding him as a Roman Emperor
Who ruled with a divine authority:
"Come see the Capulets and Montagues" –
Feuding families, neighbours who'd had words.
I sit in the Piazza delle Erbe
Which Dante saw and watch caged singing birds.

At La Lastra the Whites and Ghibellines
Lost. He went to Bologna for a span,
Until expelled, then Lucca whence, sustained
By the thought of the great work he began
In 1308, he moved on, living

In noble houses in North Italy,
Their bread bitter, tread on their stairs heavy.
Exiled, he sought a heavenly city.

After the rift between the Emperor
Henry and Pope Clement the Fifth, hopes dashed,
He returned to the Lord of Verona,
The twelve-year-old youth he'd seen, unabashed
Cangrande the First who'd now made a great
Ghibelline state of the north's ruling rooms.
I see where he stayed with Cangrande in
The castle opposite the Scala tombs.

Cangrande's military activities
Had become legendary, his conquests matched
By his tall beauty, graceful speech and wit.
Noble, courteous, clever, he had attached
Brescia, Vicenze, Padua, Cremona,
Parma, Reggio, Mantua, Treviso.
He aimed to unify all Italy,
Gave exiles homes, patroned their art for show.

II

In a letter Dante dedicated
Paradiso to him, sent him the fair
Copy, half a dozen cantos a time.
His wanderings in poverty, threadbare,
Had ceased. Now he had a base for his work.
He opposed the Pope as Cathars had done
And consorted with his foes. Cangrande
Was a hunting greyhound, *"cane"*, a pun.

Now he recalled Florence's Duomo square
Where, between 12 and 13 now, he stood
On summer evenings, walked round the corner
To the house of his birth and childhood

In his medieval street, windows grilled,
How by the Ponte Vecchio he did see
Radiant Beatrice near the splashing Arno
And was inspired to write his *Comedy*.

I stand by San Zeno's Basilica
Between a Romanesque campanile
And tower, go inside and look back and gaze
At the white-mauve rose window's shimmering ray
Suggesting ethereal heaven, glimmering,
A twelfth-century rose window that shows
The Wheel of Fortune Dante saw and used
As Paradise's "sempiternal rose".

The breach with Cangrande came suddenly.
The warlord entertained his troops crudely.
A jester told dirty jokes, did a mime.
As Dante winced, Cangrande said cruelly,
"I wonder why this stupid fellow knows
How to please everyone when you who're meant
To be wise can't please them at all." A boy
Heaped bones at Dante's feet, a mock present.

Now his last visit, to Sant' Elena.
I see where Dante, as philosopher
And scientist, debated with great minds
In Cangrande's presence, whether water –
In streams, rivers, ponds, lakes, seas and oceans –
Is higher than the earth. Dante maintained
That nowhere in the world can the level
Of water be higher than earth that drained.

I sit again in Piazza dell' Erbe
And think of how he caught malaria
In Venice and, having borne a vision
All round Italy, died in Ravenna.

How practical was his diplomacy,
How well he bridged Nature and the divine.
I gaze at the winged lion, emblem
Of Venetian rule and the mystic line.

Santa Maria Antica. I stand
Beneath the tomb of Cangrande, his dust
In his reclining figure, the ladder
(*Scala*) imaging ascent, upward thrust.
At the end he only had Verona
And Vicenze, but I admire the way
He presided over the revival
Of this city's artistic interplay.

O Dante, like Shakespeare later, you made
Universal types from historical
Figures and blended them with your vision
In 1283 of an aureole,
The Light's three-sphered Trinity, "Eternal
Light" who dwells in itself alone, and knows
Itself, the Light seen when one's consciousness
Swoons beyond thought into the mystic rose.

O mystic Dante, who spent a lifetime
In working out the deep implications
Of your 1283 vision, I too,
In 1971, had some visions
That took me decades to unfold in books,
That fill my philosophy with ferment,
My history and my literary works.
I stand by your statue and nod assent.

The Light exists within itself alone
And it is a mystery of the meaning
Of life that it can shine into our souls
In times of need or of its own choosing,

Change us with its fathomless, clear substance,
Its single, changeless form. O Living Light,
Philosophy, history, literary works
Are worthless if they ignore inspired sight!
Conceived 20 July 1998; written 5, 10–11 February, 8 August 2001
Quest theme: image of classical oneness, influence of Dante. Set in Verona, Italy.

At Catullus's Sirmione

I drive along the blue Lake Garda, park,
Walk past the della-Scala Scaligerine
Lakeside castle with towers crenellated
In square, protruding style that's Ghibelline,
Then stroll through narrow streets to a small train
And ride up past bougainvillaea to where,
In Italy's largest Roman villa,
Catullus's father breathed cool lake air.

Here he entertained Julius Caesar,
Here Catullus came "to his own front door"
From Verona, dreaming of his own bed,
Heard cicadas in the olives saw,
Gazed at the blue unsaline lake with swans,
A hedge of rosemary scenting the warm air.
The lake is both sides of the promontory,
A cool breeze blows where birds chirp in the glare.

Catullus thought this place a pearl, "bright eye
Of islands and peninsulas". I see
Columns, arches, pediments, tall "grottoes"
Which suggest baths – and some have said with glee
It's a lakeside spa, not private villa.
I ignore that, having found far from Rome
"The Lord of Sirmione", removed from
Bohemian life, here at his father's home.

The villa was built round a large garden.
On the south, cistern and spa behind blooms;
On the north, by the lake, living quarters
Of owners, servants, guests, and social rooms;
To west and east were porticoes for walks
In shade when hot, sheltered from rain, well-planned.
In the museum a fresco (Catullus?):
"A male figure with a scroll in his hand".

I see Catullus in Verona, cross
The Roman bridge on foot and make his way
To the Roman theatre on the hillside
Above the winding river Adige.
I see him in the fast set, hard-drinking
And living for pleasure till the small hours,
Writing about it and his Lesbia
In a hundred poems that come like showers.

She was married, a much older mistress.
He had met her in 61 BC
Aged twenty-two, the wife of a pompous
Consul, an aristocrat who was free.
It was a sordid affair, hate and love.
She was unfaithful with Caelius, his friend.
He could not get her out of his racked mind,
He was tormented and longed for the end.

Catullus loved her but tried to escape
By travelling to Bithynia for a year
With stingy Memmius, praetor, kept
Recalling her till his rejecting jeer –
"Let her enjoy her three hundred lovers" –
In 54, after mighty Caesar
Had conquered Britain, or was he trying
To convince himself it was now over?

I walk back down to the castle, inspired.
"There's one tradition, like the Adige,
Of poetry and history, and Catullus,
And Virgil, Horace and Ovid," I say,
"Are like old bridges we stand on, landmarks
Where we survey above one flow that's quick.
Catullus was first in the Roman stretch,
Virgil the greater as he wrote epic."

On impulse I ask our driver to go
North of Mantua, to Carpenédolo,
And under distant Alps, tall maize and rice,
To Arcadian life near Calvisano.
Somewhere between the two Virgil was born,
Who wrote pastoral verse and of Rome's world rule,
Caught rustic life beyond bawdy lyrics,
Amaryllis sitting in the shade's cool.

I lean on Verona's old Roman bridge.
All cultures, like waters of one river,
Flow from one source under many bridges,
All nations' poets one surge from Homer.
I connect myself to the flow of all
Europe's poets, my antecedents, search
Through their books, lines, places, current of art
Like centuries gushing beneath an old church.

There is one universal culture and
Tradition that includes like ripples all
Great writers of all cultures and nations
In one flow that sparkles light like a call
From the distant source of all cultures, truth
A brimming river mirrors: shimmering sun
Along with pastoral sheep, urban faces
It passes as it echoes out the One.

Western philosophy has a Greek source:
The One pre-Socratic Heracleitus,
Parmenides knew beneath the many
Leaves reflected on its moving surface.
Catullus, less skilful, more immediate,
Reflected faces in urban language,
Mirrored honestly but lacked far echoes
I glimpse now from Virgil's more massive bridge.
Conceived 21 July 1998; drafted 21 February 2001; revised 13–17 March 2001
Quest theme: image of classical oneness and one culture, influence of Catullus.
Set in Sirmione, Italy.

21

from *Ovid Banished* (1998–1999)

[Ovid opens to the Light]

(*The Temple of Apollo.* OVID *sits with the* PRIEST. *They are meditating. Both have closed eyes. They murmur to each other.*)

Ovid.

Just as a fantail dove leaves its dovecote,
Sits on a thatched roof, then flutters to grass
And explores its freedom before it flies
Back to the hole in its white-posted home,
So I have left the prison of my hut
To perch among your Temple's white columns
And savour the splendour of the sunlight.

Priest.

If you would see Apollo's midnight sun,
The Light that shines into darkness, you must
Remove yourself from this earth's attractions.
Cleanse your senses, purge yourself of desire,
Want nothing, rest content within your smile,
Live without attachment to worldly things,
Purify your inwardness, look within

At the images that will rise in you.
Apollo's Light will shine, and, illumined,
You will become a Shining One, a soul
That is enlightened and is most serene.
This is what the priests of Eleusis teach.

Ovid.

I do want to bask in Apollo's Light,
Like Prometheus steal the eternal Fire.
I have let go of Rome now I'm rebuffed.
I want nothing, I do not hope for Rome.
I've stripped myself of all acquisitions.
I have nothing and want to know the Light.

Priest.

Then let your rhythmic breathing deepen, close
Your eyes and see the Light break like the dawn
On shimmering water. Peer at the dark,
Peer into the darkness, and penetrate
Through to the Light concealed behind black cloud.

(*A silence. Then* OVID *cries out.*)

Ovid.

I can see it. A dawning in the night.
The sun's breaking. I can see its white rays.
The sun's emerging, it's so bright, ah! bright –

Priest.

The face of Apollo –

Ovid.

It's dazzling.

It's so intense. It's filling me. Ah! ah!
I'm filled with radiance of the inner sun.
It's so intense, it's –

(OVID *swoons forward.*)

Priest.

Apollo has healed

Your troubled mind, you are now whole, Ovid.
Quest theme: experience of the One.

[death of Ovid]

(*Dusk. Outside Ovid's hut the* GUARD *stops throwing dice and stands as the* PRIEST *approaches. The priest enters holding herbs and speaks to* OVID, *who is lying on his back, feeble and frail. He breathes heavily and breaks into a rasping cough.*)

Priest.   You are worse?

Ovid.   Worse.

Priest.   I've brought you herbs.

Ovid.   Too late.
          Too late for herbs.

Priest.   The Tomitans decree
          That you are exempt from all taxation.
          This is your home, Ovid. They want you here.

          (OVID *is gasping for breath.*)

Ovid.   It's come too late. I'm not long for the world.
          The Underworld, where I, Orpheus, wait.

Priest.   To lead your art back to Roman daylight.

Ovid   (*nodding*). As I look back my writing seems worthless.
          I wish I'd written epic, like Virgil.
          I loved Erato, not Calliope.
          I built my house on rock, like this old shack
          On Moesia's rocky coast, this dark waste land,
          This barren wilderness – I tried to be
          True to my art and never compromised,

Even with Caesar, whom I told the truth,
Stood for the sovereignty of Italy
Against Caesar's imperialist principle.
But now my works seem slight, ephemeral.
I built them on rock but not big enough.
They're a mere hut like this, not a palace.
I wish I'd written epic, like Virgil.

Priest   (*sitting by Ovid*). But you're not dying of despair.
                     You're calm.

Ovid.   Serene, and accepting of all that's been.
                     Reconciled to the weirdness of my life
                     And like Apollo gazing at its shape.
                     I see my life rising like a column
                     In your Temple, that supports the white roof
                     And pediment of Roman Literature.
                     And I sit in the initiate's dark
                     Chamber below the *telesterion*
                     In Eleusis, among the Mysteries,
                     A soul waiting to see Apollo's Light.

                     (OVID's *breathing is less troubled*.)

Priest   (*quietly*). Let's bring down Apollo's Light. Close your
                         eyes,
                     Relax, let go your jaw, dispel tension
                     In your feet, knees, hips, elbows, fingers, neck,
                     Breathe deeply. Become your immortal eye
                     Behind your closed eyelids. Unveil your soul
                     And peer through thick clouds for the dawning sun.
                     Look for its shafts in the night sky. Open
                     Your being to its rays. Apollo's beams.
                     Breathe deeply, let the sun, like a lily,
                     Float on the dark waters within your mind.
                     Look for the sunrise, feel the Light's soothing

As it smoothes out the creases in your mist.
Look into all that veils the inner rose.

(OVID's *breathing becomes more peaceful*.)

Ovid.   Aah, aah!

Priest   (*breathing*). You can see the real now?

Ovid.   Bright Light,
Aah! I'm flooded with sunshine. I'm standing....

Priest.   Where? Where are you standing?

Ovid.   Sulmo.

Priest.   Sulmo?

Ovid.   My family's villa outside Rome. I
Am with my brother Lucius in Light.
And now....

Priest.   Now what?

Ovid.   I'm with my new young wife.
I'm in the valley. Streams. Vineyards. Mountains.
I'm in a field of Light. Orchard. So bright.
I'm walking into the Light. Apollo!
It's like walking towards the sun, the One!
My 'I' has blended into boundless Light.
I'm leaving the manifold universe,
I'm leaving the many to be the One.
I am the One, One Light.

Priest.   And your body?

Ovid.   Illusion. Clay. Ephemeral as leaves
In autumn when they fall from trees and float

On a stream's surface, drifting in the sky.
I'm drifting in the sky, bathed in sunlight.
I'm drifting, floating back towards the One.
The stream includes what is on its surface.
I am the One, Ovid drifted on me
Like a white swan of immense elegance.

Priest   (*softly*). You've brought your art from gloom back to
            daylight.
            Your metamorphosis is now complete.
            You've been transformed from darkness into Light.
            You have become a reaped ear of ripe grain.

(OVID's *breathing is shallow. It stops.*)
Quest theme: experience of the One.

22

from *The Rise of Oliver Cromwell* (2000)

[Cromwell receives the Light]

(*Late 1629. Cromwell's house in Huntingdon.* CROMWELL *is on his knees, speaking in half-sobs.*)

Cromwell.   Oh God, I am not worthy. I'm worthless.
            I am of no more worth than a poor worm.
            I'm ruled by self, vanity and badness.
            I struggle against my inferior self.
            My mind's perplexed, it damages my health.
            I feel tense from inner self-division.
            My spiritual and psychological
            Struggle has coiled me like an unwound watch.
            I pray to you for Light but know darkness.
            I speak in Parliament but feel I am
            A miserable sinner, chief of sinners.

I cry out to you from this darkness. Lord!
Please enter me and fill me with your Light

(*There is a silence.*)
Ahhh! An explosion of Light, like a sun!
I'm filled with Light, and now I know for sure,
I'm one of God's Chosen, not a sinner.
I have a task, a destiny to work.
Providence has chosen me for its will.

Quest theme: illumination.

23

from *Classical Odes* (1994–2005)

On the Order in the Universe

The artist waits near my front door, leaning
On the sea-wall, looks out to stormy sea,
White-haired, weather-beaten, wise lines round eyes,
Holding the picture he's painted for me.
He smiles and comes into my sitting-room
And unwraps the long canvas he has done,
Which is framed in a brown frame, a picture
Of the sea, our house and a storm to stun.

A lowering sky, a menacing dark cloud,
An angry sea that pours over the pier
And fountains at the rocks and near the wall,
Our pink house sheltering from the wind's jeer,
Nuzzling in a cranny in our blown cliff,
A haven from the elements about,
Howling wind, raging sea and dashing spray,
A place of calm amidst energy's rout.

It contrasts opposites – the storm and calm –

And catches the scene outside my window
But with a perspective that's unified,
With hints of sun behind cloud, hidden glow
Breeding serenity and disturbance,
Blending sigh and roar as in a sea-shell,
Catching a universe that is varied
Between opposite moods, in which I dwell.

I watch. He stands it on the mantelpiece,
Moving the calm scene that hung there before,
Then stands back, cocks his head and looks around,
Then nods and sidles to look from the door.
We chat over a mug of tea. He says,
"I paint harbours, the Cornish sea and sky
As Constable or Turner might see them.
I paint with a traditional eye.

"I have local exhibitions. Last week
A man came down to St Ives from the Tate,
Saw work and took away a blank canvas
With a hole in the middle he thought great.
He wasn't interested in harbour scenes
Or pictures of the sea, and so my work
Is not hung in the Tate or in London.
It hangs in homes throughout England. The jerk.

"Visitors buy my paintings when they come
To my studio in Polkerris and see
Me at work and look at what I've put by.
I don't need the Tate – just the sea, the quay."
He looks out to sea. I'm awed. This artist
Who's better than the Tate but is deemed worse
Has stuck to the old landscape tradition
That shows the beauty of the universe.

Artists put the universe in a frame

And paint its order and its energy,
The nourishment it gives to beasts, birds, men,
And connect the image to unity.
Order is missing in our debased time,
Those who show parts, holed disorder and style
Chaos are ranked with those who show the Whole
And raise the eye to the eternal smile.

The artist shows how calm and storm combine
To make a rich design that resonates,
How ephemeral opposites – paradox –
Are reconciled in eternal templates.
Plus calm plus minus storm equal zero,
The order that holds creation in place.
The artist makes his own personal statement,
Gives traditional material a new face.

Poets relate experience to the Whole
So sea and house are in a wide canvas
Whose panoramic sweep shows the order
In the vital universe beyond mass.
The verse of partists neither scans nor rhymes,
And lacks meaning for chaos has undone.
Partists versify the world as a mess,
Artists, poets reveal the Whole: the One.

Conceived 15 February 1999; written 13 June 1999; revised 22–23 January 2001
Quest theme: image of contradictions reconciled within the One. Set at
Charlestown, Cornwall.

At the Osteopath: Soul and Body

I lie face down on the osteopath's slab,
His thumb pressed hard on my right shoulder-blade.
He says, "It's a myofascial nodule".
Waves of agony sear my back, then fade.

"It's not structural, it's fibrous tissue in
The muscle, gristle. You will be in pain,
Fibrositis, unless we break it up.
You stoop when writing at your desk, it's strain."

More searing. He presses relentlessly,
Squeezing the sac till it threatens to burst.
The knot's still intact like an onion core.
Once it has formed it cannot be dispersed,
Only kept small with monthly massages.
The cure is to stop scribbling, relax, loll.
I can't. Even though writing brings me pain
I am addicted as to alcohol.

So forty years of frantic setting-down
On paper's left a knot of gristly fat
That sits in a back muscle that controls
The motor movements of my right hand that
Dashes off lines as fast as I see them,
At break-neck speed, then polishes too-free
Rhymes, checks metres, tap-tapping on my desk
Like a woodpecker tapping at a tree.

I knock against dead wood and out they come,
The grubs of ideas I seize in my beak
And devour, wriggling images wrapped in
The detritus of decayed bark. I seek
An old tree, tap, when there are no more grubs
I move to another, drum rapid blows.
I have seized more than two thousand poems
Like larvae a woodpecker can expose.

Does the woodpecker suffer from gristle,
Repetitive strain from each quick beak jerk?
I doubt it. So why me? It must just be
The way I sit, coiled, hunched over my work,

My being flowing down my right arm through
The poem I'm writing, poised to dart, find
Each stray thought that may wriggle away in
The crevices of my unconscious mind.

Give it up? I can't, and do not want to.
It is my function in life to seek out
The invisible, camouflaged grubs that
Lurk in the folds of thought, squirming about,
Images most pass by and do not see
But which are my food, which nourish my sheen
As I claw at creviced bark that allows
Me to be who I am, to tap and preen.

I have risked my body for my habit,
My shoulder, neck, my lower disc and veins,
Exercised too little and sat too much,
Had varicosed legs and thrombotic pains,
Remained indoors, thus short of oxygen,
Have bronchiectasis – my lungs don't mind.
I've done close work yet still I have my eyes,
Unlike Homer and Milton who went blind.

No concessions to limiting body!
My spirit dictates that my poems must
Continue despite body's handicaps.
The soul sees, body interferes like dust,
Hinders, impedes, secretes potential pain.
My osteopath keeps me supple and fit
So my body's a willing instrument
Of the soul that lives in it and through it.
10, 14–15 January 2001

Quest theme: image of the One. Set in Queen's Road, Buckhurst Hill, Essex.

In Cornwall: A New Renaissance

I

Cornwall, conducive to poetic trance!
I stare out of my window at a sea
Half-sunlit, half-choppy that laps, below
My window, a wall twenty yards from me.
I look and spot my cormorant diving
Beneath the inky waves for fish. Now I
Have returned to my work, am lost. The sea
Helps me to concentrate and unify.

The sea is like my mind. Spread round the bay,
Reaching the horizon, it's vast and deep
Yet is ever changing, sometimes as calm
As a lake, tranquil with lights flashing, steep
Sunlight splashing off it like heavy rain.
Sometimes it is stirred up and breakers roll,
Crash, pour over the pier and dash up spray.
Heedless of its mood, my mind's a still bowl.

Sash windows up, fresh air gusting gently
From open sea – Channel and Atlantic,
Oxygenizing my poor labouring lungs
Charges me with energy so I'm quick,
Alert, write sixteen hours with little breaks,
Always clear-headed. This open-air, plain
Regime is like writing on the beach, I
Am close to elements: sun, wind, mist, rain.

I work unaware of its moves, yet sense
Its presence like a deep unconscious mind
Torn from behind my eyes, out there to see.
The tide keeps me company. I write blind
And come to and notice the tide's gone out,
People are playing on the beach, gulls stroll,

Or else, tide in, I see boys skimming stones,
Then I return to deep within my soul.

Why do I do this, spend my time each day
Drafting a poem, polishing it twice?
I sharpen my thought, hunt for precise words,
Make a statement in language that's concise,
Associate a place with a giant,
See poems as cross-disciplined, in rhyme,
Mix disciplines, felt thoughts, in a fresh whole,
Imaged perceptions that can withstand time.

But why do I do this? I have been blessed
With wives, children, worldly success and looks,
I own three schools and a large country house,
As many properties as I've done books.
Millions come in and go out every year.
I have a need to keen clarity, search
For new ways to relate to and present
The One in words, as some need prayers in church.

The One's apart from all religions, creeds.
As there is no church to which I can go
My words reveal a new metaphysic,
Channel the Light, define soul like Plato.
I embody Truth in daily poems.
While others repeat prayers, chant mantras, shout
At football matches or do hard crosswords,
I find new angles on what life's about.

I experience something that's ordinary,
That hints at the One, and reflect and frown,
Feel it more intensely than others do
So it takes root and I must note it down
And dismiss it from my immediate mind,
Like classifying and filing, a bit

Like discarding in something memorable.
It finds me, I don't go in search of it.

I see and feel with an intensity
Others don't seem to have things they don't meet,
Forget, aren't haunted by. My poems grow
Out of my sown unconscious like gold wheat
As I reflect on the experience.
Writing harvests what's thrust to consciousness,
Purges like a confession to a priest,
Wipes clean inner eye's screen and reaped *largesse*.

It's like watching seaweed and driftwood washed
Up onto a beach by a wave-led tide,
Images strewn along the water-line
To be beachcombed, picked up, brought back and dried.
Sometimes the sea throws up nothing but due
To atmosphere sends up a mist that rolls
In from the deep, the unconscious envelops
In a cloud of unknowing to feed souls.

A sea-mist is creeping in from the sea.
The Truth is hidden from the mind, concealed
When vapour separates it, comes between.
The mist rolls in upon the house, the field.
I'm a poet of sunlight seen through mists,
I flash flecks of sunlight like splashing rain.
I love it when evening sea turns silver,
Streaked orange. Now fog's obscured the sea-plain.

It is dark now, the fog is thick and dank.
I slip out for a walk, stand on the pier.
The sea-cliffs on each side of the harbour
Are shrouded, a lamppost's light gives some cheer,
It's pale in the wisps that screen the village.
I have been writing in this sea-fog cloud,

Striving for clarity at my window
As waves pound on shingle whose drag is loud.

II

Next morning in my window, with the surf,
I think of the Renaissance that combined
Christian and pagan, how Ficino held
The Light's available to all mankind
At all times. I think how I have restored
Universals to philosophy's blur,
The universal Light to a cosmos
That's been reduced, by logic, to matter.

A new Renaissance is here, new rebirth.
We look at history as a whole, reverse
Modern philosophy so it reveals
The Light that created the universe
And literature so it glows the beyond,
Shows the One in a wave's curl and tranced sight,
Sees body as the rib-cage of the soul.
A revolution's restoring the Light.

Downstairs, yesterday, I have, between feeds
And sleeps, played with my new grandson, a whole
Who lies shaking his arms, kicking his legs,
Intent, clutching a finger, a new soul;
And I also talked on the phone at length
About restoring the soul to our time.
People are gathering, a plan's being made
For a Spirit of the Age that's sublime.

The sea, a baby and my pondering soul
Are all in one accord and hail the One,
Restore purpose, show that Supreme Being
Cares for various humankind like the sun.
I scorn materialist man-made teachings

That a third of men should be starved, made ill
Or killed in war. Metaphysical love
Pours the One's compassion, its tides and Will.

The lunch-time News announces the shock news:
To this murky backwater of the south-
West, our PM, Blair, and his wife will come
To help tourism back from foot-and-mouth
(Which stopped at Devon, did not reach Cornwall).
A small crowd waits by the Pier House – young, old.
I wander over. No one knows the times.
The media circus know – they have been told.

Three cars arrive by the shipwreck centre.
The Blairs go in, sit with two Tourist Board
Reps five minutes, emerge, grinning. He signs
Autographs. I stand under trees unawed
With Matthew. Blair stops, stares at me, a look
Of half-recognition. I stare my mind.
They walk twenty yards, a small crowd round them,
To a long camera line, pose, dock behind.

The vicar's waiting at the Pier House door
To greet the visitors and serve them tea.
Drawn by him a large crowd is strung along
The road across the dock that slopes to sea,
Who to a camera resemble tourists
Among media vans, having braved the rain.
The vicar's been three hours at the wrong place.
He's wasted his time, he's waited in vain.

Open-necked, sun-tanned, embracing, grinning,
On holiday with media profiles,
They stand with their backs to the dock and preen.
A hundred flashes catch their sincere smiles.
The papers will say they had a cream tea,

Chatted to smiling folk on holiday,
That there were many tourists. Then they're off.
Government by camera. I turn away.

Minimalist – the bare-minimum time
To convey the impression they were in
The village a long while. They barely glanced
At the dock, did not tour a ship, see tin,
Get briefed on china clay, go to the beach,
Walk round. They had no interest in the place
Save to be snapped drawing attention to –
Linked with – a glossy port: image, surface.

Back in my window I return to less
Light-weight things than image and photo shoot,
Trivialising for impression, con trick
That has replaced arguments that refute.
I forget this new-world-order mouthpiece
Who sees himself as a Bilderberg sage,
Who deceives on the material system
And ignores the true Spirit of our Age.

In my mind I'm on the Lizard (*Lys ardh*,
"High place"). Sun bounces off sea with great glare,
By couch-grass I see the rocks off the reefs,
The one visible outcrop – stratum bare –
Of the Normannian plate that collided
With "Cornwall" three hundred and seventy-four
Million years back over oceanic crust
And thrust great Lizard rocks from the sea floor.

I move behind outer image, surface
To the inner mind as deep as the sea
That's filled with images like sea-creatures –
Crabs, eels, strange starfish, the anemone,
And ignore camera crews doing intros

And leave wordly distraction for the calm
Within the Light's Universal Idea
Where ideas float like jellies that alarm.

I am with the Light which lasts for ever,
Not transient puppets employed to betray.
A Revolution's coming in all thought
That will see culture as a mystic way,
Restore the view the giants lived by who
Tower above the pygmies who run our State;
A new Renaissance that will hold up quests
And question our notions of human fate.
14–15 August 2001; revised 16–18 August, 2001; 2–3 April 2005
Quest theme: image of the One. Set in Charlestown, Cornwall.

Among Loughton's Sacred Houses

I park in Brooklyn Avenue, a long
Way back from the High Road, linger, loiter
Outside the house I came to when just three,
Semi-detached with a concrete area.
I recall sitting on the stairs inside,
Could go up on my bottom, heaved and strove.
I see myself sitting in my high-chair,
My mother in the kitchen, by the stove.

I hear a deep voice on the radio
Read the war news, then see myself in bed
Listening in terror after lights-out for
Doodlebugs, and once heard in mounting dread
A knocking underneath, a broken spring.
I thought there was someone below my feet
And was too paralysed by fear to look,
And cowered in the safety of my sheet.

And I came to this gate with my father,
Where I'm standing, fifty-nine years ago.
The sky lit up with a white flash, windows
Behind broke, bits of glass fell, lay below.
I see my father turning in the dark,
Saying "Come on, back in" in a low shout,
Limping-running back towards the front door
While I chant with glee, "The windows are out."

A string of bombs had hit the cricketfield.
We lived in the V-bomb corridor then.
My father told me stories at bedtime
Of "Peter and his dog", when the siren
Went off at the police station – air raid!
And I was led by hand to the shelter
Somewhere downstairs in there, lay on a rug,
Was read to as we waited for thunder.

From here I walked to school, first Essex House,
And then to old Oaklands across the road;
And walked back with Robin Fowler's mother.
My shoelace came undone *there*, as she strode
By her bike she stooped and tied it. That night
I tried, fumbled lace and mucked up my bow.
In old Oaklands garden I lay inside
The Morrison shelter in the sun's glow.

Grandpa, white-haired, one finger missing, came
And sat gnarled by the fire, and one tea-time
Went to the shops in fog, did not come back.
I was sent out and found him, nose in grime,
Towards the High Road, lying on the ground.
He had stumbled and cut his head. I "woke"
Him up and led him back through the thick fog,
Bleeding, now wonder: did he have a stroke?

I see my father's study, he sits by
A desk, green curtains drawn, light on. I stand
While he tells me the twins have died. Will I
Help tell my younger brother, hold his hand?
Filled with importance and responsible,
Wondering if I should grieve, they'd not known me
As they'd never left hospital, I nod,
Am haunted by that room which I still see.

I drive to the school my grandson went to
And stand outside the green home we bought, see
Myself hold a grey battleship. Up there
Wires hung from the skirting-boards, ARP
Telephones had stood on the bare floorboards.
A hot May afternoon, and I hear words
From my birthday party in the garden.
Robin Fowler gave me a book on birds.

I said, "I've got this book." "No, you haven't,"
My mother said menacingly, laying
Jammed bread on a clean, white tablecloth I
Sat at with other small children, watching.
A blob of damson jam dropped on the cloth.
I see my mother in a summer dress
Pinch salt and rub it on the purple stain.
I could lean in and rub the salt, touch, press.

I see the bedroom where I used to read,
Up there on the right, where I dreaded creaks,
The streetlight reassuring on the wall;
And then I moved to the back room that speaks
Of my brother. We shared a black cupboard –
Rickety, a door catch that clicked
And whispered round it from our twin beds till
One of our parents called up, "Go to sleep."

I recall being ill and the gasfire
By which I would read all Dostoevsky.
Dr Walker came, I ate arrowroot,
A poached egg on mashed potato. I see
My mother cook on the old kitchen stove,
Red and black tiles on the floor: Welsh rarebit,
And on Sundays a sizzling sausage pie;
High tea at six, the nursery dimly lit.

As I had younger brothers and sisters
Nurses came to stay, my former bedroom
Had a bath, nurse's chair and baby clothes.
I saw a baby being bathed in gloom,
In a half-oval white bath that slotted
In a metal holder on folding legs,
Filled from a blue enamel jug's water
Boiled on the coke boiler near piled clothes-pegs.

I think of summers in the back garden,
The grey enamel tub we put pears in.
My father up a ladder hands pears down
For me to pull off twigs and leaves, wipe skin;
And also apples from the apple-tree
To take to the cellar, arrange in rows:
First pears, not touching, topped with newspaper,
Then Cox's orange pippins above those.

I recall how we dressed for church in suits –
The clock ticked too slowly on the church wall;
How we walked to my grandmother's and sat
In her large pink armchairs, while in the hall
Her clock struck each hour's quarter sonorously,
And told our news, my aunt nearby, her skills
No longer at the London Hospital
Where I saw Queen Mary by daffodils.

I stand in Station Road, mind in nursery.
I sit left of the fireguard and coalfire.
My mother holds her hands towards the coals,
I feel warmth on my cheeks as I aspire.
Coals glow red-hot, orange, I see faces
As low flames dance and sparks fizzle on soot.
To her it was normal but it haunts me:
The simple homely warmth of hand and foot.

I recall the room on the half-landing
Where my father lay during his last hours,
Grasped my hand, how when we raised beer tankards
Together, he choked out his failing powers.
I stood by him when he lay still and dead
And saw the Council Offices through glass,
The workplace he walked to, and early stars
Beyond the pear-tree's branches, twilit grass.

I see the Brook Road gate, my grandmother
Walking beside me with her stick "to say
Goodbye for the last time", at eighty-nine.
She died soon after, when I was away.
Memories whirl through my head as I stand
By the knobbly lime-trees I used to prune
With a long-arm. I was snapped on that path
With my brother, in sandals, one hot June.

I see my father and my mother peer
Round the side wall, though they are both long dead.
My father limps and smiles, smoking his pipe,
Holding a pail, and smooths his balding head.
My mother clutches the Moses-basket,
A baby lies inside, playing with hands.
They smile at me from a far place, and I
Smile back. They're gone. Only the house still stands.

The tears are in my eyes as I loiter
On the once tree-lined kerb of Station Road
And look in from outside on vanished youth,
Look across sixty years. How much I've owed
Them, I would ring the bell, go in and stand
In the same places, but all would have changed.
It's better to keep fresh in mind from then
Those faces so familiar, now estranged.

I went away, I left them, fled at first
To Oxford, then Iraq, Japan. Surely
I'd left them earlier, changing from law
(Their world) to poetry, self-discovery,
Culture, my world of walks in the Forest,
Deep ruminations by glades, leafy brooks
On literature, and a mountain of texts
On my bed, to be read, Europe's best books.

The gate to this house proclaimed "Journey's End".
It called me to a journey with a goal,
To search and research through history's ages
And find in myself, and awake, my soul.
I travelled deep into cultures and mind,
Soul-climbed through regions, religions, up stone,
Philosophers of east and west, poets
Who've anything to say and who have known,

And now I'm at my journey's end I stand
Where my climb for lost knowledge was begun
And think how the very name on the gate
Urged me to start a journey to the One.
This place was a call – poetry a method,
A trellis rose-like souls can climb and grow –
And a pledge that one day all journeys end
As mine has now I stand in sun, and *know*.

With memories like these which still haunt me, how
Could I retire anywhere but this place?
This Loughton where some houses are sacred
Holds dear and troubled memories I retrace.
And so I've come back to such memories,
Will never leave Loughton except for weeks
Here and there in Cornwall, Italy, Greece.
I embrace Loughton and have her for keeps.

Memories of one's childhood are limpid-clear,
They have the power of images and seem
To come not from this world but from beyond
Everyday's phenomenal screen – from dream:
Faces so vivid I could lean and touch,
Hands held over the nursery fire, still kind;
And coals that will never grow cold again.
The Loughton I embrace is in my mind.

20 February 2003; revised 24–25 August 2003

Quest theme: journey to the One through familiar houses. Set in Loughton,
Essex.

At Connaught House

I

An L-shaped front with chimneys, I go through
The front door, left to the bare sitting-room
And gaze across Epping Forest at Queen
Elizabeth's Hunting Lodge that's in gloom.
I pass on, saunter round the swimming-pool,
Sunset on its Roman columns, and yield
To its steamy warmth and blue. Windows look
Out on the sloping lawn to the first field.

I wander through the empty house, the small
Kitchen, study, out to the garage wing

To be a library, soak in stables,
The vegetable garden and outbuilding,
Then go back in and climb the airy stairs,
Stroll in and out of bare bedrooms, to west
At each window snatch views of late-sun trees,
The side gate that leads out to the Forest.

Below, round a fountain of three Graces,
Are the twelve wedged beds of the rose garden.
Two circles, a cross, four side paths all make
A Union Jack seen from air, the union
Of England, Scotland, Wales which Europe would
Undo for twelve regions, as if twelve beds
Had primacy over paths and Graces
In the pattern, whose threefold fountain heads

Show: Britannia with Welsh and Scot nymphs; or
Three goddesses of fertile grounds, sisters –
Aglaia, Euphrosyne and Thalia:
Brightness, Joyfulness and Bloom, three daughters
Of Zeus and Hera, bestowers of charm
And classical beauty in poetry;
Or Existence, Being, Void who, arms joined
In sunlit O, show the One's unity.

I clasp a popping stone in my right hand
A hundred and seventy million years old;
A round pebble, split in two halves, each stamped
With identical ammonites, whorled gold.
The hard surface hides two matching spirals,
Soft molluscs coiled in shells as hard as chrome
That have endured through time, one raised, one grooved:
Two hearts that fit together in one home.

This will be our new house, I hold the plans,
Trace over the pool my new study suite

With filing-cabinets, trace six bedrooms,
See each nook filled with my knick-knacks, my seat;
Stairs up to the roof space. This will be where
I grow old in my triangle of schools,
Walk down to Connaught Water, one with trees;
A Forest person looking at toadstools.

The Ching valley is spread out in the dusk.
The sloping grass falls away to the brook
Which rises in Hill Wood near High Beach church
And drains woods on its way past crow and rook.
I see High Beach spire in a tree-top sea.
Down in a trough is Connaught Tennis Club
Where I cycled as a boy and retrieved
Practice serves by Mottram, a scampering cub.

Edward the Confessor gave that Chingford
Parish, within Waltham's half-hundred's doze,
To St Paul's, gift the Conqueror confirmed.
It was known as King's Ford as the meadows
Were called King's Meads and the Lea the King's Stream.
The Normans (who wrote Kent as Chent) spelt it
Cingheford. This view is of Anglo-Saxon
Lands held by the first English – exquisite!

There's no history here, just an Essex place.
I have put off my grandeur and expense
To live simply in a large house, write books,
Contract my hand to what I know, dream, sense.
I've finished with outside things and must make
My peace with my new works, get up to date,
Think, see, imagine all that's in my head
In prose and verse like Hardy at Max Gate.

I wander down the sloping garden grass
To the long lily pools, all linked, stepped down,

And in spite of early dusk feel the warmth
Of a new summer creeping in green-brown,
Flecked buds and scent of flowers speared by rabbits;
And I have chosen this to grow old by
Near my young family, son and grandson,
All school work shed, now an observing eye.

From here I could walk through the Chingford woods
Past Fairmead Bottom, Loughton Monks and go
To High Beach church where my boys were christened,
Wheel through Theydon down to Abridge, follow
The Roding that rose near Dunmow and runs
Through marshy green fields sunsets wash with joy,
Under Chigwell Lane, out to Roding Lane
And the bridge I crossed so much as a boy.

I think of the brown river as it brims
Under that bridge, and I think back to when
I walked with Mabel to the humped-back bridge
And was a boy cycling to school again
Across the flood meadows and pushed my bike
To the other bank's towpath and shade's cool,
Rode the track past the barrage-balloon site
And up the narrow hill to Chigwell School.

We walked two miles towards the Loughton bridge.
On the far side where Chigwell Hall once stood,
Willows; our side, thistles with bearded seed,
Purple loosestrife and nettles. Life was good:
A flock of whitethroats, pipits. And we found
Viper's bugloss, teasle, burdock. I squealed:
Purple mallow! A civilisation
Is like a mallow growing in a field....

The Roding from its Dunmow source to Thames
Is fed by tributaries from this Forest

And pastures, water-meadows and marshlands
Round ancient Saxon towns, Essex's best.
This Forest clay holds oaks, spruce and hornbeam.
I love the trees that cradle my paddock,
I love the brown-sedge reed-swamps, yellow flag,
Ditches with gypsy-wort, poisonous hemlock.

This swathe is my country: I can recite
A hundred names of woods of which I'm fond:
Woodman's Glade, Magpie Hill and Cuckoo Pits,
Kate's Cellar, Peartree Plain and the Lost Pond,
Each of which has old memories for me.
Strawberry Hill, the Stubbles.... Here among rooks
I'll live like Chaucer's reeve on a far heath
And devote my last years to my last books.

II

From the pools on my land I look across
A valley our wooded landscapes thrive on.
We woodlanders live round bushed trees, old ponds
In this county where most names are Saxon –
Epping, Loughton, -ing "people of", -ton "town" –
In ancient royal forests in the wild
Among rabbits, hedgehogs, shrews and foxes
That I looked on in wonder as a child.

Here in the seventh century was the kingdom
Of the East Saxons of the *seaxe*, curved sword
Still on the Essex shield, whose Christian king
Saebert or Sigeberht found heavenly reward
Laid in a wood-lined burial chamber
To dissolve in acidulous Southend soil
Among things he took to the next world: wood
Drinking-cups, buckles, crosses of gold foil.

The Forest had a powerful lure for us.

We ran as soon as we had sight of trees
Banked, humped on the skyline, and then were drawn
By growing trunks, leaves fluttering in the breeze.
The Roding and these Forest streams and ponds
With sticklebacks and tiddlers that we caught,
And lilies, glint an ancient way of life
When cloth-capped children newted as a sport.

When this Forest ceased to be royal, was placed
Under the City of London's fat wing,
The Crown appointed a Ranger to watch
The bye-laws, rights of pasture and grazing:
The Duke of Connaught, Victoria's third son
Prince Arthur, who lives on in Ranger's Road,
Gave his name to the Water and this house,
Linked the Crown to these woods and this abode.

Exhausted like Propertius and Horace
I, with urbane and modest good humour,
Will retire from the bustle of the court
I have peeped into as an observer,
And will live in this sacred grove, less far
From London than Otley but far enough,
And hear news of those who pursue laurels,
Smile in blissful retirement, mind still tough.

When I was young we were agog: Angry
Young Men challenged the Establishment's mien
In plays and novels, questioned the icons
That were ruling us – Churchill and the Queen.
Osborne lambasted and then turned Tory.
Now I record with no little regret
The old order's long decay and passing,
Lament an England I cannot forget.

I look back at the timber-gabled house.

It is a palace of art: library
With all books in perfect order; records
In filing-cabinets, found easily;
A view between the Forest and the stars;
Apart from mankind where I can conclude
Within the triangle of my three schools;
A place where I can work in solitude.

I think of Joash Woodrow, great artist
Who withdrew from the world forty-five years
Ago and filled his family home in Leeds
With three thousand five hundred drawings, fears,
Paintings, hopes, sculptures, proof inspiration
Springs from solitude, not the public eye.
I too have known obscurity's great joy:
To write innovative works that don't lie.

What think my peers of my range, breadth and scale?
A few whose verses neither scan nor rhyme
Are indignant I took such care and feel
Affronted (threatened?) by my upstart crime:
Gigantic size, vast scope in verse and prose;
Disqualify my findings as steep hills,
Ignore my forests that demean saplings.
All should be small, doodles like daffodils.

So few know the great secret I exist.
I am ignored by all verse and prose hacks.
The press, radio, TV don't stoop to know.
All recoil from my truths like plague attacks
And quarantine them so they can't infect.
But I don't mind, like a forest that's oak
I put out leaves, shed them and then sprout more.
From this high place I see tiny men's smoke.

My purpose is my poems, my backbone.

I go about my business every day
And stanzas (like this one) float through my mind,
I set them down and understand and say
What my life means with freshness, clarity
And exactness, and measure my progress
By the growth of my work, which, now unknown,
May convey to future souls our "isness".

I've spent my life whittling at big ideas
And cramming them into eight-line stanzas
Like masted ships into midget bottles,
Trimming edges to make them fit so as
To please the eye. When books are no more read
And surface image has swept depth aside
My carved miniatures may seem messages
Like those tossed from where exiled Ovid died.

III

I amble by the pools in the garden.
Western philosophy is like a spring
From Parmenides and Heracleitus,
At first a splutter, then a trickling,
Now gushing Plato, Aquinas and Kant,
Locke, Hume and Leibniz filling pools, more near;
Now Positivists and Existentialists
And Universalism, the end one here.

Pools balance: Plato and Aristotle;
From them, Rationalists and Empiricists;
Lower down, Idealists and Realists;
Lower still, recent Intuitionists –
I love the Vitalists (Bergson, Whitehead)
And Existentialists like Heidegger,
Husserl – and Logical Analysis
That denied meaning (Wittgenstein, Ayer).

Pumps recycle the flow back to the start.
Now all's still, I see bathed in my end pool
The stars of the Western universe caught
In this puddle like flecked duckweed, the Rule
Reflected, disturbed by a webbed-toed newt,
And in its centre, distant, floats the moon
As twilight darkens into early night,
Reflecting unseen sunlight where I swoon.

I look into this mirror for a few
Of two hundred billion stars on the tree
Of our galaxy, heavenly Milky Way.
In my mind's puddle I can also see
A hundred billion galaxies that fill
The glittering universe that is missing
To man's telescopes, moon- and Mars- machines
That ply empty space and give it meaning.

O Western universe, the spring between
My sleeves flows like yours through these pools to sigh
As Horace's Bandusian water gushed
And can reflect your patterned starlit sky
And all the movements of philosophy
And can when running show the trickling run
Of Western direction, but above all
Reflect the night-sky of the darkening One.

The spring in my consciousness and these pools
Reflects the river that winds through my mind
Past the humped bridge I wheeled my bike over,
Near where a lorry knocked me from behind
Off my bike into the grass verge and past
My grandson's nursery where tots sing and bash;
Near where the Chelmer sometimes floods the road
At Great Easton and leaves a watersplash.

I see a dandelion, a yellow flower
As bright as morning sun, beyond Time's Word;
And a stem from the same root with round down,
Spores that will be blown by wind and scattered,
Seeds that will land, take root and grow new plants.
Being was once a round ball that was whole,
Then blown into planets. An artist's works
Are blown out like fluff near his golden soul.

Being was the gold Light's separate ball,
A wind blew and scattered each galaxy.
Ours has now become our stars and our earth
While the gold Light still shines eternally.
My works were once on a round ball of fluff,
A latent perfect clock beside my flower –
My gold soul – and will be dispersed, take root.
My flower's changeless, outside time's changing hour

The One pervades the twilit and night sky,
Leaks through the star holes, drips Light to the earth,
Rains on the Forest trees, frosts, dews the grass,
Constitutes all that's green, has form, had birth.
The universe is a well-ordered whole,
Cosmos that pours Being into our lives.
I love the sticky buds, chestnut candles
That light my way, show how Being connives.

I think of the Otley Hall knot garden:
Two infinity eights on their sides, twined.
I think, love and infinity are one,
A boundlessness beyond "before", "behind".
Add timelessness, a white seed hovering
Above the twisting knot of what's beneath,
And love's a tangled order whose sinews
Transcend a Tudor shape, soul's modern sheath.

The Western universe is meaningless
Unless it's seen with a poet's keen eye.
In my garden water's pumped down leats, pools
And's pumped back up to flow again. I sigh,
I watch the circular movement, aware
I pour in energy, more takes its place.
The flow within me's from Being to form
In an endless cycle that I embrace.

In Connaught House I will pour energy
Into new works, my spring endlessly new.
Like Hardy I'll do both poems and prose,
Take solitary walks to the past and chew
Down the Forest path to Connaught Water,
Reinvent myself, open to the One
That greens the Western universe's plains
And prinks the Forest flow from skull to sun.

I have a layered fourfold eye that peeps
Through body, mind, soul and spirit and sees
Past, present, future and eternity,
England, Europe, the globe, the One through trees,
History blend with politics, vision, Void
Or Great Zero, I co-exist with nought.
At Connaught House I co-naught and perceive
The trickling flux that erodes wood and court.

I stand by the bay-tree near my spring, look
In my pool still as mirroring mind, find
Dandelion and down, moon and fluffy stars
Which are all one when imaged in pure mind
Or before space-time when all was One seed
Enfolding Light, Void, Being, Existence;
Know a laurelled poet's still mind reflects
The Oneness of the universe through sense.

10–11 April 2003; revised 3–7, 9, 18 February, 3, 8 March 2004; 10, 16 April 2005

Quest theme: image of the One. Set at Connaught House, Buckhurst Hill, Essex.

After the Pisan Arno

I

I arrive at Pisa station and stand
On a number–1 bus to the Duomo.
We cross a bridge, I see the shimmering
Of coloured houses flecked in the Arno.
I get out and go through an arch, am shocked:
I'm back in the Middle Ages – devour
Round Baptistry, rectangled Cathedral
And very white, the famous Leaning Tower.

Now four days later I am back again.
I leave my luggage at the station, catch
A bus to the Arno and walk along
Lung'Arno Galileo, Shelley's patch,
See near the Ponte alla Fortezza
A plaque on the wall of his home and feats:
'Epipsychidion' on Emilia
And 'Adonais' on the death of Keats.

It's hot, I saunter to the Templar church
And then cross the bridge to the other side,
Ponte alla Fortezza, and stroll back
Along Lung'Arno Mediceo, wide-eyed,
And pass Palazzo Lanfranchi, rented
By Shelley for Byron, who came in style
From Ravenna with servants, saddled horse,
Birds in baskets, caged monkeys, dogs – and guile,

To join Teresa Guiccioli and this
Façade designed by Michelangelo,
Ghost in its upper floors, across river

From Tre Palazzi di Chiesa's glow
Where Shelley had his flat; no Allegra
Whom he'd left in a convent, where she died.
He moved to Genoa after Shelley drowned,
And volunteered to fight in Greece and spied.

I wander towards Ponte di Mezzo.
I know I could live here on the river,
Here on the Pisan waterfront, in view
Of where Shelley and Byron lived; ponder
My future in the footsteps of those two
And of Pound, imprisoned near the Arno.
I think of kindly Pound I visited
In Rapallo twenty-three years ago.

We discussed the epic I'd one day write.
Virgil, Milton both took twenty-five years
To gestate – procrastinate – their epics.
I think how Dante saw Beatrice through tears
By this Arno, in Florence. The same time
Passed before he began his *Commedia*.
I, too, have let years glide by like water.
I'm ready to give birth in one more year.

I sit outside a river bar and sip
A cup of tea and feel my future press.
Dante, Virgil, Shelley and Pound urge me
To withdraw from my active life, progress
The epic I have shirked twenty-four years.
I see I must admit the Italian
And Greek traditions into English verse
As did Shelley and Keats. I know I can.

All groups must go – philosophy, science;
They were means for me to accumulate
Encyclopaedic knowledge epic poets

Must absorb before they start to create.
I must ditch my running of schools, replace
Myself to give me time to write my works.
The epic looms, a vast struggle between
Good and evil, Sistine heights and depths, lurks.

And now my flesh creeps, my hair stands on end,
My eyes are wet and I'm trembling inside,
I'm intense, pure feeling that's overflowed,
Run through me like the river's gentle slide.
I see I must embody the culture
Of the West in a twelve-book epic, fill
It with meaning and write three hundred Greek,
Roman-Italian poems that distil.

I cannot speak, I'm blinking back my tears,
I know with awesome certainty my course.
Like the river Arno I must flow on
Between two banks to my goal from my source.
I'm single-minded, will spurn all blandished
Meanderings, calls to politics – shoo! –
Or to preach from a pulpit, mystery school.
I know with conviction what I must do.

I take a taxi back to the station,
Sit on the rim of the fountain till seven,
Then take a taxi out to the airport.
I am different, I walk with gods again.
I know I must write three hundred poems
On European and English ways and views,
Global and metaphysical prospects,
And an epic – for ten years for my Muse.

                    II
All that was then. Ten years later they're done,
Both epic and three hundred Odes like doors,

All opening to long vistas, avenues
That reveal the West's roots, its growth, its laws,
Views between trees like the spokes of a wheel;
The West approached as if it's quincunxes
That radiate outwards from a round hub –
Quite different from logical sequences.

My avenues are to make sense of things
I've seen or heard or read, and to explain
Why things have happened in the universe,
World, Europe, our nation's local terrain,
Or tiny events in my experience,
Like leaves small parts of one circular Whole;
So they can be understood, so I know
Their meaning from the pattern round my soul.

I write to achieve clarity of thought
About complexity, simplified view,
And to express classical clarity,
Reflect on experience digested, true,
Mind grappling with complex issues, precise,
Ending on top with exactness yet dense;
Catch the situation's total content,
Sense first, careful exact verse serving sense.

I sit in my situation – sea-mist;
Am somewhere else in imagining mind,
Striving for clarity; and then come to,
Am again in the present sea-mist, blind.
The sea comes in, goes out, leaving rock pools
And I drift in and out of here and now,
Leave the present for imagined elsewhere
And hone perceptions so they're clear and wow.

I think how I laboriously open
Paths through thickets I subsequently shape,

How some days it's intractable and I
Wrestle to sheer idea to form and scrape,
How some days it's quite effortless, as though
The rhymes were there, wanting to be revealed,
How I hew and conjure from air and show
A place that would otherwise stay concealed.

Now my conjuring's done, I think of my
Vision by the Arno when all was bright
And I saw two projects to take ten years
In one blinding call in tearful sunlight.
I could have left England and lived somewhere
In Europe's ruins to set it all down.
Now I am glad I chose to stay myself
And not stray far from my boyhood hometown.

I live a life of artist's solitude.
My daily flow of verse, like daily prayer,
Trickles energy from my inner spring.
I am determined, crouch with hands, scoop, snare
In rhymes the bubblings from my mind's crevice.
Is this genius? If genius is a spring
Perhaps. I have a source, a Muse. The rest's
Vistas: classical avenues that zing.

Such avenues to old sites were the norm
When I was a young man for all students.
The rounded education still assumes
A knowledge of Europe's cultural events
Which, since film dethroned the book, has dwindled
And now's confined to a minority.
You call it an *élite*? Nevertheless
Its breadth and depth keeps our culture healthy.

I spent ten years working on what I glimpsed
In one moment by the Arno that May.

Was it my Muse that gave me all that work?
Or Providence that called me to portray
The decay of the West's Establishment?
I did it to show the West's fourfold soul –
Instinct, reason, intellect, spirit – split
In England, Europe, globe and One: the Whole.

Conceived 3 May 1993; written 30 December 2003; revised 31 December 2003; 1 January 2004; 2–3 April 2005

Quest theme: images of the One. Set in Pisa, Italy.

24

from *Armageddon* (2008–2009)

[book 12, lines 3244–3262, invocation to Wisdom]

O Wisdom, you are, like Christ, an ideal
Beyond imperfect men who just aspire
And your Millennium which Christ has brought
Is an aspiration for which the Good
Work and which is for ever undermined
By the Bad in the endless interplay
Between opposing *yin-yang* forces that
Conflict and balance, order-disorder,
Just as plus A added to minus A
Equals zero, Nothing, in the silent,
Profound algebra of the infinite.
O Wisdom, you have tilted the balance
Just slightly towards peace and against war
Like a cease-fire that's often breached, yet holds.
And now Christ's Thousand-Year Millennium
Has given us recalcitrant humans
A better chance of forming a World State
That keeps the peace and restores paradise
In outer harmony where souls can grow.

Quest theme: image of contradictions reconciled within the One.

[book 12, lines 3459–3495, the poet as spider and peacock]

Just as a spider spins thread from its glands,
Silks from its spinnerets it chews to break,
And weaves and hangs a web with a centre
And twelve spokes radiating out, held in
Place by twelve circular filaments that
Intersect each spoke and form rotary
Shapes, each one larger as they spread outwards,
And, patient, waits for tiny flying things
To stick on thread where crystal drops of dew,
Condensed balls of atmospheric vapour,
Have formed in evening air; so this poet's
Gut and mouth have spun a twelve-spoked theme and
Hung its structure for Being to condense
As globules like dew on its worked silk thread,
Pure drops of truth manifesting from air,
The metaphysical condensed to form.
I wait for images to fly in and
Become entangled on its sticky mesh,
Tremble clear droplets under rosy sky,
The delicate filigree tracery
Of its design whose symmetry pleases
But is a practical, working form that
Has been shaped to catch truths and symbols that
Feed the spider-like imagination.
I hung my twelve-book web and caught my catch.
And as a peacock fans its five-foot tail –
And a hundred eyes peer, each feather tipped
With an iridescent eye ringed with blue
And bronze – and struts and quivers, rattling
Its quills, and, uttering loud screams, displays,
So I put up a quill structure I wear
On my back and carry around with me,
Whose hundred images are of the One
Fixed in a grand symmetrical order

That is patterned in a ribbed form. I show
The One in a hundred blue-and-bronze truths
And strut and rattle it in quiet display.
Quest theme: image of the One.

25
from *Sighs of the Muses* (2005)

Return to Oxford

I

I check in at the Eastgate, cross the High
By Schools to the tearoom where I sat by
Ricks twelve years ago, faced the place where he
Would one day be Professor of Poetry;
Then pass the round Radcliffe Camera's grey dome,
My classical, oh so familiar home,
Peer through glass for all the mornings I spent
Learning to look with scholar's eye, content.

I stand in the Bodleian quad where James
Looks down on William Herbert and exclaims
"WH"; see above doors "*scolae*":
Moral and Natural Philosophy,
Logic, Grammar, Rhetoric, Arithmetic,
Astronomy, Geometry, Music,
Hebrew, Greek, Metaphysics and History,
Medicine, Jurisprudence, Divinity.

In the Queen's Lane coffee-house, the oldest
In Europe, we sip tea, then cross with zest
To Schools South, a T-shaped hall where, balding,
Chubby, bespectacled, bending, peering,
Ricks stops tinkering with the sound system,
Hurries down, shakes hands, twinkling like a gem;

With "Nice to see you, thank you for coming"
My tutor smiles a changeless warm greeting.

I recall hearing Auden in pulpit,
Six hundred upturned faces inward-lit;
From the first floor's third row I craned to see.
Now forty-five years later it's cosy.
Here I took finals, Potter in next row.
For two terms I attended, just below,
Lectures on Yeats that were outside my course,
Striving to be me, become inner force.

We sit, the hall fills, then he makes a start
On Bob Dylan, no mike, concentrates heart,
Folds hands and speaks fluently without notes.
"*Blonde on Blonde* is his best album." He quotes
'Rainy Day', "a frustrated complaint, plea".
"Songs differ from poems, the eye can see
To the end, ears can't. His melisma floats:
One syllable bearing several sung notes."

He tells of the double meanings in "stone",
Quotes Shakespeare – would Dylan have gnawed that bone?
"If an artist and genius uses
The F- word it must have more than," he says,
"One meaning." Then he takes us through 'Just Like
A Woman', speaks of the bridge and – a strike –
The return to the opening: "Is she
Childlike? Patronising? Spoilt brat?" We see.

With his old precision he stops at six:
One hour exactly. The hall's like the Styx.
A few cross to the front, he hugs, I shrink;
Then comes to us, invites us for a drink
At the Balliol Buttery, and I team
Up with a Boston poet in a dream.

Ricks sets a scampering pace up the High,
We talk as he hurries, seventy-three, spry.

He's half-way through Haffenden on Empson
Whose pupil Irie's pictured, the don
In charge of me when I taught in Japan
In Empson's room. We pass the Bodleian.
He says, "It's the oldest Library in
The world." He's not jet-lagged (said with a grin),
Will speak to undergraduates – and chime
With Auden, who also gave of his time.

In his old college he buys Pimm's and wines,
An orange juice for dreamy Ted; and shines.
We stand in evening sun in Garden Quad,
Twelve of us, I talk to his friend and nod.
He taught at Balliol for forty years,
Has four volumes on Dr Johnson, cheers
With glancing chat. "Was it scruffy?" Ricks asks.
"No, it wasn't scruffy." They talk through masks.

"Some books have good titles and yet displease:
Across the River and into the Trees,"
Says one. At seven he shakes hands all round – mine –
And scurries off to don a gown and dine
In hall with Lonsdale. We leave and I chat
To his research assistant, who is at
The Lodge, donning bicycle-clips, alone.
I go back and eat, unsure about "stone".

I could have been a Doctor here and spent
My life helping the young to find their bent,
Now be retired and putting on my gown;
But I'd have not set sail – talked myself down:
Ricks' "Your epic predecessors failed, Pound,
Homer, Virgil, Dante, Milton" – all drowned –

"So how badly will you fail or how well?"
Sailing from Oxford I've rung belief's bell.

II

I'm back before my life diverged, my choice
To leave Law, find a poet's wind and voice
With Ricks. Morning. I find stairs near the Crown,
The Painted Room where Shakespeare bedded down,
IHS on fireblackened chimney-breast,
Orange mural of wind-flowers for the guest,
Canterbury bells and grapes, and, surmounting:
"Feare god above anythinge... and the Kynge".

Now we tour the Bodleian where, years on,
My manuscripts will lie after I'm gone;
The Divinity School's bossed fan-vaulting,
Convocation House and Court Room, climbing
Up to Duke Humfrey's bossed wood library,
Arts End's wall shelving with stalled gallery
Filled with rare seventeenth-century chained books,
The world's first vertical, galleried looks.

On to the church, the University
Till the house next door was built urgently.
We eat in its vaulted downstairs, oldest
University building, are impressed
By the first library up the tower stairs.
In the church I see where Cranmer, to glares,
Recanted till he met by Balliol gate –
Fire he thrust the hand that signed in – his fate.

We stand under Wren's Sheldonian ceiling –
Truth descends from a cloud of Light, holding
A sun so bright it hides Truth's face and palm,
On all "*scolae*" disciplines, all is calm;
Marcellus' theatre open to the sky,

204

Rolled-back Roman awning, Hermes' busts by.
Then from the Cupola we look down on
Spires and nine Muses on the Clarendon.

I look in on my old college and see,
From Front Quad's stones below the library,
The sunken lawn and my terraced staircase,
Ricks' cottaged window, go to Worcester Place
Where I left Law, past Ricks' college house where
I set sail, pass two more lodgings and stare
Where I became me, beyond Jericho,
And reach the bridge that curves to Port Meadow.

I look across the green fields where I walked
To the towpath by the brimming Thames, stalked
To Binsey Green's well by Arctic flood, head
Clear in bitter cold, walked back to toast bread
At my gas fire and numb fingers to life
In my bedsit before I took a wife,
And stand where I stood in those single days
When my life could have gone in several ways.

I have returned to Oxford, could live here
Round its old buildings, haunting walks, good cheer.
But could I be a scholar in its nooks,
Research in the Camera for my own books?
Waste whole evenings on glancing talk, then die?
In the last quarter of my life, I sigh,
I should complete my work, edit, compile;
Best done alone, apart from reason's smile.

Oxford, cradle of my literary life,
Magical place whose memories are rife,
Where I trickled *juvenilia*, scooping
A "Well of Truth" from Frideswide's clear spring,
How appropriate to locate my end

At my beginning, near Truth, my first friend –
As this last poem echoes that first real one:
Behind my shadow reigns a glorious sun.

But Truth, who holds the Light, the One, has shone
On this place and its faces that are gone.
Some are no more, the lanes fill with sadness
As I re-meet those dead in their old dress.
This place is, to ghosts and old books, a shrine
I've moved on from into books that are mine
And so, faces, I must remain above,
To get my life's work done, these lanes I love.
28 July 2005; revised 8–9 August, 5 September 2005
Quest theme: return to beginning of quest at "well of truth". Set in Oxford.

Epitaphs

1

Where is my home, and where my family?
As friend to friend let me reply frankly.
You know the doom war brought to Essex, boom
Of bombs like thunderbolts that made a tomb
Of ruined houses, walls torn down cruelly –
East London bore and Loughton suckled me,
Chigwell reared me and sent me to Oxford;
There and in Cornwall my young years. Abroad,
A child of Churchill's Age, implementing
His tripartite Iraq, and travelling
In Asia, Africa, then in London,
I wrote in distant places of Loughton,
I showed the human heart in prose and verse
And added in the universe, my nurse;
Penned of the One in poem and story,
In history. Then, sheltering like an oak tree,
Though I courted nearby Suffolk seven years

Yet never left its childhood smiles and tears,
Essex received me back and held me fast,
Epping Forest cradled me in my past
Amid children and books and birds, and gave
The Ching valley's warmth until this lone grave
In the clay land that brought my voice to birth
In trees and ponds and sunshine, on rich earth.
16 April 2005

2

Essex reared me through war, now holds my bones.
I, lost in this Dark Wood, trod ancient stones
And found Light on the Way, am now content
My works – deeds, words – should be my monument.
I showed soul, woods and stars are one process,
Revealed Being, to existence said Yes;
Loved my dear ones here, transformed dark regret.
A few clouds helped make a glorious sunset.
I mirrored my Age, am now dust. Stranger,
Look on *your* mortality and ponder.
Listen beneath the breeze and tick of time
To eternal silence and the soul's climb,
Peep behind the universe for the One:
Behind each shadow reigns a glorious Sun.
20 August 2005; revised 4–5 September 2005
Quest theme: life in relation to the One. Set in Epping Forest, Essex.

Part Two

Follies and Vices

1
from *A Stone Torch-Basket* (1963–1965)

The Expatriate
(A Dramatic Monologue set in Japan)

Ὦ δώματ᾽ Ἀδμήτει᾽, ἐν οἶς ἔτλην ἐγὼ
θῆσσαν τράπεζαν αἰνέσαι θεός περ ὤν.
Euripides, *Alcestis* 1–2

I. Wheel
In our Gethsemane
In the full moon of May,
Let us watch and pray.
A shadow glides beneath the *gingko* tree,
By the stone lotus; darkness swallows deep
The pool, the peace, the pleasure-woman's cry,
And in a silver sweep the roses die
In incidental scent for their release.
I too would now be there, had I not met you.
I joke – I only came to drink of course,
That is for others, drink's enough for us,
And lilies, and the intellectual moon.
We have the night, stranger; and they, the night has them,
By the stone lotus. They burn bright and fade, while we –
We glow and know our doom in our *Bhodi*-garden.
I joke of course, I joke about my life;
I joke like any fool who's left his wife.
Another shadow glides beneath.... Your question,
The *haiku* brought me and I stayed too long, that's all.
I joke, stranger. And I provoke.

And yet, as you are a discerning man,
I can confess, I am not what I seem,
Am at odds with something – an alien,
An alien pagan in an unreal dream.

My home? Oh no, I've no regret for that,
I don't miss England – that, too, is just a dream:
The Saturday shopping-spree, the cricket bat,
The City bells and the Forest, and Sunday tea.
That ringing laughter, by the willow-tree.
No. She had nothing for me to share,
Except...
        We were a very different pair.
No, I've no regrets; no smouldering leaves burn in my heart.
No, no, they're evergreens of winter, cold
Photogenic scenes, cheap holiday slides to while away our May:
The party, and after, until the break of day.

Another shadow... I joke, stranger, I joke.
I cannot hate the East. You see, my choice
Demands acceptance, yet another voice
Invokes: "You are apart from other folk."

A hundred births and deaths return through smoke.

II. Mirror

I can confide – come closer – other men
(Not you of course) corrode me with disgust.
(I felt the same when I was only ten.)
It is not just – ahem! – those fires of lust
(*Pace* Augustine), something more august:
Self-love and self-interest, hypocrisy,
Deceit and superficial pettiness,
Egoistic craving and vulgarity.
There is no doubt, mankind is in a mess.
Take Harmon at the office – he's my senior
(Junior in age) he.... No, Ivor Tate,
He was worse; a brash con-man who boasts
And never listens; "he's a must for hosts."
He has a manner.
        Once, in former days,

She knew him. There was a fire through the window-panes,
And then I was lost in the frost; and there were bicycle stains.
Another time there was a broken glass,
And two cigarette-ends stubbed out on the grass.
I envy no-one who is out for praise.

Have you known what it is to suffer that apart
With gutting gas-lamps huttering in your heart,
And thunder in your spleen?
                                You understand,
You too have seen it – don't you loathe mankind,
And long to strip aside his rusted blind,
Or long to rip behind his rusted blind?

I have endured a bitter, bitter dream.
I am a slave to other men's conditions.

But there's another question I often ask:
What is the point of all this menial farce,
Of papers on a desk – or an office dance?
Midwives, and brides; promotion, and success,
Are mocked to menial meaning by my death.
And what of children; running up the road from France.

I wear a mask: to myself I am a stranger
For all my intellectual positions.
I know; I fear. And Harmon does not care.
I know but do not show.
                         No I despair,
I cannot see my enemy
I cannot find him anywhere.

My life – my life is not sufficient.
In what – in what am I deficient?

III. Cinders

Another shadow glides beneath the tree
By the stone lotus. No, I have no creed;
I envy you your simple certainty.
I cannot deify the living dead.
I am a pagan of a needing breed;
Not daily bread.
                 I can erect no proof:
A trillion star-leaks trickle through my roof
And drown my differential coefficient.

And yet, you see that garden-temple's light
Just this side of the pleasure-lazaret?
There's still a light in my stone torch-basket.
I've not despaired; it may not burn that bright,
But it does burn, for something – some region
Glimpsed in clumsy silhouettes, my Zion.
In that kingdom of superconsciousness
There's no negation, I know a quiet peace,
I glow with meaning that I can't express
And happiness I never want to cease;
It doesn't matter that I've no redress,
To exist – exist! is no macabre caprice,
It is divine, that brief release,
Those dragging hours of timelessness.

But I have known another time, a cry
Within, a din, a shunting-ring of sound,
Of passions – not impressions – whirling round
With hunting appetites, and in vain I try
To gain control and ask them: Who am I?
Last night – last night my life dripped from a tap.
Tell me, did the earth shake at five? Seismology
Is now my hobby.
                 And sometimes I deny
All rational order as a brilliant lie,

And long to die.
             Last night, I lotus-sat.
There was a mewing cat. Six year's austerity
With five, then curds; and then the *Bhodi*-tree.
But not for me. Just words, Gethsemane:
Awake, alone, the flames behind my dome,
And eyes of coals that burn and yearn to weep,
Aslake for sleep, asweat for dawn to creep,
And a deep deep dread of going home.

These summer nights I'm apt to disintegrate,
But dawn pieces me together. If ever I kill
Myself, it will be to make my reason still.
And yet, I would rather be me than Ivor Tate.

I am attached to something that I hate.

IV. Dawn

I must leave you – this is my alleyway.
No, I see no one. Her? Oh that woman,
She's just a neighbour. Not an imposing place,
I do agree: a little too animal.
But see, the night is giving birth to day –
See in the palms how pale the moon-lamps hang –
A vast cave-chasm of indifference;
Another spasm – there it is, the face,
Ablaze with your Master's graveward grace – what sense
But this sense can consent to something so irrational?
Now go and kneel and be intentional.
I serve; but I will never make pretence.

    The loveless man from another home
      Is lost within his "neighbour's" room
      And loves himself in his neighbour's womb.
Follies and vices theme: self-love. Set in Tokyo, Japan.

2
from *The Silence* (1965–1966)

from The Silence

[lines 69–273, the nation's consciousness in six social classes]

*1   Sid Frampton, 'efficient' entrepreneur,
Took his foreman on an inspection tour.
In the corrugated hangar, piecework-Joe
Hammered the malleable metal and intoned
"'It 'im on ve 'ead wiv a fatted ba-nana."
'Sweeping' chips and metal shavings near the door
Albert called "'Ts 'e ol' man." In overalls Freeman drove
The final rivet in the hundredth frame, with a placid fury.
In a timid Essex drawl the boss directs
"Come over 'ere and bust up some of these boxes."
Assigned to help, bus-driver Harry Luscombe,
Part-timing for his nipper's education,
Pulls on the pincher handle, and extracts
A curved six-inch long nail, and pants:
"You won't want ter know me when yer at Oxford."
Having added a ha'p'ny to the district rate
By catapulting a hundred and eighty street-lights in one night,
Albert draws a nail near Freeman's bike,
Says "Hi say, hain't you goin' to defend yower property?"
Joe grinned, and his soul, beloved of a collective God,
Boggled in his opaque eyes.
                    Victims Joe and Albert Lee,
I want to weep, but is it burnt flesh I can smell,
Or a scratching of fleapits, before afternoon break for tea?

        Smears and dirty panes:
        Before the looking-glass
        Jeanie cakes on a face
        And, deaf to the wooing gram,

Dreams of the brand new Jag
That Charlie Weemack will race
Down streets that have forgotten
The whine and shattering blast
To the war memorial;
Where, parked with a greasy smile,
He will lubricate her parts,
Ignite her and rev her up
And, under the sputtering lamp,
Switch off when she's overhot
And pour in cooling rain.
From Peking Man to Yeats
We struggled to create
Her serviceable yawn
And, immune against the past,
That china-poodle taste,
That mechanised embrace.

Echoes and empty rooms:
After calling in her "pussy"
Twice-widowed Mrs. Hall
Stands by the gas and broods
On her Portslade property
And the man who rented her body
And built it round with a wall
In a jealous, free-hold decade
And nightly knelt at her grave
And paid her a monthly due
And lived respectably,
And who narrowed down her head
To an occasional trip into town
And fear of a burglar's tread
Or a crash in real values
Or a sudden fuse.
Quasars and galaxies
Sent light for millions of years

To help cheated Mrs. Hall
Brew twenty thousand tears.

The TV crackles in a thundery silence;
And as he renounces weapons I can hear
The scraping of a knife and tensely exhaled breath;
Not looking, Freeman turns the evening paper.
Then the Wing-Commander spoke, trying to provoke:
"Anyone'd think he'd had some experience, the cowardly traitor.
What is the country coming to if it's that soft?
My God, if I had my way I'd have dropped the Bomb years ago,
And I'd lock up every long-haired idealist.
They're a menace to society." (Freeman does not stir.)
Unsatisfied, he asserts himself on the dogs,
Angrily making them bark with a false alarm,
One of the Few who fought in our finest hour
For an unheroic age of education,
Who saw too clearly past the Second Empire,
Who could not see beyond conserving the status quo
And who would not disarm the status of Great Power.

At last the inheritor invades the blackened stairs,
Noctambulist Fosdick from a consultation;
And, dreaming of flaking walls like peeling loins
And of groins that are bare beneath a petticoat
He furtively reclimbs a darkened Soho stair,
And, turning the handle to his office room
Barks timidly at his secretary to resume his role.
And watch *this* ailing Knight of a Merrie day
Extend a sagging hand and fall into a chair;
An exhausted Tory, spawned in a tired tradition
One of the unlevelled gentry, with an unlevelled air!
After confirming the 'approximate' acreage
Of the pre–1810, unregistered estate
They agree the 'estimated' annual rents;
Among decomposing Pharaohs, in Phaestos ruin

Freeman is disturbed to preserve the established order,
To wall out chaos with a 'statutory' return.
Are they real, or are they waxworks from Tussauds,
These comfortable corpses in share-lined graves?
Lord, let them choke in a disinherited terror
Before they leave for backgammon at the St James!

The sun rose
Red and majestic
On the formal garden
White paths
Misty fountains
Dark grass
Empty couples
On idle glasses

                    The red sun rose,
Throwing a judgement on a squandered night.
Reclining on the pillared wall, His Acred Lordship
Regally received his departing guests,
And, mid crinolines turning for the last quadrille,
Tickled the crumpled bottom of his latest trollop.
Say what you will, thought Freeman, blue blood once swung in trees,
And reassured, superior, strode over and shook hands,
Looked through the smile to yellow-ochre eyes
And seeing, beyond, the perception choked with names
Said "It was nice" like an epitaph, saw the surprise
And smelt the decay.

Six purposeless futures for a savage "saint",
Lower consciousnesses he will not imitate.

*2 On the top of a London bus I was withdrawn,
In a City suit I broke the circuit of fragmentary dreams,
I awoke to my presence on the chesty engine,
And watched my breathing like a tired machine

219

And observed the puce flush of a strenuous dawn.

>And might not twenty years
>On tensely bended knees
>Take one to the meaning
>Of a schoolgirl's bleeding thighs,
>Or a stranger's red-rimmed eyes,
>Or a swelling universe,
>Or a nation's thrust and disease?
>Or, scaling a self till it's nothing,
>To the reason why two twisted lungs should breathe?

*3 "I believe in the Resurrection of the body, and the life everlasting."
In this sepulchral part of the decaying stronghold
Answers are chanted in an absent-minded dream
While Mrs. Purkiss, Vera Styles and Lady Black
Turn in their pews with insinserious smiles
Or put up a hand to adjust a hat.
And squared by trestle-tables in this Essex hall
A hundred ladies contract for merchandise,
See how they thumb with concupiscent touch,
Give ungrudged pennies with meretricious smiles.
Freeman refuses a glass of orangeade,
Agrees with ladies in hat-veils and gloves
Who soliloquise on new collection-plates,
Avoids the bored reporter from the local rag,
Awaiting the Minister, who is scoffing cakes.
"Would you like another piece of *child's flesh*?"
Suddenly the parquet heaved, dwarfs crawled up
With tattoed biceps, swarmed up pleated skirts,
And tore and rucked in struggling, churning thighs,
Then flung aside and burnt, deaf to the screams.
Freeman went outside.
                              Virtuously undressed!
O generation of virtuous coquettes,
Go to the brothel and be virtuously honest!

*4   No sap united the splitting English tree,
Feeling no connection, the final fruit broke free;
Beneath the iron cross lay a congregation.
A sinful nation, through lack of opposition:
What great dreams will you have, Jeanie,
In visionary ecstasy outside the record shop?
And, thanks to the nocturnal struggles of kneeling authorities,
What shattering insights will be flashed on your screen, Mrs. Hall,
To make you blink after five hours' vibrant surrender?
What great choice will you make at the church bingo, Dolly Jakes,
Putting yourself in question with one creative stake?
And, disturbed by an arresting mural, Mr Parks,
Will you feel the night gape like a bailiff's laugh?

                         Screaming gods and hoardings;
                         In a decayed time, unreal states;
                         Where is there any purpose,
                         If not in the silence of saints?

               [lines 623–648, Scrabble]

*5   A quarter stirs and musically resounds
With a lost century's languor,
The echoes curl with soporific yawns
And relapse in slumber;
Motes of dust resettle on cluttered walls
In this subconscious hall.
In fading light, three generations are engaged in scrabble.
Having approved her grandson's choice of bride
Materfamilias, with a determined glee,
Triumphantly builds OLDEN, and defies
Her daughter to consult the *OED*.
And in a brown background, on the wall I espy
Harmonious maidens in an ideal family.
With a handful of Xs, the cynosure declines
Her orthographic ordeal, and draws a Z.
And should I lay down that word, in no-one's dictionary,

Say, "Even now it could float through the window and flutter to the
floor,"
Or, "I have studied post-war graffitti on expectorated doors"
As though worms should squirm and hang from my bulbous eyes?
I see harmonious maidens in an ideal society,
And forfeit the victory.
January 1965–June 1966; revised August 1970; 25–26 July 1974 and later
Follies and vices theme of The nation's consciousness in six social classes unspec-
ified and unlisted, connected with inequalities, triviality. Set in Loughton, Essex;
Hove, Sussex; West Dulwich; Bedford Row, London; Cliveden, Berkshire. Follies
and vices theme of Scrabble: genteelness.

The original text has glosses in the margin in the manner of Coleridge's 'The
Ancient Mariner'. The positions of five glosses in the above excerpts are denoted
by numbered asterisks, and the glosses are listed below:

1.   Freeman recalls examples of the nation's perception. He feels that it is not
     enough to live at the level of everyday social triviality.
2.   On a London bus he becomes aware and sees with his higher consciousness.
3.   At a church jumble sale he feels that Christianity has nothing to offer him.
4.   Nor has the Essex way of life.
5.   He takes [his future wife] to meet his grandmother.

3

from *The Wings and the Sword* (1966–1969)

from Archangel

[lines 33–133, Communist revolution and dictatorship]

> There is a disease within
> And Revolutions breed
> Like resisting antibodies
> In an infected blood,
> To exterminate the germs,
> And leave the body healed;

Shots from the Winter Palace,
An absent Chief Commander,
A Tsarina's doting on
A haemophiliac son,
A faith-healing lecher –
Were these responsible for
Or were they symptoms of
The sickness that angered and drove
These thick-coated workers
In the queues at the bakers' shops
To strike processions and shots?
And, after the abdication,
Before the Sverdlovsk blood,
On the second disguised return
And after Kerensky's flight,
To storm the Winter Palace
And hail the Smolny cure?
Or, after a crusader drank gold leaf,
And a hundred day's reform,
Were an imprisoned Emperor,
An "Old Buddha's" mistaken scorn,
And, after the indemnities,
A retirement 'with sore feet'
And reprisals for a bomb,
Were these responsible for
Or were they symptoms of
The sickness that compelled
These thin-ribbed peasants
In their landlord's cropless fields
To arm for a republic?
And, after a twelve-year-old's twelve-day rule,
Warlords and a Sun-set,
Butchery under a hill
And a march against a traitor,
After the temple meditation
Through to the great idea,

And the three-sided war,
And after Chiang's escape,
To storm Nanking Headquarters
And hail the Tien An Mien cure?
And how can one proclaim
It is better to be diseased?

When the reactionaries triumphed, there were groans from the Party seats,
To sombre music, they were flogged to execution, the anti-bourgeois
    rebels,
But then Marx and Lenin shone up on the funereal drape,
And as the light streamed from their heads, the broken army recovered,
With shining eyes, they pledged faith in their undaunted Leader,
And, with flags and rifles, rushed across the stage to bring great
    victories,
And when the proud imperialists and their lackeys were finally driven
    into the sea
A great cheer went up, all applauded, and as the orchestra joined in,
With one accord both choirs stood up and sang out
While soldiers with joyous faces gathered under the red banner
And laughed and hugged peasants laden with fruit from a bumper
    harvest
And there was Paradise under their Chairman Leader's blessedly
    streaming head.
As the students crowded round me, laughing among the magnolias,
I felt a great singing in me, I wanted to sob for happiness
For I had gone back to a dawn and was with an original man;
But when, at a woman's command, eight hundred children burst into
    smiles and applauded,
And, after clambering like guerrillas round the barbed wire in the
    playground
And shooting imperialist bombers out of the amusement-centre sky,
When five-year olds danced 'Embroidering the Saviour's portrait' –
I knew they had put the smiles on those faces, and, for the sake of the
    future,
Taught them to be joyous and grateful at well-rehearsed signals

As if they were dogs, trained to salivate at a bell,
And although I could not say "Insincere", for can saliva be,
I said "No" to their Party, and I knew their Saviour was an enslaver of
    souls.
"Yes," said the former landlord in his pig-stye, and, when jogged, added,
"I am grateful to the Commune for permitting me to be a member,"
And he left the barn and stood outside his former house
While the peasants gawped in a silent arc, as if round a belled leper;
"Yes," said the Shanghai capitalist in his unliberated mansion,
"I came to see that capitalism should be detested,
These Americans call it brainwashing, but it is only the process
Of seeing things in their right perspectives,"
And his eyes seemed confused, as though a lobotomised mind
Had been dictated over, and bits of the old remained;
"Excuse me," said the official in the sacked ruins of the Summer Palace,
After the board of eligible 'voters' for the unopposed Party
And the barred library on the purged and deserted campus,
"Our history books say the concessions were seized in 1949,
And Romanization will not change a thing,
I know that Confucius was in a fairy tale."
And, staring into the green pond in the Empress Dowager's Garden,
Where, marble walks and bridges and tea-house pavilions,
The world was a circular quest, as on a meditating mind,
I was back in a past like the diseased Saints' Western Hell
Where children dance a plague song, and jeer and scowl
When the bell tolls for their Saviour's funeral,
Where an infectious idiot reviles Trafalgar Square
And, unremoulded, votes out a clever fool,
Where no historians expurgate our accounts
Or claim Suez was given away when the troops withdrew,
Where truth is in libraries and one's reflecting self
And we are here for more than bread and smiles
And no "protecting" Parties enforce our "health".
11, 20 June–23 July 1966; revised in 1968

Follies and vices theme: Communist revolution and dictatorship, brainwashing.
Set in Russia and China.

4

from *Old Man in a Circle* (1967)

from Old Man in a Circle

[lines 23–205, follies of national decline and British Empire's decay]

"The year is the prototype of all cyclic processes (the day, the span of human
life, the rise and fall of a culture, the cosmic cycle, etc.)... The year (or the
wheel of the Zodiac) is usually represented by the figure of an old man in a
circle."

J.E. Cirlot, *A Dictionary of Symbols*

From the heels of Europe, a low black cloud of dust
Hung like a shroud across a blood-red Greenwich sun,
And in a New York noon men counted bags of gold
While a white-flagged convoy steamed over a crimson ocean;
And now, under planes that hang like flies in a billowing smoke,
In a ghastly, red-brown light, the scorched horizon glows,
The Prince of Wales sinks, the Midway victors cheer,
And now, in smouldering ruins, while Red tanks crawl,
The protector of Europe waits like a butler on the American elbow,
Waives his indemnities under a boiling mushroom cloud;
Shivering in snow, in a power-cut early dark
A threadbare rationed people queues for coal –
I see lorries leaving Greece, and GIs trundling in,
I see flurries of dollar bills, like autumn leaves, in eighteen cities,
And flights of Allied planes heading for Berlin,
I see lights going on in Hindu and Moslem India, in Ceylon and Burma,
I see lights going on in Palestine and Iraq, and the sun setting over
    Africa,
I see a servant saying "Careful" in Korea, and piqued at his master
For befriending the plaintiff who lost him his fortune,
I see twilight in Malaya, in Cyprus, in Suez,
And a dolled-up Cnut stopping the night with a policeman's palm

And his master saying "Fool, can an old man stop the earth?
Wind up the clocks, for your dark is our morning."
I see a black cloud advancing from the East, and eyes turning West,
I see a giant and a shrivelled dwarf under a Bahaman sun.
I see deserted streets and skeletons shuddering at a car backfire,
Trapped far from Cuba between orange and white night,
I see a black cloud racing up from the South
And thirteen lights going on in Africa, as in a block of council flats,
In Gold Coast and Nigeria, Tanganyika, Sierre Leone,
In Uganda and Kenya, Zanzibar and Nyasaland,
In Zambia and Gambia, Bechuana-and Basuto-and Swazi-land,
I see lights going on in Algeria, the Congo, Libya,
I see a thundercloud over the western horizon,
Over Jamaica and Trinidad, over British Guiana,
I see twilight in Aden, in Rhodesia, and frowns in a conference chamber,
I see Hindu and Moslem embrace under a hammer and sickle,
I see Common Wealth leaders flinging dollars to their poor,
I see Marlborough House a museum, and, outside the wall of Europe,
A suffering servant in motley, rejected of men
Talking to himself, saying "Careful in Hanoi," as, with one last shaft,
On the Falklands and Fiji, Hong Kong, Mauritius, and the Rock,
The curved orb slid into the sea, and the land grew suddenly dark.
Northern Ireland, Mozambique.... Panama, Iraq....

      The golden sun set and a moon tinted all silver.
      I heard a voice cry, "Watchman, what of the night?"
      "Rise and fall," the watchman said, "rise and fall:
      The morning cometh, and also the night –
      The Habsburgs rose and sank into the night,
      The British rose and shone against the night."

      O Churchill.
      There is silence in Whitehall
      Save for the muffled drums;
      The flag-draped gun-carriage crawls;
      Sailors with reversed guns;

The launch moans up the river,
The cranes dip in homage
Under a fly-past to 'Rule Britannia'
And the passing of an Age.

Put another nickel in
In poor old Winnie's treacle tin
Screeched "a Jutland veteran" with a black peg leg
And all down Piccadilly, the indomitable Grand Fleet steamed,
71 battleships and battlecruisers, 118 cruisers,
147 destroyers and 76 submarines;
And on the dreadnoughts our guardian angels sang
"Rule Britannia, Britannia rules the seas."
O 15 St James's Square, O Edward the Seventh,
Clyde, Scott and Franklin, Burgoyne and Lord Lawrence,
Like a gallery of summer ghosts in the winter dark.
Ah Palmerston! Leaving the HQ of de Gaulle's Free French,
Sauntering down the Waterloo steps
And meandering along the Mall to the Admiralty Arch –

skyyyyboltbluewaterstreaktsrtwoooo,
A pair of F-111s skimmed like swallows underneath
Where Vulcan and Victor, coupling blue steel wings,
Droned towards the warning web at Fylingdales,
And, near Holy Loch and closed-down shipping yards,
Disregarded the fish with the independent fins,
The Polaris sub with the interdependent scales.

Aegospotami and Midway. Ah the maritime:
One blink and a whole armada is knocked to bits
Or sold abroad, or stored, as "obsolete",
And shipless Admirals' voices float from aerials
To 4 aircraft carriers, 2 commando ships,
2 cruisers and a few destroyers and frigates –
O Senior Service.
As I left Downing Street during the Seamen's Strike,

Big Ben peered over the trees and pulled a face
And Nelson raised an arm.

In an angry crown of cotton and motor workers
As I waited for the "grim-faced" union leaders,
Sighing over the *Times* front page, while, on a transistor,
A newscaster told of uproars in Parliament –
As I shook my head
An NAB man twitched my sleeve, and said:
"We're much better off now than we were after the war, mate.
Look at them all these days, with their mini-skirts and their records.
We went to Austria again this year, on the cross-channel steamer,
Why, I got a hundred quid taperecorder last week,
And we'll soon have made the last payment on the car,
And now our Jimmy's left school he's bringing in twelve pound a week
And that means Vi can go to the bingo parlour now and again for a little
    flutter,
She couldn't do that just after the war, you know, not bloody likely.
Empire meant nothing to ninety per cent of us, except wars.
I had a brother. Killed in Cyprus, he was, and what good the Empire do
    him?
No, the Empire was a drag, mate, and we was lucky to chuck it,
And you don't wanta worry about what's happening here, this is just
    stop-go.
No, we're all right, mate, we're more prosperous than we've ever been."

But round the corner on the blackened Treasury wall
Alongside RHODESIA WHITE I saw
MENE, MENE TEKEL PERES, and I was appalled.
(Many, many shekels – perlease.)
      "The-Tax-man's-tak-en-all-my-dough
      And-left-me-in-my-state-ly-home,
      La-zing-on-a-sun-ny-afternoon,"
Sang Lord Roberts the landowner with shoulder-length hair.
Beside him, under the equestrian statue in a packed Trafalgar Square,
Slouched Sir Eric Porter, the civil servant's son,

And, yawning with one hand limp on an ND banner,
The Marxist grandson of a Tory Chancellor,
Toby Long, a praefect at Winchester;
"Up the workers," shouted Roberts, "up the Viet Cong,"
And nearby a scowling nobody with a spurned and rejected air
Cocked his *Look Back* with a revolutionary's stare –
"'*Vous vous étes donné la peine de nâitre*,'" he sneered,
"Screaming Lord Roberts with your shoulder-length hair."

Said Roberts, "Could you spare three pounds?
There'll soon be nothing to do except wandering round."

From the air lighthearted London
Was like an orange star
On a holiday camp restaurant.
St Paul's dome bristled
With a Beatle's haystack hair,
Eros wore Carnaby gear,
And Queen Victoria bustled
From where a hook-nosed Sheikh
Followed a crooked finger
Into a flesh *boutique*;
Near a Soho *discothèque*
Two minidollies strummed,
"We export sixteen per cent
Of our gross national product;
Hovercraft and reactors,
Vertical take-off planes,
Computers and farm tractors,
And expensive British brains –
We export sixteen per cent,
We are not decadent."

Ya, ya, ya-ya, smashed kiosks and seafront windows,
Ya, ya, ya-ya, deck-chairs chucked in the sea,
And a horde of youths broke under the Palace Pier

And swarmed up the shingle with barbarian ululations,
Burst through the railings, dragged a man from his machine,
Poured across the road into the coffee bar,
Overturned the tables and trampled on the leather-jackets,
Then swept out after the Duke, jumped on four hundred scooters
And kicked and, like a cloud of hungry locusts, clacked away
To rip at concrete slabs, coils of wire and metal
And drop them over the bridge before the distant smudge of a train.

        Ring a ring a roses –

O how is this faithful city become a harlot.
As under purple flowers rooted in basement cellars
Your memory still shudders at a siren's whine
And breathes fresh air beneath your festering wounds;
But now you are charcoal and bubonic black, and you are weary, weary,
The skin on your face is peeling, like mildewed yellow parchment,
You are full of sores, and germs scuffle under your crumbling spires,
Foreign bodies clog your veins and choke your aorta,
Fevers throb hot and cold in your indecisive brain,
The whole head is sick, and the whole heart faint,
Your coins show an outline Queen, here are smudged Churchillian
        crowns,
And you burn to the pealing rooftops with rosy rings;
Ah London, your sins are as crimson, your silver like impure snow,
Your moons rise on feasts of indulgence, all varieties of vanity,
Two decades your ingrown flesh has turned grey and rotted with dirt,
Wash you, make you clean.

O how the Assyrians advance from the East....
I see the peoples of Eastern Europe take to the streets,
I see the Russian empire crumbling into dust,
O the Cold War. You resisted

While you rotted in bitter freedom.

Make you clean.

20 December 1966–13 March 1967; revised in 1968

Follies theme: follies of national decline, rebellion of Lord Roberts, Sir Eric Porter
and Toby Long against traditional values during British Empire's decay,
barbarism, social disharmony and discontent. Set in London.

5

from *Whispers from the West* (1976–1979)

Wistful Time-Travellers
(First Version)

Sitting here in our flat, after dinner,
We can turn on the past. One TV knob, and Lord-
-s of Time, we are back eight years at the Marathon.
It could be twelve years ago on a tape-record-

-er. Our voices will speak from that Christmas, at a touch
Of a key. Or if I put up a screen, I could be
Me as I was at a wedding fifteen years back
In a garden of celluloid Eternity.

We Westerners are all time-travellers now.
We glide at the speed of light. For a few pounds
We can put back the clock to yesterday,
Fill the present with yesterday's sights and sounds –

Football, cricket, boxing, thrillers, or songs,
Memories on tape or film or a round disc,
Available in the home, or the waves of the air,
To escape the present for a vicarious risk.

We needed the past when we were doddering.
We looked nostalgically back to the Golden noon
When the West held, baffled that the mightiest,

Most inventive civilisation, whose offshoot reached the moon,

Should, after D-Day, shrink in senescent ruin,
Retreat in a world which prefers the tyrant's prime
To our old system. Whispering disapproval,
We Westerners wistfully escape the present time.
26–28 April 1976
Follies theme: escapism.

Westerners and Desire: A Dialogue between Body and Soul
(Or: Between the Maenads and Orpheus)

'Desire', "unsatisfied appetite, longing, wish, craving." 'Lust', "sensuous
appetite regarded as sinful; animal desire for sexual indulgence, lascivious
passion."

Oxford English Dictionary

Body:
Forty years after the war, we Westerners
Have one relaxation we all admire.
Once it was hushed up: discretion or scandal.
Now it can be mentioned openly: desire.

We like to relax in a bed during the day
As if it were a hot bath. What, after work,
Is more comfortable than to climb stairs, flop on a bed
Lie back and be kneaded, fondled, kissed, then jerk

Round and begin to discharge the tensions,
Sucking nipples, limbs twined in urgent fire,
Then lie back and gaze at the ceiling, like a child
That has been fed and is therefore 'free' from desire?

In or out of relationships there's variety.
A woman will do anything to keep a man.

It is easy to bed him, hard to make him return.
She will debase herself to his wishes, do all she can.

And there is pressure on a woman these days.
If she won't do what her men want without inhibitions,
There are many who will – 'liberated' women –
So Western men can impose their own conditions.

Soul:
Did natural desire always turn to sinful lust,
Appetite yearn for one *and* many? Have we gone soft?
Or have we moved into an Age of the Body
When to have climaxed means no more than to have coughed?

Body:
Massage parlours, escort agencies, sex shops
All now proclaim: the sin of lust is good!
Video booths rent pornographic films,
Nudes scream from newsagents' covers a red light 'could';

What can be found behind certain dingy doors,
Girls in a hundred positions, girls, girls, girls!
Thumbed through by Westerners now wise to Aids,
Busty blondes and brunettes with tumbling curls.

We have the pill, and ready abortions,
And state clinics, and injections against VD.
So, short of exercise, we take breaks from work
And live on the brink of our sexuality.

Soul:
Satisfy desire, and it enslaves the more.
Deny it as sinful lust, and we can be free.
We Westerners had active values once,
But now we have relaxed, into slavery.
1976; revised 1990

Follies and vices theme: lust.

from *A Rainbow in the Spray* (1981–1985)

Orpheus to Eurydice
(A Soul-and-Body Sequence)

I sat in an airport: loudspeaker sounds
The board click-clicked arrival times, people
Stared at screens or sat with vacant faces
And leaned on luggage. Your flight was late. I gazed
And felt a rising excitement in my blood
As old memories stirred to wakefulness.
Airports are waiting-places, and I waited for you.
You came from an underworld of baggage checks,
Walking across marble under yellow neon,
Your long hair, wide smile, shining teeth.
We went to a car park, you curled up in your seat,
Knees underneath, and fell into my arms
And kissed me long and deep as if I were this world.
Soon we lay together in a curtained room
And I unbuttoned my soul, and you peeled off
Your well-cut clothes and slid inside with me,
Your thin body milk-white, your slim breasts warm,
Your hair tumbling round your shoulders. You opened your soul
"Only to you", you whispered. And I felt your darkness.
I gave you a card with two gold flowers, each filled
With light in one petal, one petal dark,
Each fresh with raindrops and the juice of love,
And I gave you a rolled gold locket with two flowers
And a separating chasm, a channel of Light.
You told me you wrote to me from your underworld bed.
I felt the tremendous orgasmic power of the earth
As if a large moth beat at my window like your soul
Imploring to be let in. But you were on loan.

The underworld still had you under its control.

We had to attend the Zeus-Pluto summit.
We sat in indecision of the devil's kind,
I saw horns above the eyes of some who said
God is unnecessary to his creation.
I felt in your fingers an electric charge.
Was that not a new form of Materialism ?
The monochord spreads from God to the lowest depths.
We meditated to my harp and bells,
We touched fingers, not of the Devil's kind
But soul and body fused, spirit with sense.
I knew I had left a heavenly mansion above
To come down here and find and reclaim you,
And lead you out, and back to Heaven.
And that you must not look round, Eurydice,
Or you would be lost for ever in time,
And so I played my music, wrote poems
To give you hearts to follow me to Light.
I could be torn to pieces by wild Maenads,
But I put my wind-harp on a deserted hill
And let the winds sing through it of my love.

I awoke at three to see the Light in my soul
I bathed in it, basked in its white shimmers,
Like sunlight reflected on water, and then
I listened to a chord and heard within
The crashing of a symphony, a roll of drums,
A swelling blast of trumpets and cymbal crash.
I came out of my inwardness to you.
You woke, I said, "Good morning, my angel."
You said, "Not angel". But I said "Angel",
I recalled when we were lying in a cloud
And wishing we had bodies we could touch;
And had we not taken bodies to meet,
And would we not always know each other as souls?

You lay beside me, I told you my destiny,
My direction, my mission in this dark world.
You said, "The years are passing, you must make haste."
I looked back to the waves, mountains and woods,
Pictures frozen like stained glass images.
You were the centre of my being, I had found you,
Knowing there is one who finds, one who would be found.
You showed me a photo in a silver frame,
You said "I carry it everywhere". I looked and saw
Myself from long ago, Eurydice,
Looking slim, with brown hair, under a blue sky.
You said "I fell in love with you that day."
I looked at your eyes and wide smile, so young,
And I did not know you had fallen in love with me then.
I thought how you came to my hotel, how hard
It was to do then what you are so good at now.
You kept your soul from me then. It was body-thirst.
A strange white-cheeked blackbird called from a tree.
I walked through deserted streets and returned at dawn,
Let myself in, tapped at your door like a ghost,
And for the last time, we lay together
Whispering, head pillowed on your hair,
Your milk-white skin ready, you opened and said
"I want my body to show you how I feel"
And I felt your soul opening like a flower;
I sank into your soft being's petals,
You shuddered and smiled with far-away eyes,
Unfocused, defenceless as you held me,
Pliant, supple, yielding, submissive. We loved
Each other's airy soul through our body's fire.
I loved you and turned to possess your soul,
And the underworld forbids unions of souls.
I saw you wave and blow a kiss and turn.

You were gone, taken from me, snatched by the power
That governs the rhythms of your body's juice.

You are lost to this world, lost in the underworld,
And I, Orpheus, who descended from my heights
To save you from your mountain slopes,
And bring you up to daylight, to the blinding light,
Have power of music and number, which comes from beyond.
I have the gift of the gods – and need you with me.
I led you upwards, playing, and you followed.
Now I look round the corner of each door –
And see you wave and blow a kiss, and turn,
Lost to me until I can raise you again!
Alone again, I drive through streets to work
Lampposts loom and recede with vacant gaps
And I think of you who fill my grieving soul,
I am now in a gap as between lamp-posts,
And a light I was drawn to has gone out.
At work I go through my day mechanically.
Solve problems, but deep down I am with you.
You have gone, my angel, and now I stare,
And the lump on my heart is heavy as stone.
I see your curled hair, eyes with a secret look,
Now baring your perfect white teeth, stretching your lips,
So neatly walking among the primroses.
An umbilical tightness under my heart.
A heaviness in my heart, like a cannon-stone.
You said, "I am a woman, I cannot live without love.
It is very easy to meet someone else.
I can have any man I want, like picking a cherry.
What shall I do? What am I, a woman, to do?"
You are of the underworld, and have left me
With a swallowed cherry-stone in my lungs,
Half-wishing the Maenads would tear me in pieces.
But I am divine and must return to the heights.

April 1985; revised 18 January 1994

Follies and vices theme: infatuation, lust.

6

from *The Warlords* (1994)

[D-Day Soldier]

D-Day Soldier. For two nights we tossed on the choppy sea.
It was full of ships and craft, surely the Germans
Would see us and bomb us from the air?
The storm soaked us as we huddled on deck.
No one said much, we waited, seasick. Then
At H-hour a barrage from our Navy ships.
We scrambled down long ropes, packs on our backs,
Clutching rifles near tied gas masks, and jumped
Into assault craft, a ribbon of shore ahead
Gleaming in the early morning sunshine,
With little puffs of smoke from our Navy's shells.
Dipping, swaying, we crouched all tense and looked,
We approached through fire, bullets whipped up the
    waves
And clanged our sides. We nosed through floating
    bodies
Towards the smoke. A German plane roared down
And strafed the crowded beach, men and vehicles.
In that moment each one of us was afraid.
Yet we all showed courage. Bang! Down went the flap,
Out, we jumped into three feet of cold waves
And waded through the bullets and corpses
To the sand at the lapping water's edge,
Then dived as the plane whined down and raked our
    path.
"Mines," someone shouted, "stick to the matting."
We ran doubled-up under sniper fire.
The man beside me on the landing craft
Fell at my side, shot through the head. We gathered
At a muster point at the top of the beach,
And I saw a German soldier dead in a tree.

We were given provisions, and then ran on
Towards a house and fields, we advanced.
Follies and vices theme: systemic killing during Second World
War.

[on Hitler]

(*17 June, morning. Margival, near Soissons, Hitler's reserve HQ, Wolfschlucht
2. HITLER, ROMMEL and RUNDSTEDT. JODL, SCHMUNDT and others.
STENOGRAPHERS.*)

Stenographer. This man is the terror of the world. Four Focke-
Wulf Condors flew him and his staff to France,
The entire fighter force along the route
Was grounded, anti-aircraft batteries
Shut down. As he drove from Metz airport to here,
Luftwaffe fighter planes patrolled the highway.
He has come to boost the Field Marshals' confidence
After the reverses in the battlefield.
All men tremble at the power his conquests brought.
I look forward to seeing what the man is like.
I am sure he will have Rommel quaking too.
Follies and vices theme: systemic killing during Second World
War.

[chorus of Auschwitz prisoners]

Chorus. What will become of us? Who will help us.
We hear that Montgomery has landed,
Normandy is a long, long way away.
How many months will it be before his troops
Have captured Berlin and reached here? Where are
Zhukov's men? Last month, eight thousand were killed.
This month, some two hundred and twenty-five
Thousand, mostly Jews sent from Hungary.
We know, we've seen them, we drag the bodies

From the gas chamber into the crematorium
Next door, we burn them and bury the surplus.
Each day prisoners are taken out and shot
Before the killing wall next to block eleven,
And more are hanged on the portable gallows.
Montgomery, make haste, help us, help us.
We cannot wait more than a few more weeks.
It will be our turn soon. Help us, help us.
Follies and vices theme: systemic killing during Second World
War.

[Eisenhower at Falaise]

(*Later in August. Falaise, the battlefield.* EISENHOWER *stands apart from*
KAY.)

Eisenhower.   Now I, the Supreme Commander, am confronted with
The reality to which my plans have led:
The Falaise battlefield, covered with tanks,
Guns, vehicles, horses and thousands of dead
German soldiers in uniform, overhung
Like a morning mist with the foul stench of death
That gets in my throat and chokes and sickens me;
A field of decaying flesh, as if the top
Had been taken from a burial ground, exposing
The rotting corpses of the hidden dead.
This is an inferno, this is infernal. I loathe war,
I despise what my plans have done,
This victory I have won over these humans.
I am disgusted with myself for being
Involved in this slaughter, this massacre,
Which falls below the standards I uphold.
War is like a cesspit that must be cleared out,
There is nothing for it but to wade in muck
And inhale the sickening stench and finish the job.
But while I do it, I hate what I am doing

And want to keep casualties to a minimum.
The odour of war nauseates me, Kay,
And I feel ashamed to have ordered that these young
    men
Should be bombed and strafed into lifelessness like this.
Civilisation is not pretty when
It resorts to war and deeds of barbarism.
Follies and vices theme: systemic killing during Second World
War.

[Montgomery demoted]

(*1 September, evening. Dangu, Montgomery's new HQ.* MONTGOMERY
sitting alone on a canvas chair, being painted by JAMES GUNN. *They are
observed by* HENDERSON.)

Henderson.   He looks like a medieval English king
                 Surveying his lands at Crécy or Agincourt.

                 (*The session is over.* MONTGOMERY *rises and goes into his
                 caravan.*)

Montgomery.   Demoted. Elevated to Field Marshal
                 But demoted as Commander, from Land Forces
                 To Twenty-first Army Group. And by a man
                 Who had not seen a shot fired in his life
                 Before *Overlord*, does not understand strategy,
                 Has failed to impose a clear strategic plan
                 On the battlefield, squandering all our gains,
                 And is therefore useless as a field commander.
                 He's completely and utterly useless.
                 Demoted after the greatest invasion ever
                 And a three-month battle resulted in victory,
                  And me, across the Seine, heading for Brussels.
                 Where is the justice in that? What is the meaning?
                 (*Praying.*) O Lord, I asked for your help for *Overlord*.

You gave it, and we were victorious,
But the task is only half-done, and now the command
Is in the hands of a man who will lengthen the war.
Is this what you want? Is this part of your purpose?
If it is, I am content, though I cannot see
The benefit to the Allies, the troops, or
The German people of prolonging the war.
Is it time for America's Grand Design?
Is it time for the British to hand over
Their imperial rule and their world role?
O Lord of Light, I accept my demotion
If it is a part of your greater plan.
We warlords tussle for power but over all,
Our Overlord, is your Providential Light
Which knows the whole tapestry of history,
The past, the future, why events happen,
When one power rises and another declines,
Why one General rises and another is demoted.
What is baffling in nineteen forty-four
May be clear fifty years later, part of a pattern.
Shine into my soul, for I do not understand.
Follies and vices theme: deviousness (of US).

[Montgomery blocked from Berlin]

(*28 March, 9 p.m. Straelen, Montgomery's HQ.* MONTGOMERY *and*
DAWNAY, *his senior staff officer.*)

Montgomery   (*devastated*). I am stunned by Eisenhower's cable.
I am shocked. "My present plans being co-ordinated
With Stalin." And no mention of Berlin.
I am speechless. "The mission of your army group
Will be to protect Bradley's northern flank."
I am devastated, fuming at his folly.
Why are they so hostile to me at SHAEF?
Who are my enemies? Public opinion?

Simpson's Ninth Army, taken away from me
And reverting to Bradley to mop up the Ruhr.
Bradley having the main role, and to Dresden.
And nothing of this said to us at Rheinberg.
And co-ordinating with Stalin, a Commander-in-Chief
With a Head of State. And did Tedder know?
Not going to Berlin, I can't believe it.
Is he blind, does he realise what he's giving Stalin?
The US and Russians must have made a deal.
There is very dirty work behind the scenes.
Until I know what Eisenhower is doing
With Stalin, the wisest counsel is silence.
Follies and vices theme: deviousness.

[Eisenhower hands Berlin to Stalin]

(*14 April. Reims, Eisenhower's HQ.* EISENHOWER, *sombre.*)

Eisenhower.   I am in agony, for I must make a choice
That will have a universal application,
Affect all mankind, and men still unborn,
Shape history, and if I become President,
Tie my wrists with the rope of my own decision.
Should Berlin be American or Russian?
Militarily, I have only fifty thousand men
Who have advanced two hundred and fifty miles
In two weeks, and have already stretched
Their lines of communication. Racing them
Are two and a half million men, who are fresh,
Who have prepared two months, and are twenty miles
Away, and who must surely get there first.
To try and lose is worse than not to try.
Politically, if I win, I present Truman,
A new President, with the choice of rescinding
The Yalta agreement, that Berlin is part-Soviet,
And, worse, I raise doubts in Stalin's mind

About American good faith over Yalta.
He is anyway quick to say we are misleading him.
Then a hostile Soviet army, like a tidal wave,
Two and a half million men against our small force,
May keep going into Normandy, to the Atlantic
And sweep over all that we have won from Hitler.
It is better not to anger the Russians.
It is wiser to stick to our agreement
And not risk what our hard-won efforts have gained.
Politically, I know, since the First World War,
There have been men in Washington, and London,
Who seek to promote Communist world rule,
Who would dearly love Stalin to have Berlin.
They follow their own agenda, not SHAEF's.
I have my suspicions about some men, including
Two who promoted me from nowhere to
This pinnacle from Lieutenant-Colonel
To Supreme Commander within three years,
Two years nine months. My career progressed
When, like Churchill, I wrote to Barney Baruch.
Now I must choose on military grounds,
As the voice of SHAEF, and shut out all interests.
I am in anguish as I must decide
A course I know to be politically wrong,
But militarily right. Judgement is like love,
You weigh everything up, and then choose heart
Or head. I must choose head, but my heart yearns.
Berlin, Kay. A leader reviews, decides,
Communicates, inspires, and then defends,
And I will have a lot of defending to do.
Follies and vices theme: deviousness.

[Stalin on Russian expansion]

(*18 April, evening. Moscow. Stalin's study.*)

Stalin.   Zhukov. Chuikov has the Heights and has broken
             The Germans' first line of defence? Good, good.
             The cost, thirty thousand men? They gave their lives
             For their motherland.

(*He puts down the phone.*)

                              Thirty thousand,
             That's war. Hitler attacks me with Barbarossa,
             Seeking to eradicate all Soviet Jews.
             And fifty million die in repelling him.
             Thirty thousand to drive towards Berlin.
             This blood will achieve territory, our rule.
             I took over from Lenin a divided land,
             I killed six million to unify it,
             Reshape its borders, rule a vast expanse
             From the Baltic to the Pacific from a strong centre,
             A union that will now expand westwards,
             As far west as the Allies allow my troops.
             If they weaken, I am ready to push on
             Till the whole continent, from the Atlantic to the Pacific,
             All Euro-Asia, will be under Red rule.
             The Byzantine Russian civilisation
             Is in its greatest extent under my Tsardom.

(*He stands before a picture of Ivan the Terrible.*)

             Ivan the Terrible, I look to you.
             You approve of everything that I have done.
             You know our Byzantine Russia must expand
             At the expense of the Holy Roman Empire
             And the Habsburgs, and their successors,
             And the British Empire, the non-Orthodox faiths.
             You know Russia's Byzantine destiny
             To rule the world through a creed that captures minds.
             Autocracy, through Communism, is our way.

I keep the tradition of the Russian Tsars,
I unite our lands and cultures with the glue of power,
And keep it stuck together by repelling force.
Thirty thousand is a small price to pay.
A human life is material which the State
Can remould into a peasant or a soldier.
It is while it is alive and then, is nothing.
Death is like a curtain drawn across a window.
It is nothing, it has no significance.
It is the end of life, as evil is the end of good.
There is no sacredness, men have bodies
That can be used like shell cases. There is nothing
Sacred about life, no good. Ivan you knew.
We have millions of material units
To sacrifice, to expand our empire.
Follies and vices theme: ruthlessness, deviousness.

[Speer on Hitler]

(*Wrecked Chancellery garden.*)

Speer   (*to Göring*). I can remember when, for his birthday
                parade,
            Forty thousand men and hundreds of tanks
            Took three hours to salute him while he stood
            On a dais. On his fiftieth birthday
            I rode with him in his car as he stood,
            Arm raised in salute; slowly we passed hundreds
            Of thousands of soldiers standing silently.
            He was like Tamberlaine in a chariot.
            The Army had increased sevenfold in four years,
            The Rhineland, Austria, Sudeten and Czech lands
            Behind, Danzig, East Prussia and the Polish
            Corridor ahead, and who could stop him?
            Each man had sworn an oath to his Napoleon.
            He was magnificent. I knew then it was war.

When he spoke the world trembled, and we were all
   proud
To follow him. Now a few SS men and
A few boys from the Hitler Youth. He's trembling
Fumbling for their hands, patting their cheeks, pinning
Iron Crosses on those Axmann points out,
He's staggering unsteadily, saying
The enemy will be destroyed outside Berlin.
It's pathetic. I couldn't bear to watch any more.
I know Stauffenberg's bomb began the decline,
And Dr. Morell's syringe has played a part,
But I can't help feeling power festers in the flesh
And infects the blood till the health corrupts.
I've seen it in other leaders. Power ruins
Like a drug an athlete takes to enhance
Performance; soon the body craves for more
And is addicted, and the doses must be increased,
And his health is past its peak. So it is with him.
Amid the trappings of power, he is impotent.
He was the mightiest in the world, and now
He looks like a drug addict who's terminally ill.
Follies and vices theme: systemic killing, power.

[Bormann's manipulation]

(*23 April, later. The Führer bunker, Hitler's office.*)

Bormann   (*alone*). A word here, a raised eyebrow there, no more.
                 I do not have to suggest my rivals come down.
                 Kluge, Rommel, Rundstedt, Model, I've seen them fall.
                 Göring, Himmler, I have had them in my sights
                 For months, no years. And others too. Burgdorf,
                 Guderian, Krebs, Jodl, Keitel, Goebbels.
                 I remember things and bide my time, put on
                 An oafish air so they do not suspect
                 My cunning, my deviousness. The way

Of advancement is to be at hand, of use,
To flatter the confidence of a great man,
And knock out the others one by one, secure
Their confidence by taking their side, suggest
A course of action here, an indiscretion,
Then undermine them by subtle reports
Which parade the misdeed unobtrusively,
Then arrange for them to have a disaster,
Then bring it, reluctantly, to the great man's eyes,
And then dispatch them on his authority,
Until in the end all have gone save you and him.
But what if I have to flee before the prize?
And flee I shall. There will be no trace of me
If the Russians put an end to my grand schemes.
Follies and vices theme: cunning, deviousness.

[Churchill voted out]

(*27 July. Downing Street.* CHURCHILL *chokes back tears and cannot speak.*)

Churchill.   They are perfectly entitled to vote as they please.
      This is democracy, this is what we've been fighting for.
      Attlee's flown to Potsdam this morning. He asked
      If I'd continue there as he's inexperienced,
      But I said No, the British people want you,
      You go and deal with Stalin on their behalf
      And make sure he keeps his word and holds elections
      In Poland and the Eastern European countries.
      You and Stalin are both socialists, you go
      And sort out Russia's misinterpretation
      Of the Yalta decisions. The Potsdam meeting
      Grew out of what I told Truman on May the twelfth,
      That an iron curtain is drawn on the Russian front
      From Lübeck to Trieste, including Poland,
      And we don't know what is going on behind it.
      Still, it's not my problem now. But it grieves me,

Because of Roosevelt's illness and death, and now this
Popular hankering for a form of social reform
We can't afford in our post-war bankruptcy,
Two inexperienced men who were not at Yalta,
Truman and Attlee, will give Stalin what he wants,
He will get away with a military empire.
The Victory in Europe was a partial victory.
In eastern Europe we've all been defeated.
What galls me most is, I have been denied
The power to shape the future of the post-war world.
It's like Monty. You give them victory and
They demote you. They are as fickle as
A woman with several lovers. In May
They shout "It's your victory", in July you're out,
They depose you....

(*Silence.*)

Now that I am in the wilderness again
I ponder that had I remained Prime Minister
I would have persuaded the Americans to use
Their new power, which is drawn from victory and
The atomic bomb, to confront Stalin,
To make him behave decently in Europe;
And I cannot help wondering, Truman has been weak
Towards Stalin, was this deliberate,
Has Marshall an understanding with him,
Is that why Eisenhower sent Stalin that cable?
I am better placed to judge than most,
And I see the hand of Zionism in the war.
At Yalta Roosevelt told Stalin he was a Zionist
And Stalin said he was one "in principle".
The Jews will have a new state in Palestine
For which I spoke in 1939,
In accordance with the Balfour Declaration
Which was made in exchange for Rothschild's guarantee

He'd bring America into the First World War
On the British side and save us from defeat.
So America entered the First World War
In return for Balfour's promise to a Rothschild
That there would be a homeland for the Jews
In the British mandate of Palestine,
And now the German Jewish Rothschild family
Have seen the Nazis fall and will have their state,
And if I were suspicious I might think
That Hitler was lured into war with Zionist money
Through House, Baruch, Schacht, Wall Street and I. G.
    Farben,
Vast sums that reached the Nazis through Warburg
    banks
So that Nazis could massacre Jews and swing
International opinion behind this new state.
But I cannot be suspicious. That way madness lies.
That way history is not what it seems, and leaders
Who appear to do their best for their nations
In fact work to another agenda, luring
The unsuspecting into catastrophic wars
That suit their own interests that remain hidden
From view. And what the history books describe
Is wrong, for history is what a cabal intrigued.
I do not want to believe that, I prefer
The view that leaders do their best for their peoples
Without pressures they know nothing of.

(*Silence.*)

I want to believe that Eisenhower chose
On military grounds not to go to Berlin –
Not that there has since Lenin been
A Zionist-American-Communist joint front
Which engineered the rise of Roosevelt
And, also, the succession of Stalin,

And that Eisenhower was under orders
To make sure that Russia's post-war position
In Europe will be the dominant one,
That he therefore had a political objective
In making sure that Stalin was first to Berlin
By vetoing my wish to attack the soft
Underbelly of the Reich, and then Monty.
I rose after writing to Baruch in thirty-nine,
And after speaking in the House of Commons
In favour of setting up a Zionist state
In Palestine. I fell at the hands of
Public opinion, which can be manipulated.
I do not want to think I fell through a plot,
Because I tried to stand up to Stalin
And was felt to thwart a hidden alliance
Between Zionists, Americans and Russians
Who influenced public opinion against me.
I prefer not to believe that Zionism
Was behind my rise and engineered my fall.
I want to accept the surface of history
And not stir the muddy depths which cloud the
    reflection.
I prefer not to know about "groups" that would run the
    world.
I stood up to the two most terrible tyrants
Mankind has ever suffered; and I fell.
I am full of questions that will echo
To the end of this century and beyond,
As we regroup in a United States of Europe
And eventually in a United States of the World.
Follies and vices theme: ingratitude, deviousness (of Zionists).

[report from Hiroshima]

(6 *August. The cruiser* Augusta *returning from Potsdam.* TRUMAN *and*
AIDE.)

Aide.   I have an eye-witness report from Hiroshima.
                The uranium bomb was two thousand times the blast
                Of the heaviest bomb ever used before.

Truman.   Describe what happened.

Aide.   A flash and with a roar
                A yellow and orange fireball rolled and shot
                Eight thousand feet into the sunny air
                And turned into a ten-mile high column
                Of black smoke, a mushroom cloud rose and hung,
                And as the great wind dropped, on the ground
                A flat desert where there had been a city,
                The roads like tracks across endless waste ground:
                Hiroshima has disappeared, and in its place
                Rubble, ruins, twisted metal and people
                Horribly burned, lying still, stirring or
                Groaning and crawling or just sitting dazed.
                Over ten square miles a thousand fires blazed,
                And a hundred thousand may have died at once.
                Birds had burnt up in mid-air, and people's brains,
                Eyes, intestines burst, their skin peeled, and some
                Burned to cinders as they stood. Others had
                The print of their clothes burnt onto their naked backs.
                It was awesome. Sir, this new weapon which
                Makes a thousand-bomber firebomb raid look
                Insignificant, has in one blast outmoded
                Six years of war, which must now be strikes like this
                That can wipe out half a country without warning.
                A new terror has arrived, that makes one yearn
                For the sort of world war we have just seen
                Where hatred has a limited radius,
                That of a conventional high explosive bomb.

Truman   (*with awe*). This is the greatest thing in history. We had
                To drop the bomb, I had a report that

Half a million Americans would be killed
If we were to invade Japan. General
Marshall and I are quite clear it will stop
The Pacific war before the Russians reach
Japan, which we can occupy alone.
We have learned from Berlin, where the Russians
Occupy half to our quarter. The hope is that
This bomb will abolish war because no one will
Invade another's territory and risk its use.

Aide.   So long as Stalin doesn't steal it from us.
                   Follies and vices theme: systemic killing.

[Stalin reviews his success]

(*November. Stalin's Kremlin HQ.* STALIN *and* BERIA.)

Beria.   Our agents Vasilevsky and Terletsky
                   Received answers to their questions from Niels Bohr
                   At two meetings with him in Copenhagen
                   On the fourteenth and sixteenth of November.
                   The twenty-two questions were put by Kurchatov.
                   Bohr had the blessing of the Americans
                   Oppenheimer, Fermi and Szilard for
                   This leak of the American atom bomb.
                   He said there must be international control
                   Over atomic weapons, hence their leak.
                   Kurchatov, Khariton and Sakharov
                   Are now confident that there will be a
                   Soviet uranium and plutonium bomb.

Stalin.   Good. We want our well-wishers in the US
                   And Britain to find out the technology
                   To make comrade Sakharov's task easier.
                   (*Exit* BERIA. STALIN *is alone.*)

(*Satisfied.*) I did it. All along I had my own agenda
To transform the Soviet Union from a nation
Of backward peasants with horses and carts
Into a major world power all would fear.
I terrified them into the twentieth century,
Then I allied with Hitler to carve up part
Of Poland. I made overtures to Britain to
Keep pressure on Hitler from the western side.
I counted on Hitler to attack me.
He fell into my trap, he readily obliged.
Then my main thought was a Soviet empire
In eastern Europe and the Balkans. I delayed
Taking Berlin until I had overrun
Eastern Europe. At Yalta, I used their fear
Of Hitler, who was already finished, to redraw
Occupation zones and Poland's borders,
Knowing my stooges would seize power, invite
Russian troops in and give me indirect control.
The Allies were too trusting, they believed my words.
I made them honour their mistake, and took
Berlin. If I were Montgomery I would feel
Aggrieved, but imperial diplomacy
Is about power and achieving your interests.
The Russian civilisation is in a stage
Of union, of reunifying its own lands.
It has expanded to control its parts,
All its territories. It has always claimed
Poland and Eastern Europe, there has been no conquest
Of the European civilisation, which is younger than
　　ours,
Merely a readjustment of our borders.
I secured the Soviet Union's interests –
I needed less than a week to invade
Japanese-held China and secure our
Interests at Port Arthur and at Dairen –
And will go down in history as the ruler

Who, like Ivan the Terrible, held the union
Together and expanded it to its greatest extent.
I have been a Genghis Khan, a Tamburlaine
Over a greater area than they conquered.
Berlin was the key, for with it came Poland,
Czechoslovakia, Hungary, and all the rest.
Occupation is nine points of the law.
And now, thanks to Niels Bohr, though he barely
Knows it, I am about to have the atomic bomb.
I shall challenge America and spread
Soviet influence throughout the rest of the world.
Man is material, which can be raised
Like clay a potter shapes on a turning wheel.

Follies and vices theme: ruthlessness, unscrupulousness,
ambition, deviousness.

[Montgomery and UK marginalised by US]

(*December. Lüneburg Heath.* MONTGOMERY *standing alone on the heath.*)

Montgomery.   Marginalised, I was marginalised,
And with me Britain, and as a result
It's an American-Russian world now.
Did the Americans do it deliberately
To advance their power, or were they just blind?
In not going to Berlin, was Eisenhower
Just being fair, too trusting and naïve?
Or honouring a deal that Roosevelt made
At Teheran with Stalin, to secure
A Russian offensive that would coincide
With my *Overlord*: Berlin in return for attack?
If I had led the Allies into Berlin
Before Churchill met Stalin at Yalta,
I could have held back the Communist tide,
All Europe would be Anglo-American.
Now the Soviet Union surrounds Berlin

And controls Poland. If my way had prevailed,
This would not be so. Does it matter now?
Yes, for many millions will not be free.
Or is there a stability I don't know about,
Is there now a secret east-west accord?
I can't believe that. Once again, I have been proved
    right.

(*Silence.*)

I sometimes question what my battles were for.
Was the world a better place for what I did?
Yes. I pushed back Fascism in North Africa
And Italy and North Europe. But as fast
As I rolled it back, Communism took its place.
Hitler was Overlord of Europe till
I invaded Normandy. Who's Overlord now?
Not Eisenhower; not Churchill, nor me, we
Were marginalised. Europe is now divided
Between Truman, all-powerful with his new bomb,
And Stalin, whose huge Red Army has occupied
The east and who cannot be dislodged by
An atomic bomb. Stalin is Overlord –
Apparently, for the real Overlord is you,
My guiding, Providential, loving Light
Without whom Hitler would have won this war.

(*Silence.*)

Now America is an atomic power
Thanks to German scientific insight,
And Russia will soon be one too, warfare
As I have known it is of the past, finished:
Operating from mobile caravans through scouts
Close to the battle front, like Marlborough
Or Wellington or Napoleon. War

Is now a distant nuclear missile threat.
And where does that leave Great Britain? Not great.
The body of our European civilisation
Has suffered a malignant cancer, which has been cut out
With our consent by the surgery of two other
Civilisations: the American and the Russian.
Now, after our civil war, we are convalescing
And our health will be restored.
But no more have we the energy for empire,
No more is our role in Africa or Asia.
Empire is at an end. We have ended
An imperial phase in our long history.
If that had to happen, then the civil war had to too.
Now the British Empire will collapse for we've
Bankrupted ourselves to recover from Hitler,
And a new Europe will grow out of this ruin.
I, who rule a quarter of Germany, consent
That German people should be in our new Europe
In which Britain, an island, will be different....

For over a year I implemented a plan.
Now there is no need for it any more
I feel slightly lost, a warlord without a war.
I must live again without a plan, I must find
My meaning in God's world, beneath reason.
I must look for the plan in the universe,
Rather than Rommel's, and there is as much
Deception and subterfuge, God is a General
Who guards his secrets from his troops' eyes.

(*Silence.*)

Under the atomic bomb the world will draw together.
There is a need for a new philosophy
Which embraces all mankind, all religions,
A metaphysic for the United Nations.

The only way I can live without a plan
Is to piece the potsherds of the universe
Into the tessellated urn from which they came
And, like an archaeologist, know its pattern
In the fresh air of the universal sunshine....
But I have moved beyond war and conflict,
I look for opposites being reconciled.
I hope my son and Rommel's become friends.
And I ask of future generations
Not glorification or triumphalism,
But sober assessment, and credit where due.
More than Lawrence of Arabia, like the moon I drew
Tides of men, and flung them like a stormy sea
Up the beaches across the Channel, towards here.
Like Marlborough, I never lost a battle.
I stood for a Britain that had greatness.
I was a potsherd in the larger pattern,
A fragment, an episode, a chain of events
In the unfolding process of our history;
But I am proud of what our deeds achieved,
How our courage transformed our time, our Age,
And in the stillness of the trees, round this heather,
In the ghostly moaning of the winter wind
Which sounds as if the dead are gathering,
I hear the million men of *Overlord*
Roar their approval for a job well done.

Follies and vices theme: ruthlessness, deviousness (of US,
Russia).

7

from *Overlord* (1994–1996)

[book 1, lines 1–49, 102–151, invocation to Muse on Overlord]

Tell, Muse, of tyranny and millions killed,

Of the pinnacle of the world's power
Among mountain peaks and green slopes, of cruel
Destruction of cities, and whispers of
A Nazi atomic bomb. And tell of
The rise of Eisenhower and, with Christ's help,
The defiance of his supreme command
And opposition on the battlefield
Of Montgomery and Zhukov which led
To the liberation of Europe from
Nazi tyranny, the fall of Berlin
And the defeat and death of Hitler, who,
With counter-symmetry and chiasmus,
Plunged earthwards when he lost Satan's support
Like a falling star with a burning trail.
And tell of Light's triumph over Darkness
Though Satan's guile nearly outwitted Christ
Through his wily disciple, Stalin, and
Near spoilt God's plan for the millennium.

Tell, Muse, of plans and battles, commanders,
Of ambition and conflict, as the day
Of decision approached that would decide
Who would be Overlord of the whole world,
Whether Hitler, Overlord of Europe,
Commander-in-Chief of German armies
Whose genocidal rule of gun and noose
Conquered his neighbours in a new empire
Till tyrannicides challenged him, to bring
In a post-Nazi regime with Rommel
Or Beck as Head of State to end the war;
Or divine Hirohito, prisoner of
His murderous Army Generals, Overlord
Of Asia, Hitler's sole ally now that
Mussolini was gone; or Eisenhower,
Supreme Commander of Allied Forces,
The man who more than any other ran

The war and planned an Allied victory
And brought about American world rule;
Or Montgomery, implementer of
Operation Overlord; or Roosevelt
Or Truman, leaders of the world's foremost
Rising power; or proud Churchill, who still held
The British Empire that ruled a quarter
Of the colonial world, and who had stood
Alone when Europe fell and, brave, defied
The cruel dictators' might; or bland Marshal
Stalin, co-ordinator of Russian
Forces which were led by Marshal Zhukov,
Who sought world power for a land of peasants....

O shades of my forerunners, o Homer
Who showed gods beside heroes on the plains
Of Troy; o Virgil, who told of the dark
Fortunes of Aeneas, both on earth and
In the underworld; o Romancers, who
Sang of the search for the Grail, the chalice
That shone with pure Light; o Dante, who with
Virgil passed from dark Hell to Paradise;
O Marlowe of the warlike Tamburlaine,
O Shakespeare of *Henry the Fourth* and *Fifth*;
O Donne, who judged the new philosophy
And science of a sceptical new Age,
And abandoned *The Progresse of the Soule,*
An epic work on the scale of nature
(From first apple to Queen Elizabeth);
O blind Milton, who lamented the lost
Paradise of Satan-Cromwell's England,
Who justified the ways of God to man;
O Marvell, whose Garden was Paradise;
O Dryden, who showed Monmouth's rebellion;
O Pope, whose sylphs guarded Belinda's lock;
O Goethe, whom Weishaupt called Abaris,

Who created Faust as illuminate;
O Blake, whose Hell was a great energy,
Who wrote of Milton and of higher worlds;
O Coleridge, who opposed Newton's mind
As passive, "mere materialist", and
Reconciled physics and metaphysics;
O Wordsworth, who pondered an epic on
King Arthur and, listless, recoiled and drooped;
O Shelley, who revealed the One as Light;
O Tennyson, who wrote of Arthur's wars;
O Hardy, who recreated the wars
Of Napoleon – I beg you, help me.
O Pound, who saw the decline of the West
And hinted at a deeper meaning, you
Who sat under a Rapallo full moon
And urged me to begin this task which I
Have now pushed aside for twenty-five years,
Who stood and gripped my hand, passed on the power
Of Calliope's art – I salute you.
And all who wrote of the great battles of
History: Troy, Actium, the Spanish
Armada, Trafalgar, Waterloo and
The Somme; as I gaze at a hedge I see
I grow a white vision like a wild plant –
Please come to my aid with heroic verse
In twelve books like twelve leaves on the stem of
Jack-by-the-hedge (garlic mustard) which grows
Wild in hedgerows and ends in a white flower.
Follies and vices theme: tyranny, systemic killing during Second World War.

[book 1, lines 939–946, 989–1041, D-Day]

The greatest invasion fleet ever sent,
Five thousand ships, bobbed in the still dark waves
Off the fortified coast of Normandy.
From the shore it resembled a distant

Flock of dark sea-birds caught in the storm and
Riding out danger on the choppy sea....

D-Day, day of decision, departure,
Disembarkation or defeat, D for
The Day (*en Français J-Jour*) and H for
The Hour, which fluctuated on the coast
Like high tide. Half light, the tossing sea was
Filled with assault craft. Sea-sprayed, men hunched in
Helmets and packs, rose and fell, surged forward.
Hearts in mouths, none spoke. All looked at the beach,
A distant line of sand, holding rifles,
Moving forward stealthily as a fox
Approaches a farmyard, creeping at night.
Who would be dead in a few minutes as
H-hour approached? What hand-to-hand combat?
The infantry went in, silent heroes.
Splash! Down went the flap into a ramp. Choke
With admiration and awe as each stood
Up and jumped into three feet of water,
Rifle held up, the cold chill of the sea
Shuddering through, and waded forward as
Machine-guns chattered like awakened geese
That honked indignantly in the silence.

Omaha beach, a long bluff and a height,
A hundred and seventy feet, above
A strip of shingle vehicles could not cross
And five defended exits through the cliff,
An infantry division well dug in.
Bad weather and great surf. Aircraft bombed blind
And missed, naval gunners saw few targets,
Sherman tanks and guns launched over three miles
Out sank, as did ten infantry assault
Craft, while more had their bottoms ripped out by
Rommel's underwater obstacles, and

Laden infantrymen drowned. Currents pushed
Some troops ashore two miles off their target
On defended beaches; without tanks or
Engineers they were pinned down, equipment
Lost in the surf, units mixed up. Some troops
Crouched in their craft under a hail of fire,
Fear in their stomachs as each bullet whipped
Up the rough sea beside them, and then bang!
Down went the flap – the ramp – and they stood up,
A Hell of smoke ahead from the shelling,
And jumped into three feet of cold water
And waded past corpses of their comrades,
The sea dark with blood in crimson patches,
And staggered, wet, onto the sand and – "Mines" –
Followed a path through, ducking constant fire,
Under the cliffs of the bluff which rang out,
And huddled under what little cover
They could find, unable to leave the beach,
As crabs left high and dry by an ebb-tide
Crouch under stones or burrow into sand.
Two or three thousand were wounded, or killed.
Follies and vices theme: systemic killing during Second World War.

[book 2, lines 502–709, Hell]

In seven rings of increasingly dim dark,
Seven Hells lurk like dark descending caves
To which all souls are drawn by the degree
Of shadow or darkness in their nature,
Seven levels, each veiled from the last one,
Each miles wide and merging into the next
So seven seem one, as seven caves appear
Part of one long cavern in Wookey Hole –
Through which, underground, flows the River Axe
Whose million-year old swirl has carved chambers
Where clear green pools lie under stalactites –

When seen from the path that leads down into
The fissured limestone walls of the last cave.
Beyond a dark wood and a vestibule
Where slump, heads bowed, the souls of the futile,
Who, rejecting and rejected, wait, bored;
In the first Hell, in gloom, among horseshoe
And pipistrelle bats hanging from the roof,
Dwell those who can be rescued, virtuous
Heretics with rational-social outlooks,
Who were proud with a high opinion of
Their merits, exalted and arrogant,
Novelists, dramatists and poetasters,
Rationalists and humanists, scholars,
Positivist philosophers, their dupes,
And reductionist scientists, and theirs,
And sceptical materialists, who,
Though agnostic or atheist and not
Aware of the Light have led blameless lives –
Democritus, Newton, Darwin and Freud –
With souls of pallid greyness, along with
School inspectors, teachers, doctors, dentists,
Police and all who ran the State system,
Insurers, traffic wardens, the blameless
Church-goers who sang hymns and said rote prayers
And missed the Light, the essence of all faiths,
Because the vicar was not mystical,
And here dwell many vicars in this murk,
Archbishops, Cardinals, ministers, priests,
Who recited mechanical prayers from
A book, and missed the vision of the Light.
Here each endlessly proclaimed his creed and
Knowing it was wrong, felt dissatisfied.
In the second Hell, in darker torment,
Dwell in dampness the lustful, all who have
Been attached to their sensual desires,
Slaves to the need for gratification

Rather than masters of their deep passions,
All who had self-indulgent appetites –
Messalina, Casanova, Harris –
The incontinent who lacked discipline,
A ring of whores and Don Juans, whose itch
Or ache kept them in body consciousness,
Which used others as objects, instruments,
So their souls were never lit by a ray
Of Light and never grew. And also here
Were lovers and mistresses whose desires
Distracted them from truth during their lives,
Who broke up others' unions, brought grief
To others and deprived them of the Light,
Government Ministers, Princes and Kings,
Nobility and workers side by side,
Their souls unreachable like nuts in shells;
Here they itch, twitch and ache without relief.
In the third Hell, in still dingier gloom,
Dwell the gluttonous, all who preferred food
And drinking and loud laughter in taverns
To contemplation which opens the soul
To the Light and starts its growth, like a shoot,
All who surrendered to their appetites –
Lucullus, Henry the Eighth, De Quincey –
A ring of social hostesses and guests
Addicted to alcohol, nicotine,
Drugs and time-wasting, passing many hours
In hazy consciousness, an illusion
Of togetherness: here hunger and thirst
Torment them in their perpetual fast.
In the fourth Hell, in even darker murk,
Dwell the hoarders and spendthrifts, all who had
A selfish appetite for money, and
Were avaricious, greedy for their gain,
Were misers or extravagant spenders –
Midas, Rothschilds, Rockefellers and Ford –

Attached to their greed, too busy earning
Fortunes or shopping, using merchandise,
Cars, computers, lazy sun-holidays –
Profiteers, property developers,
Bankers, stockbrokers and solicitors,
Stock exchange players and estate agents,
Lawyers, accountants and tax inspectors –
To contemplate and open to the Light
And journey up the Mystic Way, progress,
Their acquisitive consciousness having
Barred them from growing their souls; here, endless
Craving to hoard or spend, unsatisfied,
Leaves them in permanent numb frustration.
In the fifth Hell deeper in darkness and
Egocentricity and selfishness,
Dwell the wrathful, all who have assaulted
Or attacked others in fits of anger,
Who did not learn to control their temper,
Disputed heatedly, felt bitterness,
Felt scorn and yearned for revenge, and believed –
William Conqueror, Philip the Second –
Humiliation must be answered, who
Were quick to take offence, so did not seek
Quiet or meditate to bring in the calm
The Light gives, serenity and peace that
Passeth understanding, political
Agitators, demonstrators, MPs,
Football crowds and players, beer-drinkers and
Revolutionaries whose consciousness
Was too much on society or men
To be transformed by Light; here, endlessly
Stirred to rage by no cause, and unable
To express it, they boil and seethe within,
Simmer as if insulted, discontent.
In the sixth Hell, in deepening darkness
And self-assertion, caring for no one

But themselves, as if locked in a dungeon,
Envying the good fortune of others,
Resenting and coveting beauty, wealth,
Dwell the violent, all who have struck a blow
Against their neighbours, robbers, murderers
Who have injured fellow human beings
By theft or bestial bodily assault –
De Sade, Dick Turpin and Jack the Ripper –
And the fraudulent who out of malice
Have tricked their neighbours, cheated or swindled
Them of their earned savings, being attached
To advancing their own interests and not
Opening to the Light's gentle calm and
Loving their neighbour in the unified
Vision, violently separating
Themselves from the Light's truth; here too are found
The tyrants who had tens of thousands killed,
Who could not complete their divine mission –
Robespierre, Napoleon, Lenin and Haig –
And suicides, who out of self-hatred
Ended their own lives, ignoring the Light
Which reveals to all men their destiny,
And all who have been violent towards God,
Nature and art, who have gouged out the earth
Or damaged paintings, both God's creation;
Polluters and wilful hewers of trees.
Here an endless desire to harm fills all,
But they cannot express it and so feel
Frustrated, murderous and unhappy.
In the seventh Hell, in night darkness dwell
The spiritually slothful, the most
Ignorant who deceived their neighbours, who
Were not misguided but deliberate,
Fraudsters who falsified reality,
Who corrupted and perverted others,
Panders, pimps, seducers who degraded,

Flatterers who exploited rank desires,
All who made money out of the pure Light,
All fortune-tellers who used psychic powers
And magic to foretell the future known
Only to the Light and who stole money
Out of public office, betraying trust,
All hypocrites who misled others' souls,
All thieves who stole from others, all who
Advised others to practise fraud and sowed
Discord in religion, town, family,
All falsifiers of accounts, and all
Who were brutal with a deceiving smile,
Who authorised foul genocide, all who
Were separate from mankind, practised Satan's
Deceit and so are closest to Satan,
To the Lie which would falsify all truth –
Cagliostro, Marx, Illuminati –
And farthest from opening to the Light,
Their attention on corrupting others.
Here a perpetual yearning to gull
Others fills their minds without expression,
And their craving to chat is unfulfilled
And leaves them endlessly discontented
And miserable. In all seven Hells
One glimpse of Light can take a spirit out
Of Hell and put it in the first Heaven;
As in the dark regions of Hell no light
Penetrates, redemption by Light cannot
Be expected.
       Beyond these seven Hells
Is pitch darkness of chaos, where light is
Absent, where Satan dwells in the centre
Of a thorn, guarded by prickles, hanging
Like a bat (as his form Odin hung on
The World Tree), near a cesspit where all waste
Matter decays before, recycled, it

Flows back into existence; surrounded
By Arch-demons, forms his emanation
Spawned in fornications, incarnations
Both aliases of himself and children,
Such as Baal, Sammael, Beliar, Abaddon,
His Hindu-like manifestations as
Idol, seducer, fornicator and
Destroyer; and by all his disciples,
Simon Magus, Roderic Borgia (Pope
Alexander the Sixth), Adam Weishaupt,
Eliphas Levi, Aleister Crowley,
Rasputin; in a thicket of Darkness
Whence, like the Axe through underground caverns,
Decomposed, broken down into new forms,
Its force and consciousness again released,
Matter flows out into the universe,
Polluted with deception and falsehood.
Follies and vices theme: vices found in Hell including pride, lust, gluttony, greed,
anger, violence and sloth.

[book 5, lines 3298–3359, Auschwitz]

In life as well as camps such as Auschwitz
Individuals achieve the greatest fame
Or notoriety when position
Lifts them above anonymous faces.
Roza, the organiser of the theft,
Was now as famous as the camp hangman:
Jakob Kozelczuk, who, having arrived
From East Poland over a year before,
Was now the bunker's attendant, jailer,
Who kept the cells in order and led out
(When they had undressed in the lavatory
And their name in indelible pencil
Was written on their naked bodies, to
Facilitate identification

Before the crematorium ovens)
The victims to the Black Wall, named from its
Black cork insulating plates, in the yard
Between blocks Ten and Eleven, where, before
Grabner, the Political Head, they were
Shot in the back of the head in pairs. He
Grabbed each pair of skeletons by their arms
And at the double hurried them over
To the Wall of Death and stood between them,
Still gripping each at the scrawny elbow,
And made each kneel on one knee, then one rise,
Head to the Wall, not looking to one side,
Unable to stand upright after months
Of crouching, famished, in a stinking cell.
As a pied wagtail on a sea-wall bobs
And dips its tail and bobs again and then,
Running, dapper, wags its tail up and down,
So, to and fro fussed dapper Kozelczuk.
Nearby a prisoner stood, holding a spade
And, strutting slowly like a carrion crow
In black plumage, in black above his prey,
With short air pistol or small-calibre
Rifle so no sound carried to those who
Lived on the main road just beyond the Wall,
The executioner, generally
Gestapo chief Palitzsch, menacing with
His gun behind his back, shot each in turn
In the back of the neck where the spinal
Cord enters the skull. When each had fallen
With a groan, as blood ran in a thin stream
The executioner put a boot on
His forehead, pulled up an eyelid to see
If the eye was motionless, and if there
Was a gurgle, shot him again in his
Eye or temple. The corpse-carriers, with
Fear in their alert eyes, and with speed, then

Loaded the corpses on wooden stretchers,
Ran them to the other end of the yard
And threw them, blood still trickling down their heads
And backs, on a mounting pile of corpses
By a far wall where a swarm of flies buzzed.
The spade-holder shovelled sand on the blood.
Kozelczuk fetched and led out the next pair.
Most guards saw men as vile material that
Could be stilled with one shot and in an hour
Reduced to its component atoms and
Returned to the earth mixed with clinker and
Ash.
Follies and vices theme: systemic killing, executions, cruelty.

[book 5, lines 3428–3468, hanging of Roza Robota]

A cold early January evening,
And a cold hanging at the women's camp
In Birkenau, as four Jewish women,
Roza Robota and Ella Gartner,
Then Regina Safir and Estera
Wajsblum, were brought to two floodlit gallows,
Crunching across the sparkling frozen snow
In the bleak snow-covered assembly square.
The first two were hanged during roll call in
The presence of all prisoners who worked in
The night-shift at the Weichsel-Union
Factory, male as well as female prisoners,
Their breaths like mists above the crisp deep snow.
Roza and Ella were led to wooden
Gallows – post, bar, crossbeam, hook and white noose
Above a platform with a trapdoor. All
Were silent as sentence was read out by
First Protective Custody Commander
Hössler, who screamed: "These women assisted
In the October seventh uprising

By stealing and providing explosives
To the Special Squad. All traitors will be
Destroyed in this manner. Hangman, proceed."
Jakob Kozelczuk looped nooses round necks
With gentleness hidden from the Nazis.
Shivering from the cold as much as fear,
Roza called out, "Vengeance will come," and her
Organisation's words, "Be brave and strong,"
As the trap fell. She hung, eyes closed, floodlit,
Neck askew, limp, turning to left and right,
Her last breath floating in the floodlit frost
As Ella, with a haughty look, followed
Her to a more friendly world where being
Floats like a cloud of breath, beyond all cold.
The night-shift left to work, silent, each man
In his thoughts, each woman indignant as
The slack bodies were thrown into a cart.
The day-shift returned for roll call, and then
The second pair were led to the gallows
To end the last public execution
Before the evacuation of Auschwitz...
Follies and vices theme: systemic killing, executions.

[book 9, lines 2884–2938, Stalin sees human life as material]

In Moscow that evening Stalin was rung
By Zhukov. "Chuikov has the Heights? Good, good.
The cost, thirty thousand men? They gave their
Lives for the motherland." He rang off and
Slowly paced the high-windowed Kremlin room
And brooded as if wading in their blood:
'Thirty thousand. That's war. Hitler attacks
Me with Barbarossa, to liquidate
All Soviet Jews, and fifty million die
Repelling him. Thirty thousand to drive
Towards Berlin. This blood will achieve it.

I took from Lenin a divided land
I killed six million to unify it,
Reshape its borders, rule a vast expanse
From the Baltic to the Pacific from
A strong centre, a union that will now
Expand as far westwards as the Allies
Allow my troops. If they weaken I am
Ready to drive till the whole continent
From the Atlantic to the Pacific,
All Euro-Asia, is under Red Rule.
Byzantine Russian civilisation
Has reached its greatest extent under my
Tsardom.' He stood before his picture of
Ivan the Terrible. 'Ivan, I look
To you. You approve of all that I've done.
You know Byzantine Russia must expand
At the Holy Roman Emperor's expense
And the Habsburgs' and their successors' and
The British Empire's – non-Orthodox faiths.
You know Russia's Byzantine destiny
To rule the world through a creed that captures
Minds. Autocracy through Communism
Is our way. I keep the tradition of
The Russian Tsars, Alexander the First's
Imperial lands. I unite our lands and
Cultures with the glue of power and keep it
Stuck together by repelling all force.
Thirty thousand is a small price to pay.
A human life is material. The State
Can remould it into a peasant or
A soldier. It *is* while it's alive and
Then is nothing. Death is like a curtain
Drawn across a window. It is nothing,
It has no significance. It's the end
Of life, as evil is the end of good.
There is no sacredness, men have bodies

That can be used like shells. There is nothing
Sacred about life, no good. Ivan, you
Knew. We have millions of material
Units to sacrifice, to expand our
Empire.' He gazed at his reflection thrown
By the electric light on the window.
It was the image of the main victor,
And seemed to stare at him like a horned Beast.
Follies and vices theme: systemic killing.

[book 10, lines 1620–1652, Hitler floods Berlin tunnels]

Now Berliners found horror underground.
That night Chuikov's scouts entered the U- and
S-Bahn tunnels, seeking a route under
The Landwehr canal. Next morning Krebs told
The conference, "Soviet troops are using U-
And S-Bahn tunnels." Hitler, in a rage,
Shouted, "The tunnels must be flooded. Blow
Up the watertight bulkheads that keep out
The canal." Krebs protested, "But, *Führer*,
Our own troops use them and trains take the sick
And wounded to hospitals, and thousands
Of refugees live in the tunnels. It
Will be a human disaster. A wall
Of water will pour through the tunnels and
Many will be killed." Furiously Hitler
Ordered, "Flood the tunnels, they don't deserve
To live."
        As pinched Berliners crouched in their
Underground command posts in the stations,
A cascade of water swept through the dark
Tunnels, boiling, frothing, carrying all
Before its foaming roar, knocking men off
Their feet. Struggling, thrashing, swallowing foul
Canal water, trying to stand up in

The flood, stumbling over rails and sleepers,
Spluttering, choking, gasping in the swirl,
People fought to reach the ladders, many
Were trampled underfoot. The torrent rose
A metre, then dropped. Many had drowned and
Their bodies floated face down. There were screams
And cries in the dark, and bafflement. Who
Had done this to them? Who had flooded them?
The Russians, or was it an accident?
Follies and vices theme: systemic killing, cruelty.

[book 10, lines 4149–4171, news of Hitler's death spreads in Berlin]

Word spread through Berlin that Hitler was dead.
In ones and twos people came out from their
Cellars and breathed the air, stunned at the piles
Of rubble, ruined buildings, heaped up streets,
Smashed plant and services, the mounds of stones,
But overjoyed the Russians and Allies
Would now liberate them from senseless war.
The Jews were safe, no more the killing wall;
Gone the extermination camps, the gas
Chambers and chimneys. The people were free.
They dreaded the Russian conquerors but
Were relieved they had survived endless war.
In twelve years he who would create forms that
Would last a thousand years had vandalised
A thousand years of German history. "*Si
Monumentum requiris, circumspice*",
Wren's epitaph his son carved in St. Paul's:
"If you seek his monument, look around" –
At the burnt ruin of Hitler's Berlin.
A church bell rang out over the city
Calling all Christians to light candles and
Pray to the God who watches like two eyes
Peering from air on a Byzantine coin.

Follies and vices theme: systemic killing, destruction.

8
from *Classical Odes* (1994–2005)

Pastoral Ode: Landslide, The End of Great Britain

I

I wander round this Tudor, timbered Hall.
The setting sun shines spangles in the glass
Of leaded windows set in a brick wall.
I feel it in the air, eighteen years pass
Like the long shadows on the croquet lawn.
In the still evening I detect beside
My open study window and calm scorn
A shifting in the nation, dark "landslide".

Night's shadows creep, the sunlit garden fades.
Eighteen years of a certain kind of rule
Are ending. Cold war and armed truce are shades;
In place of missiles, hospital and school.
The country needs renewal, a safe switch
To a fairer society, have-nots
Doing better without hurting the rich;
A new energy, free from backbench plots.

I feel it in the breeze, a mood for change.
The people have turned against long tenure
For a fresh approach, rejecting as strange
Smears, lies, divisions and corrupt behaviour,
Impatient with State cuts and expecting
An end to cash shortage and mass pay freeze,
Certain taxes will go down, resenting
Division, splits, scandals and endless sleaze.

The people have forgotten it went well,
How unions were tamed, the pound made strong,
How living standards rose, inflation fell,
The victories won in wars against the wrong,
How privatising, market forces so
Transformed the weather they prolonged daylight
Till this illusion that the sun must go
Spread across the land like these shades of night.

A peacock honks from dark silhouettes, tense.
A world government Group has planned to scoff
At and steal our national independence,
To break up the UK by splitting off
Scotland and Wales as European states,
Finishing with the pound, stopping our boom,
Bringing back union strife. A tame press baits
One side with its scandals and foretells doom.

The gloom is real, the vision has now gone.
The regicides ditched conviction, belief,
Loyalty to an idea and passion
For the pragmatic posture of a chief
Who linked with personalities and hoped
For human loyalty and was let down
When they, still fighting for an idea, moped
And betrayed him with this pretender's frown.

I think, walking under the early stars
(Looking for a man in a ruff, his head
Tucked under one arm), knowing *their* press czars
Manipulate opinion round their dead,
Surely the public cannot trust this dressed
Demagogue who has like a hatched cuckoo
Pushed all the other eggs out of their nest
And opened his mouth to devour and chew.

I rest on centuries' quiet in the Great Hall,
See our nation's history in adzed beams, bide
Time. I switch on the television. All
Exit polls predict a Labour "landslide" –
Into the sea towards Europe. I go
To bed, watch a screen and count swings, like sheep,
Of eleven to fifteen per cent. I know
What the outcome will be, and fall asleep.

II
A cuckoo calls. I wake and grope a hand
To the bedside radio and now hear
That this upstart who has said "Trust me" and
Has hatched by policies already there
In the old, reused nest, has won with ease
By a hundred and seventy something seats.
The people sought to punish splits and sleaze,
Not give unchecked power to these pious cheats.

I walk with painters and a builder, chat
With an electrician and leaded glass
Repairer, who do not refer to that
Result as if nothing has changed the grass.
Bees swarm round their queen on a white post, twined.
A beekeeper lifts them with his bare hand,
Puts them in a box and leaves some behind.
So Providence removes a clustered band.

A blazing day and on my lunchtime screen
In the moat room, French windows wide open,
Our Prime Minister calmly ends a scene
And says that he will leave the stage; and then
The pretender arrives and grasps raised hands
That happen to wave issued Union Jacks.
A hired crowd: such "public opinion" bands
Bode fierce manipulation, and the axe.

Late afternoon. A cockerel struts and crows.
Small midges dance above grass by the moat.
I sit in the open study windows
And recall a Shetland ram and a vote
At a show for first prize in a rare breed.
Penned in by sycophants, with two curled horns,
That scornful long-haired ram waited to lead.
So had our lost leader waited on lawns.

Wild bees and wasps nest in our viewing mound.
We have a trusting public, who believe
There is no danger in our hillocked ground,
That well-strimmed promises do not deceive.
Our new society hums like wild bees
That menacingly buzz to guard their nest,
Which looks harmless in an afternoon breeze
But contains lethal stings that can arrest.

A Bilderberg agenda rules this crowd.
Like actors politicians recite scripts
Under the direction, as from a cloud,
Of a global *élite* in bankers' crypts
Who want a European Union
And urge our politicians to agree
To hand their power to bankers to bring on
A single European currency.

I walk past the nuttery urn and stand.
A bunch of Scotsmen now hold all the main
Offices of State in the UK, and
Will give the Scots and Welsh Parliaments plain
Self-rule, break England into regions – eight
Linked to Europe through county councils to
End all national borders and integrate
Our nation in supranational EU.

A naïve optimism is abroad,
Settling the Irish problem is now right
As if IRA hard men, overawed,
Will surrender, give up their century's fight.
They will seek a united Ireland in
The new United States of Europe, scent
We now have leaders who will not bargain
With realism, but with wish fulfilment.

Here by the moat under a chestnut tree
With candles I ponder. Our nation's gold
Will now go to Frankfurt, and there will be
Nothing to back our pound, which must be sold
For inflated euros as we unroll
A Union of fragmented nation-states.
I see a country Rockefellers stole
From Rothschilds while our Englishness deflates.

By hanging fragrant wisteria I mourn
The New World Order's rule, towns ringed by moats,
Motorways where tanks can move in at dawn,
Besiege the people, keep them out like goats
If they are driven to the countryside;
Where, hospitals and camps heaped in ashes,
A populist leader with a landslide
Reaches out to a crowd he oppresses.

Indoors I linger on the landing by
My framed seven-foot chart and print of Canute
Commanding the sea to retire. Now my
Nation-state is provinces in a mute
Centralised Europe which floats a slick top
Of grants, policies, laws that all seem strange,
Like King Canute I see but cannot stop
The tide that creeps in and wets us with change.

The UK this momentous day has been
Sold to a United States of Europe.
I take no pleasure in having foreseen
On my chart twelve years back the sickening drop
To our civilisation's newest stage,
Along with Communism's end. I see
Our tradition invaded and rampage
Like our fishing fleet into slavery.

Will the change last or perish with the hours?
The purpling of meadows is seasonal.
The rarest minds, like the rarest wild flowers,
Are ephemeral and perennial.
See a thousand faces droop from stems, blow
Like purple snake's head fritillary bells
In Framsden's mottled green water-meadow
Where each spring hang transient, perennial smells.

Time creeps as on the face of an old clock.
Cogs turn, pendulum ticks and lowers weights,
The longcase hand moves discreetly, tick tock,
Past painted peacocks, floral scenes, estates,
The moon a woman's red-lipped face half set.
The hand ticks with the tyranny of time
And on the hour, with a whirr of cogs met,
The ting-ting-tinkle of a high-pitched chime.

Ducks swoosh by white lilies, quack their advice.
Like Marvell and Voltaire I will retreat
Into my garden, Suffolk paradise,
This end of Great Britain, sit on a seat
Put the moat between myself and the world,
Leave the affairs of State to come unstuck
In an impostor's hands, Euro-flag furled,
And feed chickens and peacocks, and breed duck.

I will retreat into the distant past,
Recreate history as a Tudor knot
And medieval herb garden, contrast
The apothecary's rose and the shot,
Splashed blush-white of Tudor *rosa mundi*,
Learn falconry and Tudor bowls and thought,
Study the Virgin Queen's progresses, try
To ignore the dreadful things done at court.

I will keep hawks and bees and watch wheat grow
In farmers' fields by bridlepath and lane,
Listen to the cuckoo where cowslips blow,
See gold fish spawn in splash-ripples like rain,
Look for rabbits at dusk, savour the balm
By ponds aglow with lilies, gaze at stars,
Write odes as if this were a Sabine farm
And ignore conquered ninnies' blind hurrahs.

1–26 May 1997; revised 2 July 1997

Follies and vices theme: disguised tyranny, self-importance. Set at Otley Hall,
Suffolk.

9

from *The Tragedy of Prince Tudor* (1998)

[UK seen from 2100]

(*United Nations building, New York, AD 2100. Enter the* MINISTER *of*
WORLD CULTURE *for the United States of the World. He speaks in an*
American accent.)

Min. of World	Friends of Europe's most northern isles, good folk
Culture.	From regions dear to Brussels and New York,
	Citizens of our great World Government,
	As the Minister of World Culture, I
	Invite you to leave your enlightened time

And make an imaginative journey
Not to a distant age or place – not Rome
Or Abyssinia – but to an era
In Europe's recent past when there was still
A nation-state called England, far advanced
In its death-throes like a convulsing lion,
That kept subservient in hegemony
Three other regions – Scotland, Wales, Ireland –
And its own muttering English people
In a hated Union, suppressed by
An archaic electoral system that
Ignored proportional representation
And kept in power an oppressive Commons
And Crown remote from subjects in unrest;
An unfamiliar Age of Kings and Queens
Guarded by an unelected Chamber,
The feudal House of Lords, that cared about
Quaint notions: sovereignty, independence,
The purity of transient currency,
The pound which is now a collector's piece.
In our reformed, federal republic
We unveil this newly discovered work
As an example of the paradigm
Under which the oppressed English suffered
As Anglo-American heroes like
An English PM, US President
Struggled to create our New World Order
Which is the epitome of world rule
And sets an example to all mankind,
The four billion the earth's food can sustain,
Who've earned their right by work to be alive
And not be classified "useless eaters".
This social document from a passed Age
Catches the moment when it ceased to be
And our Order was born and monarchies
Lost sovereignty and sanctity, and passed

To our republican World Government
Like baubled jewels left in a codicil.
Go back to the end of the Windsor line
When crown and pageantry spoke for London –
Hanover, rather, for they were German
Until the First World War when they disguised
Their Germanness and took their castle's name....
Good people, leave our secular time for
One when a sunburst meant more than the sun,
And though our tale stops just short of the time
When quaint England abolished itself for
Eight regions within polyglot Europe
That include Picardy and Normandy;
And though it tells of narrow-minded men,
Leave our time of correct attitudes and
Be amazed at the struggle to resist
Our first movers' visionary exploits;
Applaud our Founding Fathers' brave efforts
And the leadership of Rockefeller
And Rothschild who pioneered – despite huge
Odds – our vast United States of the World
Which towers like a mountain, superhuman
Olympus above mankind's tiny towns.
Follies and vices theme: spin.

[Rockefeller on population reduction and New World Order]

(*Inside the hotel.* ROCKEFELLER *addresses the Bilderberg Group's conference. He is an old man. He speaks monotonously in an American drawl.*)
Rockefeller.   Olympians, we are the gods who control
Human events from this Mount Olympus,
Decide the fates of leaders and dispose
As Zeus and the immortals did on crags
Where eagles nest and swoop, peaks streaked with
    snow.
We are apart and look down on the world

Whose lands resemble wastes of parched desert,
Chaotic rocks and tranches of wasteland,
And our lofty concerns order its mess
As unhooded falcons hunt for quarry.
From our great height, omniscient eminence,
Hawk-eyed observation, omnipotence,
We see an overpopulated earth
Riven with borders like rivers. Our cure,
Malthusian local wars, famines and plagues,
Disasters delivering quotas of dead,
Will stop our six billion rising to ten,
And checking of libido, this restraint
Has a new ally, WMDs
Iraq has stockpiled, which can kill all men
Twice over. Olympians, this last year we
Have made progress in not resisting culls
Among multiplying useless eaters
By allowing natural disasters scope.
Since Bosnia, the New World Order rules.
NATO has become the UN army,
Globalism's triumphed, WMDs
Offer new options for good management.
And, Olympians, we have made some progress
In dissolving borders like dried rivers,
In merging differences like currencies
And monarchies, so everywhere's the same,
A multi-cultural global unity
Of egalitarian republics.
We welcome our new English leader's vision
In loosening the United Kingdom
So Scotland, Wales, Ireland and London rule
Themselves and leave the English Crown weakened,
Its sovereignty reduced (the Dutch model),
Set to give up its currency, the pound.
England will have eight self-governed regions.
He'll deliver the monetary union

His predecessor was unwilling to.
Follies and vices theme: population reduction through
war.

[Prime Minister on modernising the monarchy and vacuousness]

(*The Royal Palace, London.* QUEEN *and the* DUKE. *Enter the* PRIME
MINISTER)

Prime Minister. Ma'am, sir, sir, I've come on just one issue.
    We are a modernizing government
    And the people demand a new approach
    To the State opening of Parliament.
    To be popular is to be perceived
    As being of the people, one of us.
    The people want you to be one of them.
    No pageantry, no glittering, no crown.
    They want to see you as more ordinary.
    Just come in a dress and read out my speech.
    That is the way to make you popular.
    Of course it will only be surface change.
    Perception is all, old can seem quite new
    If it is perceived so. We are not now
    A country in decline but coming back,
    Progressing, dynamic, energetic.
    The monarch can seem full of energy
    If wearing modern dress and slickly shown.
    Just as truth can seem a lie to liars
    A lie can seem truth if properly dressed.
    A monarch will seem popular if shown
    As a mirror-image of the people.
    I recommend we do the people's will.

Queen   (*icily*). And how have "the people" expressed this
       will?

Prime Minister. Why, through the mandate they bestowed on me.

Queen.　　　　And did they know they were expressing it?

Prime Minister. Why, yes, we said we'd reform Parliament.

Queen.　　　　And did they understand what "reform" meant?

Prime Minister. I'm their elected leader, I can do
　　　　　　　Whatever I wish if there's a mandate.

Duke.　　　　The Queen is Head of State, not you. Not you....

Prince.　　　　You think the way to save the monarchy
　　　　　　　Is for us to adapt, become modern?

Prime Minister. I do, and I recommend compromise.
　　　　　　　Change and the Crown's secure. Don't and it's not.

　　　　　　　(*The* PRIME MINISTER *bows and comes to the front*
　　　　　　　of the stage.)

　　　　　　　(*Aside.*) Like a chameleon who takes the colour
　　　　　　　Of his surroundings so he is not prey,
　　　　　　　I take on the personality and
　　　　　　　Opinions of others to be all things
　　　　　　　To all men, whose "Proime Min'star" I appear,
　　　　　　　At ease with golfers, pop singers and film stars,
　　　　　　　One of the lads sipping a pint of beer,
　　　　　　　Having a laugh, not thinking seriously
　　　　　　　About interest rates or atomic bombs,
　　　　　　　In tune with all men, criticized by none,
　　　　　　　With high approval ratings from voters,
　　　　　　　Able to be natural with royalty.
　　　　　　　I appear vacuous. Vacuity's
　　　　　　　My secret weapon – public's vacuous.

I tune to their wavelength to win their votes,
Act a calculating vacuousness.
I am a good actor, can play a part,
Now firm, now hesitant, now near-tearful.
I agree with all men – bosses, workers,
Eurosceptics and pro-Europeans,
Liberals and hardliners, I love them all,
And include their opinions in my own.
Republicans and ardent royalists,
Conservatives and clause-four socialists,
Scottish, Welsh, Irish or just plain English –
Inclusiveness means adopting their views
And changing my colour for camouflage.
I support both sides of the Olympians.
All views blend in newness, modernity.
Follies and vices theme: popularism, usurpation, vacuousness.

[Prince on Kingship and duty]

(*The* PRINCE *in the garden of his principal estate and country house, holding a hoe.*)

Prince.   The Crown rises to a point, divine Light
Whose rays descend and enfold a King's head,
Infusing wisdom and guidance so touch
Can heal the maimed, remove a leper's scars.
The divine steals towards my garden peace
Like sunlight spreading across clouded grass.
The Crown is shaped like the Light pouring round
A King's judgement, which heals a nation's soul
As does the power that channels through a priest.
A King's High Priest of the Church of England.
I would that I lived in the Tudor time
When a King had direct contact with all
Like a priest at communion, blessing each,
Not through the barrier of the alien State.

The King is the spirit of his nation
And channels divine Fire to its leaders....
The Crown on my head is the divine Light,
And my Kingdom will be like this garden,
I plead for its soil to be organic,
Pure, uncontaminated by science,
Free from all pesticides and nitrogens
That destroy health and stimulate cancers
As much as nuclear waste. This garden's earth
Is like this Kingdom's culture, for it blooms
Self-controlled flowers and waste, profligate weeds.
The King, like a gardener, nurtures the earth.
The King must purify the soil with Light,
So from its metaphysical ferment
Grow herbs, roses, herbaceous borders
That reveal the perfection of the One
In individual forms, God's Universe.
The King is God's anointed, crowned with Light,
And his Kingdom nurtures the finest growths
Which riot colour like a spring hedgerow.
This garden is a miniature landscape,
A Kingdom where organic souls unfold.
The Sovereign guarantees sovereignty in
The nation and in souls, both soil and flowers,
And loss of sovereignty is spiritual loss.
A nation without sovereignty becomes
A cultural desert that knows no Light
Or tangled undergrowth of thistly weeds
Without order, morality or soul.
True aristocracy is in spirit,
True Kingship is illumined consciousness.
I will be the Defender of the Faiths.
I stand for the Tudor time, old England,
When Kingship was mystic and understood.
I'm rooted in the Tudors though German.
And so have nicknamed myself Prince Tudor.

I'm opposed to our anti-English time.
I must inform my people of this threat
From the Olympian Group. I must and will
Mobilize the nation to save the Crown,
Defend the monarchy so it survives....

I've given my life to duty just as
A player gives his evenings to the stage.
I am an actor who has to perform:
Being a bland Prince from the royal train,
Stopping at stations, being cheered by crowds
And waving back, walking up muddy fields
In boots, discussing the countryside with
Farmers (who're in suicidal despair)
In seventeen-hour days with little food
And not much sitting down, keeping to their
Tight schedule, shaking hands, meeting people
Who toil in difficult, unrecognized
Lives, over whom I will soon reign as King.
It's a gruelling round of hard work, and I
Do it without complaining and I now
Must beg that preening flibbertigibbet
Who trumpets charity and loves to hear
The adoration of the mob, to live
With my sons (and me), out of duty. I
Long for the peace of this garden where I
Do not have to impersonate myself,
Where duty is a morning with a hoe.
I am apart from my people, who glint
From a great distance with their chilly smiles
As on a crisp evening a host of stars
Wink and twinkle in frosty, friendless air.
I am alone, am solitary in crowds
As a timid tree sparrow on a roof
Looks nervously around and then flies off,
But I am ruled by duty to the Crown.

Follies and vices theme: eccentricity, impersonation.

[Rockefeller on coming world government]

(*A hotel at Turnberry, near Glasgow. The annual Olympian Bilderberg Group meeting.* ROCKEFELLER *faces the delegates which include* ROTHSCHILD *and the* PRIME MINISTER.)

Chairman.	Our President, Mr Rockefeller, will
	Summarize our progress during the year.

Rockefeller. Olympians, another year has passed
And from our god-like vantage-point on high
Our over-populated earth seems ripe
For our impending global rule. We have
Resolved the divisions which have racked us.
Israel will give up land to Palestine,
The question is, how much? Northern Ireland
Is moving towards union with the south
Thanks to the implementing of our plan
By the PM, who has courageously
Released bombers and killers from jails so
They can fight on. Our coalition's firm,
And we will progress through the euro and
Economic and monetary union
In Europe, which must be speeded up, to
One global currency, so long our dream.
The world is now grouped in zones and regions
That can be garnered into our great blocs.
Our administrative work's nearly done.
The UN army exists and has teeth.
No state will dare take arms against our will.
We have outlawed guns in restless countries.
Most cities have a by-pass or tank-route
So we can blockade rebellious peoples.
We can dispose of all insurgents who

Challenge our authority, in the camps
We have secretly set up, and we have
Perfected surveillance on citizens
Through the guise of traffic-control cameras.
We will soon introduce in Britain
Cameras mounted on bridges that will take
Photos of all cars' number plates and so
Monitor the population's movements.
The most satisfying *coup* has been seen
In Britain, where, after decades of work
Against the world-wide British Empire, we
Have split its Kingdom into four countries,
Three of which will be states in New Europe
And the fourth, England, is now nine regions
Or Euro-administrative units.
The Titans among us have long pressed for
The survival of sterling, but they (our
Anglo-Israelis) have now conceded
That a millennium's currency will be
Replaced to expedite global control
And we pay tribute and thank them for this.
This change is due to the leads of PM
And his predecessor, who puffed our cause,
And it is with great joy I now present,
Just flown up here to join us at Turnberry
From the G8 meeting at Birmingham,
Soon to be joined by US President,
Our "moderniser" of Britain, the PM.

(*Applause. The* PRIME MINISTER *appears and grins.*)

Prime Minister. Olympians, I'm now wearing your hat
And, speaking among friends within these walls,
I can say openly that we are all
Opposed to national sovereignty and are
Committed to transcend the nation-state

293

For a union of federal states that will
Start in Europe and end with global rule.
As our host has just said, the hard part's done.
We are modernisers, we sweep away
The past and emphasize a popular
Present. PR perception's everything
In today's world, the image and soundbyte.
So that our iconoclasm can be
Perceived we are eclipsing royal power .
And we have cancelled bowing to royals
And curtsying to the Queen. We attack
The mystique of royalty, so we show
The Queen at ceremonies formerly
Private, admit cameras where they've been banned,
To garden parties and investitures,
And show her as an ordinary person –
Running, laughing – and so reduce her power.
We promote popular culture – pop songs,
Fashion, rock music – not highbrow culture
(Elitist Shakespeare and opera) which is
Of the past and lacks popular appeal.
This will be the culture of New Europe.
We want pop music at the Albert Hall,
Rock lyrics at poetry readings in pubs,
And blockbuster writers at Festivals.
Olympians, we are preparing for
A devolved Britain of quite separate states
To be ruled by Brussels and Strasbourg, with
The euro as the currency of each.
I am proceeding as fast as I can
But nationalism is slowing me up.
We're doing all we can to introduce
A United States of the World formed of
The United and European states
And all the global regions and their blocs:
South America, Africa, Asia,

China, Oceania and the Russian states.
That is our truly international aim –
Dream of Rockefeller's Olympians!
Follies and vices theme: dictatorship.

[Prince's distaste for glossy England]

(*A mental hospital, London. The* PRINCE *sitting in a dressing-gown beside his bed. The* PRIME MINISTER, *with* WORMWOOD.)

Prince.   Your glossy England fills me with distaste.
                 I am a King in waiting and I see
                 Institutions that have lost their meaning
                 In false, caring language and compassion;
                 Schools where children are not educated
                 With discipline and judgement of what's good
                 But indulged with warm praise, play and high marks;
                 A welfare system that serves dependence,
                 Not self-respect, responsibility,
                 And a health service ruled by sentiment;
                 Churches empty of doctrine, tradition
                 And rules that seek cosy self-esteem in
                 Modern services of banal words through
                 Happy-clappy, touchy-feely smiling,
                 Hugging neighbours, not confronting dread God –
                 Hence church attendance halved in fifty years.
                 Our Foreign Office trumpets ethical
                 Policies yet still arms dictatorships;
                 Our Agriculture Ministry proclaims
                 That eating meat is safer than it was
                 When nothing's changed except your caring smile.
                 I want real institutions in my land,
                 Not fakes that look good and are images
                 Of caring, niceness and popular smiles;
                 Real policies, not gesture politics.
                 I lambast your fake society and

Its fake institutions. I want what's real,
What includes reason, bears grief with restraint,
Is moral rather than sentimental.
Something is rotten in this dear green land.

Wormwood.   That's a scurrilous piece of defiance.

Prime Minister. Your jaded view is dangerous to our cause.

Wormwood.   You're in no position to say such things.
            The clampdown has happened. It has gone well.
            Your mother, the Queen, is our puppet. You
            Will soon abdicate in favour of Prince....
            Your son. Our dictatorship is in place,
            Though we call it "increased democracy".
            It has the world government's approval,
            The UN will accept it. You – shut up.

Prince.   You intimidate like a hunting owl
            That hoots before it swoops upon a mouse.
            Your bird-of-prey instincts threaten terror.
            Shouting and abusing cannot convert
            What's wrong into what's right. When I am King
            I will be King until I die. But you
            Are just in power till the next election.

Prime Minister. You say you have distaste for our England.
            You're of the past – deluded, out of date.
            We will by-pass you. Our futurist dream
            Has no place for royals in new England.
            We are against history as that is past.
            We are for the future and the people.
            What you call conspiracy's our future.

Prince.   The present is what has flowed from the past.
            The future's what will flow from the present.

It's all one river and you've built a dam
Against the current. You will be submerged.
You cannot dam the current of history.

Wormwood.   It's not a river, it's a state of mind
And how we are perceived in people's minds.
You are irrelevant – *élite* and past.
We will know every movement that you make.
Follies and vices theme: faking images of institutions, self-
delusion, false language.

10

from *Ovid Banished* (1999)

[Augustus on *Pax Augusta*]

(*Augustus's house on the Palatine. The Room of the Masks. AUGUSTUS, who
has just turned 60, is with LIVIA, his Empress.*)

Augustus.   I have brought peace to a divided world.
Julius Caesar chose me to succeed him....
I, *divi filius*, son of a god,
Became *divus Augustus* but I kept
Julius Caesar on public buildings like
The Pantheon and Mars Ultor temple.
I wear his mantle on Prima Porta.
I am called Caesar by all, as he was.
And yet, and yet, I've charted my own course.
My way's different from Julius Caesar's.
He usurped power to end the Republic
And rule as king, dictator, dread monarch.
After the civil wars and Actium
I restored the Republic as *Princeps*
And gave Rome back the freedom she had lost.
The Julians would revive dictatorship

And civil wars would break the peace I brought.
The Claudians must continue my way,
Maintain the meaning I have restored to
The *Res Publica*, free from oppression.
I welcome all mankind to our city.
I keep the peace of the *Pax Augusta*.
My heir will preserve the Principate's peace.
Follies and vices theme: power of Principate.

[Ovid's frivolity]

(*Ovid's house in Rome, near the Capitol.* OVID *is with* MESSALLA.)

Ovid.

I live for pleasure, also to amuse
The fashionable world of wives who peep
At others' husbands, who have roving eyes.
I've no time for religion or the gods,
Only to laugh. I am really shallow.
Rome's blinded me to all the deepest things.
I live from the rational, social ego,
For literary success, creature comforts.
I satirize, poke fun, play it for laughs.
I live where our secular people live
In surface sunlight, not the darker depths.
I am the norm. I am their consciousness,
A raconteur and wit with epithets.
I plead guilty to frivolity – though
My frivolity is just a mask – and
Levity, the Italian *levitas*,
In contrast to old Roman *gravitas*,
And to new mock-didactic parody,
But not to being seriously engaged
Or political towards Augustus.
I tell truths about human nature but
Do not oppose the *imperium* with deeds....

I don't like the civilised life of Rome,
Its pleasure-seeking, hedonistic smile
Which I have to flatter to get across
My poems – otherwise I'd be silent.
My mask is of frivolity and mirth
So I can draw an audience, who bore me.
I would gladly forego my audience
And live for real behind this mocking smirk.
A poet, like a singing bird – tit, finch –
Flies to a patron's bird-table and swings
On hung nuts, pecks, then peers through a window
To thank the helping hand that put them there.
Poets are best when countryside creatures.
As a green woodpecker squats on pasture
Near the galleries of a deep ants' nest
And catches prey with its long sticky tongue
Until, startled, it shyly flies off, so
A poet feeds on Imagination,
Which is as universal as turfed loam,
And extracts images like crawling things.
I'll heed your words and attempt to transform
As ploughed earth's transformed into a wheatfield.
I'll begin by proposing to a girl.
Just as a plain, unprepossessing herb –
Sage, hyssop, thyme, spiked rosemary, wormwood –
When pinched, leaves a fragrance on the fingers
That lingers and is revived with each sniff
Of the nostrils at forefinger and thumb,
So her fresh cheek, which I jokingly pinched,
And her pert charm's left traces on my mind
Which I revive when I recall the scene.
She'd be a good countryside influence.
Follies and vices theme: frivolity.

[Julia and Julian dictatorship]

(*AD 7. Messalla's house.* MESSALLA, OVID. JULIA, *Augustus's grand-daughter, is present along with* IBIS.)

Messalla.   Tonight we are honoured as Ovid will
               Tell us about the work he's laboured on
               For seven years in epic hexameters.

               (*There is applause.*)

Ovid.   Thank you Messalla. My new work is called
               Metamorphoses, or "transformations".
               Parthenius, tutor to both Virgil and
               Tiberius, has a work of that name.
               Mine is very different. It collects myths
               Found in Homer and the Greek dramatists
               Into one volume, some two hundred and
               Fifty tales woven in one tapestry
               In fifteen different books of epic length,
               All on one theme: Protean transformation.
               It still awaits its final polish but
               I will later read some finished excerpts.

               (*There is applause.* JULIA *approaches.* IBIS *hovers
               nearby within earshot, pretending he is looking
               elsewhere.*)

Julia.   What does it say about the *imperium*?

Ovid.   Nothing, Julia. It's a volume of myths.

Julia.   Oh come, it must suggest that there's a need
               For transformation in my grandfather's
               World rule? Don't you suggest that there should be
               A transformation of Principate Rome
               Back to the old Republican virtues?...

I believe in Julian dictatorship.
In *Metamorphoses* you show Caesar
As the god he became after his death,
As the fiery-tailed comet all gazed at;
And Augustus as the son of the god.
Five years ago you paid a tribute to
My poor brother Gaius, and I am pleased
That you have spoken for the Julian line....
I want to know your attitude. And if
You won't tell me now, tell me tomorrow.
Please would you sign my copy of your *Art*?
I'm free tomorrow afternoon at three...

Ovid   (*aside*). I wear a comic mask like a player,
As a strategy to survive this time,
And appear naïve to the foolish throng,
Gullible, innocent, easily duped.
In fact, I'm shrewd behind my buffoon's mask,
And ambitious for my own preferment.
If I visit the Julians tomorrow
And they succeed Augustus when he dies,
I will have advanced my fortune. If I
Don't go I'll lose an opportunity.
I have a quarrel within myself that
Enhances my art but hinders my life.
It's a risk but I have to take it for
Playing safe does not make for getting on.
I won't tell my wife. Julia's colourful
Reputation makes all wives defensive.
A fool knows best when folly makes him wise.
Follies and vices theme: heedlessness, rashness.

[Julia's conspiracy]

(*The next day. Julia's house.* A SLAVE-GIRL *admits* OVID.)

Julia.   Dear friends, the celebrated Ovid's here.
He's come out of sympathy with our cause.
We are all very honoured. My mother
Would be so pleased that he can share our news.
A most reliable Palatine source
Informs us of a grave development.
My grandfather's chosen Tiberius
To succeed him as Roman Emperor,
And wants to banish my brother and me
To remote islands, worse than far-off towns,
So the succession's from Livia's line
And not Scribonia's or Agrippa's.
The imperial secret is out. We must
Prevent our banishment by striking first,
Release my mother, involve the army,
Overthrow Augustus, restore ourselves,
Prevent Tiberius from inheriting.
Who will depose my ailing grandfather
And install Julius Caesar's pristine line?
Who will release Julia from Rhegium,
Agrippa Postumus from Surrentum?
My mother championed the Julian line
As I do now, and all you who are here
Have said you'll help the Julians succeed
So the next Caesar is a Julian
Who looks back to Julius Caesar's Rome,
And not a Claudian of world empire
As is my grandfather, who has allowed
Livia to bully him into her view.
We will discuss our strategy for power.
But first we will mix blood as a proof that
We are in one group with a common aim.
Stand in a circle, each put out a hand
Over this bust of divine Augustus
And as the blood flows clasp right hands and place
Them on the head of my dumb grandfather.

(*The conspirators pierce their fingers with a knife*
PAULLUS *has been holding, pass it round, and stand
in a circle.* IBIS *holds back.*)

Will you join us, Ovid? You encouraged
My mother, will you now encourage me?
Follies and vices theme: naïvety.

[Augustus banishes Julia]

(*Augustus's house. The Room of the Masks.* AUGUSTUS *sits.* LIVIA *stands
near* JULIA *who is under guard. An* OFFICIAL *is present.*)

Julia.   What has happened to Paullus?

Livia.   Beheaded.

(JULIA *collapses into tears.*)

But first he took the full blame on himself.

(JULIA *stops crying and stares at* AUGUSTUS.)

Caesar has decided your punishment.

Augustus. I overlook your role in Paullus' plot.
You have committed adultery with
D. Iunius Silanus, and others.
You've taken after your wanton mother
And must share her fate. In accordance with
The *Lex Julia*, Julia, I banish you
To the barren island of Trimerus.
I have no daughter and no granddaughter.
The safety of the *imperium* is all.

(JULIA *is led away weeping.* THE OFFICIAL *remains.*)

Livia.	Caesar will now rule on Agrippa's fate.
Augustus.	By Senatorial decree Agrippa
	Is moved from Surrentum to an island,
	Planasia, near Elba, where he will
	Live out his life in solitary exile.

(*Exit* THE OFFICIAL.)

Livia.	You have done well, Caesar. But there's one more
	Decision you must take. Look at that wood.
	As death-watch beetles enter wood and gnaw
	For eighteen years and then emerge to die,
	But perhaps fly into another beam,
	And in due course riddle a roof which falls,
	Some poets eat into the State's timbers
	And threaten the protective roof of State.
	They are noxious insects and must be sprayed.
	They must be extracted. I will leave you
	So you can think about what you must do.

(*Exit* LIVIA.)

Augustus	(*alone*). As a great-spotted woodpecker taps trees,
	Drumming on decayed wood with rapid beak,
	Pecking the crevices to extract grubs,
	And dominates an early spring morning,
	So an Emperor picks out harmful plotters
	And rids the State of insects that make rot.
	There's public sympathy for Julia
	And her brother, scorn for the *imperium*.
	I will stab all opposition. I need
	A pretext for preferring Tiberius
	To Julia. I banished her mother for
	Political reasons, but gave the cause
	As sexual. I must do the same again.

I need a public figure to take blame
For the banishment of young Julia.
A scapegoat whose banishment will silence
The public clamour and associate
Julia with erotic misdemeanours
And mute gossip about the succession.
Someone known for erotic love who will
Scamper like a chased fox away from Rome
And draw the baying public from the truth.
A known opponent of the *imperium*
Whose links with Julia will seem scandalous
And divert attention from Tiberius.
A dissident who's scandal-prone and *louche,*
Who opposes world government and who
Will leave the *imperium* healthier for
His ostracism and his banishment.
I bear him no ill will but need: Ovid!

(*Re-enter* LIVIA.)

Livia.   Caesar, you know what's next. I read your thoughts.

Augustus   (*aloud*). Now bring me Ovid, the *imperium's* foe.
                Follies and vices theme: manipulation (by Livia), deviousness
                (by Augustus).

          [Augustus banishes Ovid]

(*Augustus's house on the Palatine, Rome.* AUGUSTUS *presides over a private court in the Room of the Masks.*)

Augustus.   Information has come to me, that you
                Were present when Julia, my granddaughter,
                Spoke to the plotters about killing me,
                And that you did not report this to me.

Ovid.   Caesar, I admit that I was present.
               But by accident, not by design. I
               Was invited by young Julia to sign
               A book. I blundered in at the wrong time.
               And nothing was said about *killing* you.

Augustus.   You knew my granddaughter Julia wanted
               To overthrow me for the Julian line.
               You "blundered" in on the conspirators
               But took no part. You blundered out again.
               I know. My spies have informed me. I know
               Julia invited you to talk with her.
               But you did not report what you stumbled
               On by accident. That was a mistake.
               Now some of those you blundered in on have
               Attempted to free both Julia and
               Agrippa Postumus from their islands.
               Enough is enough, I must sort you out.

Ovid.   I can't deny it. I will tell the truth.
               I admit it, I stumbled in on them
               By accident, as she'd invited me
               For what I thought would be… a private talk.
               I did not know the plotters would be there.
               I took no part in their Julian plot,
               And nothing was said about *killing* you.

Augustus.   Why did you not reveal this plot at once
               That you stumbled in on by accident?

               (OVID *glances round the room.*)

Ovid.   I will tell you the truth. I'll speak plainly.
               I greatly respect the stability
               That you have brought to Italy and Rome.
               The plotters worked for a new order that

Could improve the world after your demise.
I sympathized with their long-term goals, for
I was born a year after Caesar died,
I grew up in the Republic when Rome
Was a metropolis for our nation,
With Latin Italy's supreme language,
Not a cosmopolitan melting-pot
With a *lingua franca* of many tongues,
A corrupt, impure, polyglot Babel.
The mixing of peoples has weakened Rome's
Beliefs and secularized Rome's culture.
What was Roman's now multi-cultural –
Diluted, contaminated, confused.
You cannot be imperial and retain
Rome's belief in traditional values,
Rome's belief in itself, and so the seeds
Of self-doubt, decline, disintegration
And conquest by barbarians have been sown.
I warn you that your Empire won't survive
The *oikumene*. Inevitably
Barbarians will enter the Roman home
And destroy what greatness your conquests built.
It is the law of imperial grandeur –
That an *imperium* gets infected
And can't resist those tribes it once suppressed.
Your Empire is like a child's tower of bricks:
One swipe from tiny fingers, down it comes –
Or else it crashes when the balance goes.
Rome will fall. I foretell the fall of Rome.
My allegiance now's to you, Caesar. But
My future support's for the Julians,
Not for a militarist succession that
Would use conquest to build a World Empire.
I question a new world order which is
Enforced by Roman legions carrying
Statues of Roman gods, which they impose

On all parts of the imperial Empire.
I believe all parts of the Empire have
Their own cultures, which they should all retain.
I am opposed to massacres of tribes
And any calculated genocide
In the cause of brutal Roman conquest,
Torching towns in the Danube hinterland.
The *imperium* is a killing machine.
I write for all mankind, affirm the right
Of all to live at peace in their own way
In villages outside the *imperium*.
I am a writer, I work in Latin,
My attitudes are shaped by Literature.
I do not want the Roman culture mixed
With barbarian cultures in a world State.
I stumbled in on them and kept it quiet.
This is about my literary posture.

(There is a stunned silence in the room. OVID *has
spoken too honestly for his own good.* AUGUSTUS
speaks very quietly, but he is shaking with rage.)

Augustus.   This involves much more than mere Literature.
You have questioned the public policy
Of pacification of all regions.
I've been a peace-maker, a peace-bringer.
I've presided over the expansion
Of our Empire. I, who rode with Caesar
At his African triumph and served him
In Spain, in civil war conquered the West
(Italy, Sicily) and then the East,
Won Egypt from Antony and became
Master of the Roman World – to bring peace.
I defeated the hostile Alpine tribes,
Took Galatea in Asia Minor and
Mauretania in Africa, and then

Pacified Gaul and Spain and erected
My *Ara Pacis* to glorify peace.
I took Noricum so the frontier moved
From Italy to the upper Danube,
Then pacified Pannonia and crossed
The Rhine to invade Germany as far
As the Elbe, and took Bohemia, and
Judaea. Now much of Europe, Asia
And Africa are under my peaceful
Rule. Our legions imposed this peace. I've used
Troops to subjugate for the greater good
So there could be peace throughout the Empire.
I have continued Julius Caesar's Peace.

Ovid   (*quietly*). A lot of killing's gone into your Peace.
                Pacification's something to be feared.

Livia.   How dare you speak so bluntly to Caesar!

Ovid.   There's a language of peace and one of war,
                And poets use language to tell the truth
                And speak of peace as peace and war as war
                And not of war as peace and peace as war.
                Literature cares about human beings....
                I saw Virgil, heard Horace read his *Odes*.
                I have a new way of writing which you
                Do not appreciate or understand.

Livia.   This is outrageous and intolerable.

Augustus.   I understand more new writing than most.
                I have presided over the greatest
                Period in Latin literary history.
                After the Golden prose of Cicero
                I encouraged patrons (Maecenas and
                Messalla Corvinus) and polished verse

On patriotic themes, love and Nature.
In one decade I was presented with
The greatest Roman works: Virgil's *Georgics*
And *Aeneid*, Horace's Odes and his
Epistles, Sextus Propertius's and
Tibullus' elegies, Livy's history
And Pollio's chronicle of events.
I can't think you are in their league, surely?
Is Ovid really in this Golden Age?

Ovid.   It's said I'm the last Golden Age poet.

Augustus.   I can't understand why, you're ordinary.

Ovid.   A poet of the ordinary life,
As recognized by all your citizens.
What it comes down to is, I learned by chance
That you have chosen Tiberius as heir.
You did not want the Julians to know this,
And say I should have denounced them to you.

Livia.   He's both arrogant and impertinent.
Enough of this defiance. Sentence him.
He wants to live outside the *imperium*.
Grant his wish. The place for him is Tomis.

(AUGUSTUS *speaks with a quiet, cold fury*.)

Augustus.   The charge against you is high treason, that
You conspired with others against the State
And opposed the world-wide *imperium*.
I have examined all the evidence.
We have witnesses who have denounced you.
By your own admission you are guilty.
You were implicated in my daughter
Julia's intrigue which led to banishment.

I spared you then. Now you're implicated
In my granddaughter Julia's intrigue by
Seeing treason and not reporting it.
I will now proceed to my judgement. I
Sentence you by imperial decree
To banishment from Rome for ever. You
Will be taken under guard to Tomis
On the Pontus, beyond the *imperium*
And you will live with the local people
Outside the Roman Empire till you die.
This is a *relegatio*, so your lands
Are not confiscated. Your wife can stay.

(OVID *is deeply shocked.*)

Ovid.   Tomis. They don't speak Latin there, do they?

Augustus.   Greek and barbarian tongues, which you deplore
But which will only be Latinised when
Moesia's "pacified" by Roman legions.
My *imperium*, world government, can bring
Great boons to all mankind – peace, freedom from
War, famine, plagues, disease and starvation.
The *Pax Romana* is its greatest gift.
Barbarians raid across the *limes*
And have to be repelled to guard the whole.
Local wars preserve the *Pax Romana*.
They're a necessary evil, a means
That is justified by the precious end.
The writers of the Golden Age grasped this.
They all understood Rome's world destiny.
You have opposed the *imperium* now;
See if you like life among barbarians.
You must depart by early December.
A guard will sail with you to dark Tomis.
Your *Ars Amatoria* will be banned

311

From Rome's three famous public libraries.
It has not been condemned by a decree
From the Senate, and so it can't be burned.

Ovid.   And my other writings?

Augustus.   They'll also be
Withdrawn from the libraries and you will
Have no audience in Tomis, your escorts
Will ensure that your writing's at an end.
Death by silence – we'll wall you in with quiet,
Cut off your audience so you are not heard.
That's our response to all who challenge us
And oppose our *Lex Julia*, and publish
Works that mislead the young, like my daughter.

Ovid.   This is a drastic form of censorship.

Augustus.   It defends moral reforms I'm proud of
And purges Rome of dubious verses.
Like Socrates you've corrupted the young.

(OVID, *still shocked, musters himself for a defiant exit.*)

Ovid.   What I've written will be circulated
In all times. My works will outlast my life
And will be read when your *imperium*'s gone.

Livia.   Take this insolent man back to his house.
Guard him while he packs for life-long exile.
Follies and vices theme: manipulation, deviousness, vindic-
tiveness, tyrannical censorship.

[Messalla pleads for Ovid]

(*Augustus's house. The Room of the Masks.* AUGUSTUS, MESSALLA.)

312

Messalla.   Caesar, I thank you for your attention.
I do not excuse Ovid. But I know
That deep down he admires the *imperium*,
And if he sometimes professes not to,
Then, though the sentiment is culpable,
A Caesar as powerful as you may feel
Rightly indignant, yes, but with your famed
Noble magnanimity may still waive
Severe punishment, recognizing that
Literature is the temple of free speech,
Purified language that is handed down
From generation to generation,
Where all worship as if at your Altar,
Ara Pacis of the *Pax Augusta*,
Where high culture is guarded like a flame.
A Golden Age such as yours can withstand
A free proponent of the other side.
All opponents and dissidents can be
Accommodated in your greater State.
The Augustan virtues of tolerance,
Reason and sensibility must shrink
From censorship; rather they listen and
Put right a perceived wrong that's criticized.

Augustus.   The *imperium* has spread to all mankind.
I've built a United States of the World.
Very soon the Roman *denarius*
Will be the single Earth currency that
Embraces Parthia and the German tribes,
Pannonia and African Numidia,
Even India, which Alexander reached.
Once my world order is established, yes,
I can be generous to all my critics.
But until then the legions' action has
Precedence over urbane discussion.
I am a man of action. You're learnèd.

Action requires censorship that will shock
Learnèd scholars of Egyptian and Greek,
Persian and Roman knowledge and wisdom.
I am universal in my choices,
Which are made for the *imperium*'s good.
You are universal in your reading,
And take in all cultures and see all sides,
But your task is not like mine, to extend
The *imperium*, and if any of your
Client-poets blatantly undermine
The *imperium*, then they must be silenced.
I have to act decisively to keep
The world Roman and suppress all revolts.

Messalla.   You're quite right, Caesar, as in everything.
But is Ovid against the *imperium*?

Augustus.   Yes. I have evidence.

Messalla.   I see him as
A poker of fun who makes Literature,
Who does not know his political views.
He deals in situations and reflects
Philosophically in what he writes.
He is a man of letters who absorbs
History, mythology, philosophy
And displays them as a peacock displays
A many-eyed fantail to impress mates.
He's not a serious opponent of
Your *imperium* and what the legions do.
His way's the pen, it's not wielding the sword.

Augustus.   But the pen is as mighty as the sword.
It influences minds. Each book he writes
Is a political act that affects
The *imperium*. I do not like his work:

Pornographic advice, subversive myths
And provocative, jesting attitude.
Virgil's better – he wrote epic that can
Be compared to Homer, and pastoral verse.
But I fear him, for people look to him.
He cannot be ignored. He will be read.
I have walled him round with silence, and banned
His work from public libraries. He's ceased
To exist as a poet. I will not
Be deflected from crushing opponents
Of the world-wide *imperium*, my great work.
State power must swat ephemeral artists
Who whine and bite like maddening insects.

(*There is a silence. AUGUSTUS indicates that the discussion
is over and that MESSALLA should leave. Exit Messalla
after a bow.*)
Follies and vices theme: showing-off.

[Ovid rails against Augustus]

(*Ovid's hut in Tomis. The GUARD is sitting outside. OVID is with
CONSTANTIA, who is taking dictation.*)

Ovid.   On my journey I wrote some "Sad Poems"
                   And now I want to dictate another.
                   It's addressed to Caesar. First some ideas.
                   I am angry that I've been exiled here.
                   Caesar's thunderings are random, like Jove's
                   Whose lightning strikes a dead tree, then a vine
                   That droops with grapes – does not discriminate
                   Between a barren heart and an artist
                   As vibrant and as creative as me.
                   No less random are Caesar's flirtations,
                   Which are as many as his arch rainbows.
                   He takes his pleasure, then pontificates

Against verses on the art of pleasure,
Hypocrisy that cries out to be mocked.
He has corrupted the Roman ideal,
Turned the eagle into a cruel vulture,
Used the high gods to keep himself in power,
And fostered secular profanity.
As geese honk near a pond, heads in the air,
And a male scoots forward, its neck stretched out
To shovel off a foe that's after food,
So Caesar chases off all those he fears.
I resent what he's done to me. Avoid
Great men, live a quiet private life and thrive.
Why did he pick on me? I did not know
What they were doing when I blundered in.
An error and a book.... I don't make sense?
Write it down. He, the mightiest in the world,
Will stand up to all plotters who want change.
He stands for the blinkered world government
That wants all countries to be provinces
Within the great Roman Empire.
Follies and vices theme: hypocrisy.

[Augustus dying]

(*AD 14. Nola. Augustus's sick-room.* TIBERIUS *enters the sick-room.* LIVIA *hovers behind him.* AUGUSTUS *is lying on a couch.*)

Augustus.　　　Who's there? Is it Tiberius? I'm quite blind.
　　　　　　　I'm glad you've come. You will be Caesar soon
　　　　　　　And I can hand over the world to you
　　　　　　　Like this orange. Excuse my lower jaw.
　　　　　　　It has to be propped up by a pillow.
　　　　　　　I've got worse very fast. I don't know why.
　　　　　　　You see, I've had my hair combed. I am still
　　　　　　　Ruler of the known world. Rumours of my
　　　　　　　Illness may cause popular disturbance.

My father Octavius died in this room.
You must always remember, it's a play.
You are an actor with an audience.
Did I not play my part in life's farce well?
If I pleased you give me a warm good-bye.
I can't move my lower jaw. There will be
A lot of soldiers from Actium and
The battlefields that brought me into Rome,
Waiting for me. I have no regrets. One.
I wish I hadn't banished Julia,
Your sister. I loved her.

Livia.   Nonsense, Caesar.
She plotted to kill you with that Ovid.

Augustus.   I don't know, I don't know. Not with Ovid.
I think Ovid was blameless all along.
But he opposed the *imperium* and so
He had to be banished. I feel dreadful.
My mausoleum has long awaited me,
My deeds inscribed on the two bronze pillars
That flank the entrance doors – my *Res Gestae*,
And now I am ready to enter it
And dwell in gloom with the shades of Hades.
I, master of the Greco-Roman world,
Am mortal, and it is time I must die
And be cremated on a funeral pyre
In the Campus Martius and be scooped up
As two handfuls of powdery cinder-dust,
And, lord of riches in this Roman life,
Must sit with Pluto in the Underworld,
Twin umbrarchs of that dark sinister realm.
Leave me, I need to think about my life.
Follies and vices theme: wrongful banishment.

[death of Augustus]

317

(Ovid's *hut. Enter* CONSTANTIA *hastily. She pushes past the* GUARD.
OVID *appears within.*)

Constantia.	Caesar dead. In market they say he dead.
	He die quick. Livia hasten his end.

Ovid.	It will not make any difference to me.
	The world government's a system, it's not
	At the whim of a personality.
	The system has a policy on me.
	It's consistent, to keep me in Tomis.

Constantia.	Forty Praetorian Guards carry his
	Body from Nola, where he die, to Rome.
	Caesar a god. They say he now a god.

Ovid.	A god! The man who banished me a god
	Now ranked alongside Apollo's pure Light?
	That is the logic of humanism.
	Man equal to the one Creator god.
	When civilisations turn secular
	They die. Augustus' rule was secular,
	Secularisation's the death of Rome –
	Write that down please. Rome rose with the sacred
	And declined when it lost its true vision.
	The Rome I dreamed of has a worthless core.
	Now I understand, Rome was secular,
	A barbarous place of noise and raucous cries.
	This Tomis is more civilised for here
	There's a tradition of the deeper self
	Where all can locate their being's well-spring.
	In Tomis time is the season's progress,
	A natural rhythm of the days and nights.
	In Rome time wears a helmet and marches
	With shield and ruthless stride to world conquest.
	Imagine, Rome with all its fine togas

And pillared temples, soaring aqueducts
And marbled villa courtyards – barbarian!
And Tomis with its hovels open to
The wind and babblers in a foreign tongue –
Civilised! Sound, silence. City, Nature.
I, poet of sounds and warm city crowds,
Prefer the solitude of silence and
The steppes and skies and frosts of cold Nature.
A metamorphosis that's surprised me!
Now I see Rome was just a shallow place
For all its glitter and bright elegance,
And my frivolity there was a mask
That blocked my own development and growth.
If Caesar's dead, I don't want to return
To Rome. I'm happy here, writing poems.
Follies and vices theme: shallowness (in Rome).

[Ovid criticises the *imperium*]

(*Ovid's hut. The* GOVERNOR *enters the hut. The* TOMITANS *crowd and press behind him.*)

Ovid   (*surprised*).   Have I offended –

Governor.   The Tomitans know what you think of them.
They are indignant. They made you welcome
And you repaid their hospitality
By writing disparagingly about them.
They did not like some of the things you said
At the Temple of Apollo. They are
Angry, and you should now apologise.

Ovid.   I will speak in Getic. My friends, I am
A warm-blooded Italian who grew up
In the hot sun, in orchards and vineyards.
I can't pretend that your climate suits me.

I find it cold. That is no fault of yours.
But I like living among you. I find
You kind and caring, unlike my own Rome.
I've learned Getic, I defend our Tomis
Alongside you when raiders fire arrows,
I share your lives, I am now one of you.
I would not want to return now to Rome.
It would distress me greatly if you felt
Any animosity towards me.
You are my friends. I have no friends in Rome.
I am heartbroken if some words of mine
Have been misconstrued as criticism
Of you, your province or the life you lead.

(CONSTANTIA *nods her approval and adds words in Getic.*)

Constantia.   You heard the Roman, he loves being here.
              He's against Rome. He's been misunderstood.

(OVID *turns to the* GOVERNOR *and speaks quietly to him in Latin.*)

Ovid.   Who's set me up? Who's turned them against me?
              Was this an order you've had from Caesar?

Governor.   I will not dignify that last remark
              With a comment. Caesar's above reproach.
              (*To the Tomitans.*) My friends, Ovid has apologised if
              He's inadvertently offended you.

              (*To Ovid.*) You have a gift for offending people.

Ovid.   Only Emperors who want to crush the *plebs*
              As if they rode a chariot through a crowd.

Governor.   I will ignore that last remark. I did
              Not hear what you just said.

320

Ovid.   I speak the truth.
                     The poet speaks the truth and Emperors quake
                     For though they rule through lies, they cannot still
                     The freedom of a poet's tongue. They may
                     Ban all his books from public libraries,
                     Make sure they're not reviewed and surround him
                     With silence – place him among foreign tongues
                     And under house arrest – as a danger
                     For truth is dangerous, but poetry
                     Is mightier than their guards and Governors' spies,
                     A poet's words will outlast their regimes.
                     My words will live for ever, I will be
                     More famous than Tiberius Caesar
                     In a thousand or two thousand years' time.
                     And I say the *imperium* crushes
                     Non-Roman peoples who've a right to live,
                     I say military power's a blight on all
                     Who live on the *imperium*'s borders.
                     You bribe barbarians with luxuries
                     And then crush all resistance to your rule.
                     You make a desert and then call it peace.
                     Augustus Caesar sent me to witness
                     The policy that's already begun
                     To destroy the mighty Roman Empire.
                     I see Caesar's outlook is ruinous
                     And speak the truth, and he cannot stop me.

                     (*The* GOVERNOR *turns and leaves without a word.*
                     The TOMITANS *follow him.* CONSTANTIA *with* OVID.)

Ovid.   ... I'm a bit frail, I agree. Don't tell Rome.
                     Rome brought me up to emulate great men.
                     Rome gave me noble qualities, but time
                     Has pocked and blotched my face like a statue.
                     Ahead's old age, creeping decrepitude.
                     I will be ready for Death when he creeps

Down our lane like a hooded peasant who's
Swinging a scythe through a swathe of long grass
And takes a wild rose with his sickle blade.
I am at peace with myself and my life.
I had to write, it was a compulsion,
An unstoppable force that made me sit
And scratch and fill wax tablets with verses.
My early work was poor stuff, but it took
Me into great men's salons, so I met
Caesar's daughter. That was my great mistake –
To catch the attention of a great man.
He did not like my work, it challenged him.
Poetry ruined me and brought me here.
And yet I am still a slave to my Muse.
For eight or nine years I have persevered.
I've destroyed much of what I wrote. The rest
Is one long lament, too monotonous
And full of rhetorical artifice
And barbarisms, for I've little chance
To speak in eloquent Latin save with
The Governor and my jailer, and they see
Me as an outcast who's better ignored.
I have no public and have been suppressed.
Yet still I write, for no one can control
My words, which now defeat the *imperium*
That put me in this Jove-foresaken spot.
I never thought, when Rome rose to my words,
I would be buried in a distant land
And lie in a grave in Sarmatian soil
Outside the city wall, far from the gate,
Trampled on by the thundering hooves of
The horses of barbarian bowmen
Who shoot arrows at huddling Getans.
Follies and vices theme: vindictiveness, tyrannical censorship.

[Rome receives news of Ovid's death]

(A Roman salon. Many people. COTTA, Messalla's son, claps his hands.)

Cotta.   My friends, I have had news from Tomis that
           Ovid has died, and with his death has passed
           The Golden Age of Roman Literature.
           He was the last of a line of poets –
           Catullus, Virgil, Horace, Propertius –
           Who brought glory to Rome. We shall not see
           His like again. Lesser talents now walk
           Where once strode those who perfected the ode,
           The epic, the love elegy – all forms.

           *(Those listening turn back and resume their
           conversation. They are indifferent to the news of Ovid,
           and their own concerns have taken over. IBIS comes
           forward and addresses the audience.)*

Ibis.   He opposed the *imperium*, his work
           Was bad for Rome and for our world mission.
           He encouraged loose-living, undermined
           Marriage and poked fun at religious myths
           Which Caesar revived for the good of Rome.
           The *imperium* needs marriage and the gods.
           He had to be silenced. What a poet
           Writes is not important. What's important
           Is the spread of Rome's rule throughout the world.
           The Golden Age is when the world is one –
           Britain, Gaul, Judaea, Parthia, Egypt,
           India, China, any land mass that's found,
           All in one vast well-governed territory
           Where citizenship's cosmopolitan
           And, under the aegis of mighty Rome
           Which protects the known world with a hundred
           Bases for legions who with spear and shield
           Hold back barbarians massed on the frontiers,
           All nation-states suppressed for common good.

Rome bombards barbarians near the Danube
So Rome's *imperium* lasts a thousand years,
A good sight longer than a poet's verse.
My friends, the Golden Age is yet to come.
Follies and vices theme: ruthlessness (of imperial rule).

11

from *The Rise of Oliver Cromwell* (1999)

[Hartlib describes Cromwell]

(*1627. Flanders. A public place.* MENASSEH BEN ISRAEL *of Amsterdam.*
HARTLIB. *Hartlib is a Polish Jew who speaks with a German accent.*)

Menasseh.   Tell me about this fiery Calvinist.

Hartlib.   He is a Unitarian, he sees
God as One, not a Catholic Trinity,
And he denies Christ had divinity.
His outlook's Deistic Freemasonry.
Of all my English friends he is the most
Visionary and ambitious. When a boy
He dreamed he would be King and I believe
That one day he'll be ruler of England.
He's strong enough, he has a woodman's gait.
He'll hunt prey like a hawk, swoop from a height.
He is your man. He has Jewish cousins:
His uncle's wife's first husband was the Jew
Palavicino who funded the Dutch
Rebels. They have their own lands in Holland.
Follies and vices theme: ambition.

[Cromwell criticises the King]

(*1627. Hinchingbrooke.* OLIVER CROMWELL, *aged 28, and his wife*

ELIZABETH.)

Cromwell.   I well remember standing as a boy –
              The King sat there. I was just four and I
              Bloodied the nose of Prince Charles Stuart, who
              Was two years old. And where have those years gone?
              And now this place of childhood safety – sold!
              We gentry are in terminal decline.

Elizabeth.   Your father entertained the King, but you
              Have nothing good to say about him now.

Cromwell.   No, he's a secret Catholic who likes Spain.
              He went to Spain with Buckingham to woo
              Philip the Third's daughter, but left when told
              He should become a Roman Catholic,
              Then pressed his father for war with Spain, then
              Married the French King's Catholic sister,
              Henrietta Maria. The Spanish war's
              Turned out to be a thundering failure.
              He has no appetite to defeat Spain.
              I don't trust him. I don't trust Buckingham.
              He ought to be impeached. And what's happened?
              The King's dissolved Parliament to prevent
              Impeachment! And now judges have declared
              His act illegal, what's he gone and done?
              He's sacked the Chief Justice! He's a tyrant!
              He's put himself above the rule of law.
              And now he's stuck for funds he's forced a loan –
              He'll tax us gentry into deep decline.
              Under this King, our State's like a garden
              That's been put into shade by an oak-tree
              Whose massive branches block the sunlight and
              Prevent plants from growing. It must be felled.
              This home of my uncle, Sir Oliver,
              And his Dutch second wife Anne Hooftman – sold!

Sold to the Montagus because of tax.
Follies and vices theme: tyranny.

[Menasseh bribes Cromwell to oust the King]

(MENASSEH *nods and takes* CROMWELL *aside.*)

Menasseh.   I have come specially from Amsterdam
Where there's support for you against the Crown.
Funders have been impressed by your proud stance
In Parliament, the country and this place.
Know that you have been chosen to foment
Revolution. I am to assist you.
Amsterdam Jews will fund a new army
So you can forcibly eject the King –
And when you take power, your new government.
There's unlimited funding – all you need....
The Jews were all expelled in 1290.
They'll want to return and settle again.
You must resettle the Jews in England.
And to do that, you'll have to oust the King.

Cromwell.   Unlimited funding from Amsterdam
For my Army, and in return I must
Admit the Jews to England once again.
Follies and vices theme: bribery. For this view of the funding of
the New Model Army by Amsterdam Jews and for Cromwell's
letters to and from Ebenezer Pratt of 16 June and 12 July 1647,
see Hagger, *The Secret History of the West*, pp.125–126.

[Charles faces his martyrdom]

(*29 January 1649. London, St James's Palace.* CHARLES *and* BISHOP
JUXON.)

Charles.   I feel so peaceful now.
I have relaxed my grasp on life, honour
Is more important than saving my life.
I die for a principle. The monarch's
Above the people's law, he's appointed
By divine right, not human agency.
If I have fallen short, God will judge me.
But I am God's anointed, my nation's
Shepherd. I've raised funds to lead it forward.
I'm no more tyrant than a shepherd is.
The people will learn that the usurpers –
Cromwell, Ireton, Bradshaw and all the rest –
Are working with Dutch Rosicrucians who
Are seizing our Kingdom with virtuous
Protestations, as pirates deep in prayer
Resolve to storm aboard a ship of State.
A monarch cannot be abolished by
A people without a massive change in
The constitution, for man then leads man
As pirates lead the crew they have captured,
Divorced from God's great purposes and Light.
The monarch's the illumined leader of
A nation that needs guidance. Puritans
Think they receive guidance from God by prayer.
They are deluded if they think that God
Is inciting subjects to regicide.
The monarchy in England will survive.
No Cromwell can abolish King or Queen
Just as no pirate can the captain's rank –
The people will restore a Prince of Wales.
I must be martyred for the monarchy.
Follies and vices theme: usurpation (by Cromwell), delusion.

[Cromwell resolves to execute the King]

(*30 January 1649, 11 a.m. London, an apartment in Whitehall Palace. Sound of banging as the scaffold is erected.* CROMWELL *moves to one side.*)

Cromwell   (*aside*). Now I must be resolute one more day.
                    I have pushed all into this course – Ireton,
                    Fairfax, Bradshaw, the judges, many more –
                    And now I must carry through my design
                    Which began before the First Civil War
                    And has brought me to the brink of sole rule,
                    Of Kingship, which through guidance from Holland,
                    The Lord I should say, is now in my grasp.
                    I must be as calm as a watching owl
                    That calculates his silent swoop and strikes
                    With a prolonged and terrifying shriek
                    That's out of character for a wise bird,
                    And clutches a rat in his sharp talons.
                    I must be as sly as a fox near hens.
                    The executioner will wear false beard
                    And wig to conceal his identity.
                    It will seem I'm absent from the scaffold,
                    As it will appear Ireton is also.
                    I must steel myself for this final act.
                    It must not be botched, I need nerves of steel,
                    As keen as the sharp edge of a block-axe.
                    It's no more than striking the final blow
                    To fell a rotten oak that has leaf-blight.
                    From the outset this has been a contest
                    Between Charles Stuart and myself. Now I
                    Must smite the final blow and kill him clean.
                    Follies and vices theme: regicide, murder, slyness.

                    [Charles speaks on the scaffold]

                    (CHARLES *steps forward and addresses the vast crowd.*)

Charles.   People as far as I can see. (*Aloud.*) I say
                    To the people that I regret nothing.

I am innocent, I did not begin
A war with the Houses of Parliament.
Their militia began the war on me.
Ill instruments have come between them and
Me and are the cause of all the bloodshed,
The conquerors of world imperialism,
Rosicrucian Freemasonry. Conquest
Is never just. Alexander the Great
Was a bigger robber than a pirate.
He and the pirate were two of a kind
And separated only by degree.
The refuge from imperialism is
The Church of England kept in good order.
I wanted the people to be prosperous.
I desire the people's liberty and
Freedom as much as anybody, but
They cannot have liberty and freedom
Without government and laws, that make sure
Their lives and goods are untouched by others,
And are safe from pillaging imperialists.
The people should not share in government.
A subject and sovereign are clean different.
It is to make this point that I am here.
I am the martyr of the people, I'm
Their shield of sovereignty from all robbers.
Follies and vices theme: ruthlessness (of world imperialism,
i.e. Rosicrucian Freemasonry of Amsterdam Jews).

[Bishop Juxon on the Restoration]

(10 December 1660. London. Bell-ringing. Enter ARCHBISHOP JUXON.)

Juxon.   Cromwell was embalmed, yet his coffin stank.
His filth broke through. He was swiftly interred.
A wax effigy filled his coffin at
His lying-in-state. It had glass eyes, and

After some ten days it was stood up, and
A crown was put on its head to suggest
His soul had passed from Purgatory to Heaven –
A Popish custom Cromwell abhorred when
It was used at James the First's funeral.
A kingly, Popish end – the hypocrite!
After Charles the Second's restoration
Broke on the land like a warm summer day
After the misery of a cold spring,
And all the churchbells pealed and all rejoiced,
In fact just six days ago at Captain
Titus's suggestion, his body was
Exhumed with Ireton's. Both corpses were lodged
Overnight at the Red Lion Inn, Holborn,
And joined by Bradshaw's corpse, which had been found
(Unlike Colonel Pride's). At dawn all were dragged
On hurdles to Tyburn, and hanged, Bradshaw
(President of the court that killed the King)
In the centre, from ten till four, and then
Had their heads hacked off by the hangman, who
Threw their trunks into a pit dug beneath
The gallows. Their heads were then taken to
Westminster Hall and stuck high up on poles,
Where they will stay throughout our new King's reign.
Cromwell's changes were all reversed by Charles.
The Protector's institutions perished
With him and his work ended in failure.
The monarchy and Lords will last centuries.
The British don't like change, and they don't like
A foreign power ending our monarchy
And closing down our ancient House of Lords.
Let this be a warning to all men who
Sweep away English institutions: their
Heads will end up on poles in Westminster.
Cromwell strengthened the English monarchy.
Follies and vices theme: hypocrisy (of Cromwell).

12
from *Summoned by Truth* (2000–2005)
Three Political Poems expressing Humanitarian Concerns

from Zeus's Ass
(A Mock-Heroic Poem and Warning)

[lines 397–692, Blair heckled by the Women's Institute]

Canto III

The morning dawns, a bright ethereal day,
Zeus shines on Blair a special, strengthening ray.
The Bilderbergers, who have just met at
Belgium's five-star Château du Lac, to chat
And speed a European superstate
And raise the European interest rate
("Euro-soccer" explained their block-booking),
Back in their countries, have sent supporting
Messages, for all women must be for
The European superstate and law.
Now long queues pass into a chilly hall;
The star attraction waits behind a wall,
The first serving Prime Minister to address
A WI conference (and the press)
In its eighty-five-year-old history.
Aware we're living in a new century,
The Chairwoman wants to be challenging
And apolitically thought-provoking
For members. All are wary, many see
Blair as an air raid on their committee.

With puffed-up pride, proud chest out like a toad,
Blair swaggers to the stage as up a road.
Before him, ten thousand grey-haired housewives,
The WI, bees in honeyed hives;
Home-made women, makers of home-made jam,

Supporters of worthy causes and ham;
More conservative than a Tory glare,
A no-go signal to a man like Blair.
The women stand and sing 'Jerusalem',
Some are flattered the PM's come to them
And look forward to talk about his son
And how his wife coped with today's school run.
Some, farmers' wives, have seen their income slide,
From European quotas, set-aside.
Some sit on pillows, on a waiting-list
Years long for an op for a hip or cyst.
Some have made up their minds about this man:
All things to all men, with warm words that tan
Like a warm sun on an African shore
Where the blue sea gently ripples once more;
Keen to please, all presentation and spin,
He hides his promises behind his grin.
He'd promised better schools and health service,
Partnership with business, eternal bliss,
As if he'd guaranteed sunshine each day
And every month would be as warm as May!
These ladies have seen services run late,
Education system deteriorate.
Rural communities? There is no bus.
You'll wait all day, should we now make a fuss?
The cars are all priced out – why, petrol tax
Is now eighty-six per cent, where's the axe?
GM-contaminated seed in rape,
And the streets are not safe from men who gape.
Agriculture? The farmers are all broke
Protect the fox? To kill hens? What a joke!
These ladies see he has not delivered,
Grandmothers whose wise instincts never erred.
Surely he won't lecture them on subjects
They know more about than he does: effects?

Row after row, receding into shade,
Wembley Arena's daunting lit tiers fade.
Beyond eye contact, with the grey-faced crowd
A soccer pitch away, Blair says, now bowed,
It's the most terrifying audience
He's ever faced. Its scale is as immense
As if he were Billy Graham preaching
On a turfed football stadium's decking.
He refers to a topless calendar
Of Yorkshire WI ladies, far
From these grandmothers' thoughts, and says, "At least
I'm fully dressed." There's laughter far away.
"I thought today might be my lucky day."
He speaks of civic opportunity,
Responsibility, community,
Three themes in Clinton's book, which worked for Bill
But, blindly copied, sound vapid and shrill
For he lacks Clinton's belief in such things
As a young bird flies before it's grown wings.
He is no more in tune with struggling, rooked
Middle Britain that now feels overlooked:
Ethnic minorities receive reward
While they themselves are stealth-taxed and ignored.

Blair perseveres, repeating key words that
Spread confusion like a wandering cat:
Twenty-five "values" rub against a leg,
Eighteen "communities" dolefully beg;
Fifteen "opportunities" scratch a wrap,
And fourteen "changes" leap into a lap.
"Community can't be rebuilt without
Opportunity." Does it mean a pout?
"Tradition is a bedrock of change." What
Does it mean? Is it an arched back that's hot?
He repeats "tradition" like a fixed stare.
Where is "tradition" in the Dome? The air?

How does "responsibility" now square
With the increased budget for all welfare?
"Family" – if he cares about it, why
Does he tax it, tear at a stockinged thigh?
"New Labour's values" – what on earth are they?
It's easier to tell next week's cat's-play!
He can't mean what he says, say what he means
As a cat seeks a jumpy soul and preens.
"Change", "opportunity", "new" and "reform",
"Change", "opportunity", "modern" the norm.
So many slogans in opaque English
That cry out to be petted like a wish.
So much vacuity in his language,
Like water frozen to ice in a fridge.
So little contact with the actual world,
As if his lap-top was now sere and curled.
Empty catchwords and empty phrases tell
A mind that shines in catching a sweet smell
As if he were selling bottled fresh air
As an antidote for people's despair.
Indignation boils in each female breast
And turns to anger as his lies molest.
He pesters on the things they hold most dear:
Work, family, health, children, crime, and fear;
Education and telling children off;
Hospitals and breast cancer – now they scoff.
Safe streets and hooligans, improved transport,
Asylum-seekers, drugs – he gropes their thought;
Interest rates and pensions, red tape, business.
The rape of our countryside stirs distress.
Rural post offices and crops, PC,
Fifty words on each – but no delivery.
He touches up on *élites* and envy
To appease Brown, distance himself and flee.
"Falling unemployment." It's rising, sage.
"Billions to be spent on health" – now there's rage.

Stakeholding was good till the PM saw
Big business would not change company law.
The government lacks substance beneath spin
It is light-weight, and no deeper than one's skin.
"Class size too high", "hospital lists too long".
He has not delivered on either wrong.
Now fury mounts and questions seethe below
The troubled calm of woman and widow.

Eyes narrow as he hawks his bag of sweets,
Each shiny, chewy toffee that entreats,
But once you've bitten in and softened it
It sticks to your teeth and annoys your spit
Until you scoop it out on a finger
And stick the policy on a low fir.
The NHS? Wasteful in the extreme,
Waiting lists are enough to make you scream.
There are too many administrators,
Too few nurses and surgeons – and doctors.
Blair's spent six hours a day reforming it,
And given us swimming sessions and keep-fit.
State schools? They're shrines to failure of the tongue,
Their mediocrity impedes the young.
The Dome? It's cost nigh on a billion pounds
To stand empty, where emptiness surrounds.
Police? The courts and law won't touch ethnic
Muggers, their PC softness makes you sick.
Transport? Congested roads where cameras hide.
Community? Contempt for countryside.
History and cultural heritage? The Dome
Holds less history or culture than a home.
Labour's ashamed of our imperial past.
Empire, monarchs, democracy spread fast
To lands that were benighted far away.
Tradition? Parliament and the UK
Emasculated and carved up for foe.

The pound? He'll replace it with the euro.
He'll surrender England's monetary
National sovereignty for a tyranny.
Britain, a once powerful nation with norms,
Is rent asunder by half-baked reforms.
His uselessness has a subversive use.
O senselessness, so much beloved by Zeus!

Like an ice-cream man at a children's fête
Blair holds out scooped cornets, enticing bait,
And like an adult bending near a child
He offers sweetened policies he's styled.
Now like an adult standing by a pram
Saying "You're lovely. Would you like this lamb?"
He speaks with condescending of his wares,
Talks simply of concepts by which he swears
And communicates in abridged ideas
To smuggle understanding through their ears.
Has Blair's brain been addled after two weeks
With a baby that goos rather than speaks?
Or does he feel they cannot understand
A more sophisticated contraband?
They see him floundering in heavy deceit,
In waves of waffle, promises that cheat,
And do not throw a life-belt, but rather
Prod him with an oar to push him under.
The WI's seen through Labour's spin
And reject the candy-floss in his grin
That whisks strands of sugar into a fluff
And claims it's beef with such disarming bluff.
They want action and not a salesman's smile,
From which, repelled, they want to run a mile.
He has not kept election promises,
If he's not out of touch, Mid-England is.
He's patronizing, talking down – a bore.
One lava seethes in each volcanic core.

Canto IV

Sing, Muse, of erupting anger and shock
As Olympians became a laughing-stock
When Zeus, Hera and Rockefeller saw
The triumph of new Amazons in war.
A silence as before a thunderstorm
Echoes round rural post offices, warm.
Along the serried ranks the twinsets gleam.
Blair turns page 5 and does his best to beam.
Marion Chilcott rises and shouts out,
"This is political," like a firm clout.
Blair says the NHS is improving.
The ground shudders with distant heckling.
The stewards who pass mikes and oversee
Seat numbers glare: up jumps Chris Short, JP
From Sunderland, and waves her agenda,
Irate that political statements are
Being thrown at a neutral body's ears.
Heckling? Not a walk-out? In vain Blair peers.
To left and right, falteringly at first
A slow handclap rumbles, begins to burst
Like a volcano when all are surprised.
It is spontaneous, not organized.
And now the slow handclap begins to swell
The hall. Surely *against* each heckler's yell?
He fails to connect as in a nightmare
When a laugh sounds no different from a jeer.
No, me! Powerless to stop it or retort,
Panic in his eyes, like Ceausescu caught
By the headlight glare of a slow handclap,
Realizing he had been caught in a trap,
Blair senses he is like a fox at bay.
The Chairman Mrs Carey cries out, "Hey,
Let the PM speak out of politeness."
Blair stands, awkward, at the lectern, a mess,
Bewildered by his reception, smiling

Uneasily as at a prank, frowning,
A look of bafflement like Ceausescu's
On the presidential balcony, boos
Punctuating rebelliously slow hands,
Rueful expression on face as he stands.
Mrs Chilcott shouts, "It is against our
Constitution. We've been used by his power."
Disdainfully she edges past turned knees
And exits to a sound like humming bees.

Struck dumb in surprise at the slow handclap,
Blair hunts to find his place as on a map.
Strong faces, pinched lips, disapproving stares;
Are not the hecklers hooligans? He glares.
He attacks all hooligans who disgrace
Our nation. The applause now stops the chase.
He promises to be tough on crime and
The hue and cry's now on a neighbour's land.
He says he'll not impose his candidates
On Welsh or London assemblies. He waits,
But no applause. He has apologized
For the British Empire he has despised,
The holocaust (and no doubt beating up
Germany in the '66 world cup,
Winning the last war, and the one before,
And defeating Napoleon, and much more).
Now he apologizes on new grounds
For foisting Dobson, and hears closing hounds.
Speaking faster, frantically dabbling, deft,
He says the birth of his fourth child has left
Him in contemplative mood, more relaxed.
"Reflection leads to a renewed, untaxed
Sense of purpose." Fathers should help raise their
Children – despite anti-marriage tax laws,
Support for Lesbian adoptions, no pause
In promoting gay rights in schools. These aunts

Hear a lack-lustre speech that disenchants.
And now boos ring out round the Wembley hall,
And slow handclap vies with heckler's cat-call.
He speaks to several audiences in stress.
His set text has been handed to the press.
He cannot change a word, and stumbles on
And, rattled by the barracking, pale, wan,
Quickens his pace when he should have slowed it
And balanced subject matter with some wit.
He does not make contact about his son,
Convey a mood or a message – just one.
It seems the force for change has been slapped down
By the force of the conservative frown.

Hermes is appalled. The spell's neutralized.
Middle England's no longer mesmerized.
He wings his heels to Zeus who's watching scenes
From world trouble-spots on a hundred screens.
Zeus is huddled over the Wembley stage,
Despondent at the hearing, in a rage.
Dionysus' asinine touch has worn
Off, a Brussels superstate will not dawn
Into world government unless the rude
Middle English women can be subdued
Enough to vote Blair in a second term.
Zeus asks who's to blame and makes Hermes squirm.
June–July 2000
Follies and vices theme: vacuousness, deception, spin.

from Attack on America

[lines 1–104, 9/11]

I

I see New York's World Trade Center with smoke

Billowing from the top on TV, for
A plane's flown into it, see waved white shirts
From windows on the hundred-and-tenth floor.
As I watch a jet plane swoops down and flies
Slowly like a missile at the south tower,
Flame spurts, the glassed tower cracks and dark smoke seeps.
Holding hands, two leap and flail as I glower.

I realise it was a deliberate plan.
Hijackers took over each plane, flew it
Into each of these towers at an angle.
I watch, with a roar the second tower hit
Slides down, floors loosened from their concrete case
By fireballed fuel, sinks down with intact walls
Into black smoke, one thousand people crushed.
Smoke rolls as the building implodes and falls.

I see figures wave from the other tower,
Fire below them, all trapped. A groaning sound,
The mast sinks, with a roar the first tower hit
Slides down in thick billowing smoke to ground.
More than one thousand more have been buried.
It snows white dust, covering faces that cower.
The centre of America's finance
That took eight years to build – gone in an hour.

Now in Washington a third plane's dived at
The Pentagon in a fuelled air attack.
Five floors have come down, the building's ablaze,
Smoke billows high above the Potomac,
The West's military centre, the HQ
Of the forces of the one superpower.
A fourth hijacked plane has crashed in Pittsburgh,
En route to the Capitol's Rotunda.

I see Bush speak at a Florida school

After the second attack, a pundit say
No US pilot told by hijackers
To fly into a packed tower would obey;
Therefore they had their own pilots – the first
Suicide pilots since *kamikaze*.
Who is responsible? The screen now shows
Cheering in Kabul, Baghdad, Tripoli.

Now the truth sinks in. It's an act of war
Even worse than Pearl Harbor for its blow
Struck at the heart of the American
Civilization, a raid by a foe.
News comes through that Bush is in Air Force One
At Nebraska, phoning near the cockpit.
The voice of anger swells. This must have had
Support from governments – who should be hit?

Bin Laden is the number-one suspect,
A Saudi sheltered in Afghanistan
Who'd killed Americans in Africa,
Who'd make the Mid-East non-American,
Rid Mecca, Medina, Jerusalem
Of non-Moslems, corrupt Arab regimes,
And establish global Islamic law.
He sees Americans as rats, it seems.

He has eleven thousand trained men across
Fifty countries. Will war against them work?
Will missiles on the government that hosts
Two thousand men in camps who hide and lurk,
Catch the guest? Will retaliation, war
On regimes that have sustained terrorists
Stop terrorism? Where's the evidence?
They had it coming for raising their fists?

And now the hurt and indignation's turned

Into anger, thoughts of revenge, to rage.
We're at war against world terrorism
And mountain lairs are targets to engage.
Unfolding on our screens, retribution.
Questions are asked about security.
Isolationism is now futile,
Missile defence could not set seized planes free.

The financial consequences unfold:
Sixty-seven billion pounds wiped off markets.
Now three thousand who made world markets work
Won't be at their desks, must be replaced. Threats
Of a world recession are now actual,
All confidence has gone. Travel, like cash,
Is now risky; who'd fly? It is as though
Someone has manipulated a crash.

Once again the Anglo-American
Allies and Israel are taking on clans
From rogue states who've breached the new world order,
The Taliban, Iraq, barbarians
Across the *limes* whose terror threatens,
Who must be crushed to stop future attacks –
Palestine, hosts of shadowy groups – and why's
Europe not condemning the maniacs?

A crash has been half-expected, a new
Bout of population decrease through war.
Can a strike from an Afghan mountain cave
Leave the West on the verge of ruin? Or,
Have there been sinister dealings? Who planned
It, did internal forces send torment
Through proxies to put up the price of oil
And weaken strong national government?

Has the world government intrigued these things?

The doubts begin to rise; the nation-state
Under assault, its institutions razed
So world leaders can level what they hate?
Dark questions shriek from under the rubble.
Why the pilots' sacrifice in each tower?
Were they Muslim martyrs for paradise?
Brainwashed to die for Rockefellers' power?
Follies and vices theme: ruthlessness (of self-interested expansion).

[lines 577–640, oil and the New World Order]

Then suddenly the cat's out of the bag.
A news item shows Turkmen and Kazakh
Oil and gas pipelines through Afghanistan
To Pakistan and India. The attack
On al-Qaeda was to free a north-south
Flow long planned the Taliban took over.
This *gung-ho* war's for the commercial gain
Of nations thwarted by Islam astir.

So the Global Coalition's between
Suppliers; consumers; and providers:
Russia; Pakistan and India; Britain
And the US – Rothschilds, Rockefellers.
There must be pipelines to supply backward
Regions in the coming world government.
The Taliban obstructed, were expelled
By fervour from a Pearl-Harbor event.

I see too deeply. It's been about oil
From Turkmen and Kazakh fields. Hence Moscow
Attacked Afghanistan, and the US
Formed the Taliban to guard the oil flow
From the republics, go to Unocal
In Texas and agree a pipeline rent
Of a hundred million dollars a year.

They turned against the West – and so they went.

Once railways spread Western empire, funded
By Rothschilds in the nineteenth century.
Neo-imperialism's spread by oil
Pipelines from ex-Soviet territory.
Bin Laden, like Saladin, Guevara,
Stood up to the West with a master plan,
But then discovered he's a pawn in it
As the West gets the oil, the gas – its man.

Tora Bora's fallen! Al-Qaeda's gone –
Dead, rounded up or fled – and bin Laden
Was seen riding a white horse on a pass
To Pakistan, into legend, beaten.
The trail's gone cold. It's said he's in Iran,
Plotting to nuke New York. And on hillsides
North-west of Kandahar tribesmen hunt down
Mullah Omar, to hang him where he hides.

The Stars and Stripes fly over Kabul from
The US Embassy, closed for twelve years.
I ponder swollen *hubris* and *arté*
Crushed by Americans across frontiers.
If bin Laden had not attacked the Towers
He'd still be wielding a potentate's might.
I admire how the reach of our new Rome
Put this Pontine Mithridates to flight.

Epilogue

The New World Order protects us from foes,
From squalls, strong winds, ogres in any form.
From my window the Cornish sea rolls in,
Wave upon languid wave after the storm.
Now the thunder released from Afghan skies
Is as past as Mylae or Nelson's day.

We have survived this gale; out there the world
Has changed, lands are governed in a new way.

I wonder at the language we've been sold,
The words and deeds of leaders' double-speak,
See "self-defence" means "grabbing oil", "spreading
Freedom" "hegemony over the weak".
Our new Rome thunders through the skies and rides
The clouds with the Olympians' dread might,
And "attack on America" means "war
On terror, conquest, oil – to bring peace, *fight*"!
September–December 2001; January 2005
Follies and vices theme: ruthlessness (of self-interested expansion).

from Shock and Awe

[lines 217–320, attack on Baghdad]

III

Now Baghdad is on fire, huge percussion waves
From thousand-pounders, fires from many graves,
Palls of red smoke, ack-ack above the pyres.
In the Presidential complex, ten fires.
And tears roll down my cheeks for my Baghdad
Is on fire, I pity all good, bad, mad
Humans caught in those terrifying blasts,
The poor who cower in rubble, shield their pasts.

The world's seen and heard the awesome display,
A firework show that beats any past day.
The New American Century has shown
Washington's might, power, reach is hard as stone.
This new warfare's uneven overkill –
Giant versus dwarf – that's terrorist and shrill.
I am shocked at its heartlessness and awed

By those caught in it, forehead to floorboard.

It's sent out a message on US power:
"A firestorm round Saddam's HQ, so cower" –
Strikes against his command control compound
And microwave bombs that kill underground.
It's "illegal" (the UN), a war crime.
Palms silhouetted against fires like time
Against the hot night sky's hellish red light,
Loudspeakered Saddam urging all to fight.

On our screens Rumsfeld says they've struck with great
Force and on a huge scale that demonstrate
To Iraq's people that Saddam's regime
Is finished. "Our objective – indeed, dream –
Is not to conquer or to colonize
But to liberate Iraq, that's the prize."
I sit in tears at American power
And cry within for all in their last hour

For I contributed to that war crime,
Which was to terminate a tyrant's time
And more Twin-Towers attacks. I gave consent,
I did not vote for my own government
But took part in the election, feel shame
That RAF planes did this in my name.
More news. Surrender talks have continued,
So *Shock and Awe*'s suspended. It's been viewed

By the world, that's what counts, its message clear.
Will *Shock and Awe* deter? Has it brought fear,
A surrender, or stiffened resistance?
The regime's out of control, for instance
A missile has been fired at Iran's oil.
Who's leader? Who is in charge? I recoil.
They are acting strangely, poorly advised.

The Intelligence HQ's vaporized.

I think of Dresden, though this is not aimed
At civilians but leaders; feel ashamed.
Now more jets fly low across the Tigris,
Three white flashes, a mushroom-cloud abyss.
Ambulances scream, hospitals have filled
With groaning casualties and densely killed:
People caught by shrapnel or glass blown in,
Children at play or shopping in frail skin.

An entire division – eight thousand men –
In charge of Basra has surrendered. Then
The British are in full control there now.
This evening I ponder *Shock and Awe*, how
It's already been superimposed on
Our image of Twin Towers and Pentagon
Flown at by planes used as Arab missiles:
The boiling smoke's higher than Towers by miles.

Baghdad is hit by dawn firestorm maelstroms,
A thousand cruise missiles and guided bombs.
Three more large daylight strikes, gunships take out
Iraqi resistance, killing about
Three hundred civilians. Our screens show tank
Battles, and US tanks secure each bank
Of the Euphrates crossing. Men take down
Pictures of Saddam in Basra, and clown.

Three hundred and twenty Tomahawks, more
In the first wave than in the first Gulf War.
Umm Qasr's waters may be mined, the sole
Deep-water port where food ships reach a mole,
Vital for aid. After a good night's sleep,
From my armchair's comfort I watch dusk creep
And tired troops clear the port's town street by street,

Watch war live on television, and bleat.

Where is Saddam? It seems he's still alive.
The regime's still convinced he will survive,
It's still broadcasting his speeches, it's said,
Calling the action evil and wicked.
He was hurt in the first attack – don't doubt;
Was dug out of the rubble, carried out,
Oxygen mask on face, on a stretcher.
We're told all this – is it propaganda?

Eerie silence in Arab capitals.
Will fury create insurgents, rebels?
A convoy trundles through, as slow as carts
Challenger tanks, carriers with bridge parts.
Boys, thumbs up, hold banknotes with Saddam's head
For the cameras. No one believes he's dead,
People are supporting the dictator.
Tougher troops fight with conscripts in Basra.

Columns of black smoke over Baghdad, lit
From oil-filled trenches, form two towers with wit
And counter *Shock and Awe* in broad daylight
To confuse aircraft, turn day into night.
In a hospital, a head-bandaged boy,
A girl with swathed feet, strapped baby with toy –
All dead in a caved-in ward's smouldering fires.
A pall of black smoke hangs over their pyres.
Follies and vices theme: ruthlessness, mendacity.

[lines 1065–1256, oil and the West]

Falluja's fallen! In cellars are found
Chained hostages blinking in light, minds bound.
A few snipers must be flushed out, grim tasks;
But no more can lawless men in black masks

Flout the occupation force from this place.
Now it rules this town, and without a base
Rebels must hit-and-run in a near town:
Samara, Ramadi, Baquba frown.

Now mopping up: marines in a mosque find
Four Arabs shot and dead, and a fifth blind,
Propped against a wall, bleeding from his head.
One shouts, "This man's f—g faking he's dead."
One fires, blood and brains spatter on the wall;
Says, "Well, he's dead now," shrugs, life's cheap for all.
Near where stray dogs eat rotting flesh and preen
A booby-trapped body kills a marine.

Falluja's shattered for freedom; unarmed
Prisoners killed for democracy – both harmed.
"He's f—g faking he's dead." Troops acting
Like animals to liberate bleeding
Zealots within a mosque just nullify
The West's moral fitness to occupy,
Leaving the enlightened dawn of new Iraq
A flash of thunderous lightning in deep dark.

All this was done in our name – you and me;
Though we can't damn the whole US army
For one jumpy marine's view of diehards,
A few untrained Abu Ghraib prison guards.
It's like Vietnam: "We had to destroy
The village so as to save it, cowboy."
Iraq, like Falluja,'s now rubble streets,
Black oil piped into West-bound tanker fleets.

X

This pipeline being repaired by Bechtel
So oil can flow again from near Mosul
To Haifa so Israel can have cheap oil,

Export it to Washington as war spoil,
Smash-and-grabs on a small state in the name
Of liberty, democracy – the aim
Of a plan urged by the Bilderberg Group,
Which gives orders, then questions them, to dupe.

What should be done? Chop Iraq into three?
So Sunnis, Shi'ites and Kurds are all "free" –
And Iraq suffers Yugoslavia's fate
(Serbia, Bosnia, Croatia split from State)?
It's the pattern, divide and rule for oil:
Impose tripartite statehood on its soil.
Churchill, who drew Iraq, and, with firm rule,
Kassem, who kept it one, wince at a fool.

Contrast the Caliphs' Round City of Peace
Where I served nine months until my release,
Which I drove through between palms in sun-shafts
At dawn, from Mansour (and loved the *souk*'s crafts),
The City of the Arab Golden Age,
And this scarred battleground for oil, this rage.
Churchill, Kassem – whose unity had rules;
Your graves turn at blunders by naïve fools.

I think of the Syndicate's plan for oil,
Spun as "elections help the poor", recoil;
Then balance Saddam's criminality
Against the price to end his tyranny:
A hundred thousand dead, worsening chaos,
Civil wars, partitions and no one boss,
Freedom as liberty to spin, lie, gore
Which conned the West into supporting war.

News. Blair visits Baghdad.... The "war leader",
New World Order/Syndicate rep, partner
Of Bush, creeps in during a news black-out

Is helicoptered from airport redoubt
To the walled-in Green Zone where all must wear
Flak jackets, a "conqueror" ignoring fear,
Preening before troops, claiming Iraq's free,
That democracy's won – in fantasy.

And that's the Shock: the sheer mendacity
Behind the West's crusade for "liberty",
Its overuse of might, the ruin caused,
The wrecked buildings, all reparations paused,
Carving-up of a Churchill-designed state
So oil is piped three ways, now Western freight;
And the pretence that Baghdad's streets are safe,
That where Iraqis vote no rockets strafe.

And the Awe's not wonder at US power
Whose precision-bombs make the whole world cower,
But admiration for a freedom-fight
By spirited people subdued by might,
Resisting being occupied, a bought
Small nation wrecked in one-sided war fought
For no better reason than to keep cars
And the West's engines turning like the stars.

Can the West last for ever? The US,
Syndicate-led, rule the world and progress
(After it's looted all the oil) to run
Its vast pretence, contain China? The sun
Would never set on British Empire, on
The thousand-year Third Reich, yet they are gone.
Illusions? What seem *folies de grandeur*
Can, if there's *élan*, rise to world order.

A crystal hung in sunlight fills my room
With twenty-five rainbows that brighten gloom.
Like rainbows, civilizations are all

Curved parabolas that first rise, then fall.
We see rainbows when sun's rays are dispersed.
They fade into the "now", their pattern burst.
So civilizations are always there,
We live in "now" and on a curve in air.

America's still moving up its curve
As Rome was when she ruled the world with verve.
Europe's declining into foreign rule.
This is the Shock, that the US will pool
All her seized oil and rule the world from home.
The Awe: wonder that Liberty, like Rome,
May fill the sky, her torch light all rainbows
Which she'll hold till a New World Order shows.

Epilogue

The Capitol. Crowds line the steps – the free;
Tens of thousands as far as eye can see
Below, freezing, honour their Head of State,
Sixty thousand line the parade route, wait
In bitter cold for bands and the first float.
Bush strides down steps under the dome in coat,
Is sworn in and, Caesar with a world reach,
Wows all with his inauguration speech.

Freedom must spread. (The eagle now takes wing.)
The cause of 9/11 was simmering
Resentment under tyrannies. Freedom
Must go there, break tensions and tyrants, bomb.
Freedom rolled back Communism, will cease –
Roll back – tyranny. The best hope for peace
Is to expand freedom. Now I chill, for
Freedom brings peace – through invasion and war.

Freedom and democracy must conquer
The world's darkest spots: Iran, North Korea,

Cuba, Myanmar (Burma), Zimbabwe,
Belarus – all "outposts of tyranny".
Later China? Tyranny breeds violence.
Will freedom beat it with the commonsense
Of diplomats or economic health?
No, by force: marines, bombs and war: the Stealth.

He speaks so reasonably, the drift's all deed:
Arabs resent their tyrants, and if freed
Will live at peace, not bomb; dance to our tune –
We extend freedom by conquest, and soon
A New World Order will control all air.
Rule the world, Roman; grab oil everywhere!
It's said "Free" Officers "liberated"
Iraq from "imperialist tyrants". Instead,

Those tyrants seized power, banned democracy....
He has not mentioned Iraq once, strangely
As a hundred and fifty thousand troops
Of his are battling, with searches and swoops,
To contain a rebellion. No doubt he
Does not want his six enemies to see
Disorder there as a sign of weakness.
The caravan's moved on to the next mess.

Scared Iraq's "elections". The Shias have won –
Not what the Americans would have done.
It's rule by Ayatollahs' bigotry.
Democracy or voted tyranny?
I look back to Kassem's time, when Sunnis,
Shias and Kurds smiled in my class – Suez
Set aside – where there was freedom of speech.
Now, Shia Iraq's within Shia Iran's reach!

(And I was sent out to hostile Iraq
To help hold fast with English glue three dark

Ottoman provinces, a land still raw
That Churchill hewed out forty years before.
I worked to make work what the Master drew –
Churchill, who guarded us from bombs, who knew
Us, spoke in Loughton before Potsdam's freeze
And smiled and signed my book, my Pericles!)

Shia Iraq and Shia Iran are at one.
Would-be prime minister al-Hakim's spun.
He wants an Islamic state, hear him bark
That US troops must withdraw from Iraq.
Security? Iran, Syria will send
Shias to crush the Sunnis, and defend.
So "freedom" stunned all with *Shock and Awe*'s clout
To bring democracy – and be kicked out?

Liberty, ending tyranny,'s brought in
Freedom for bigots, Shias' deadly spin.
Saddam could have restrained them, but he's gone.
Without a strongman to take the two on,
Ahead are Sunni riots, civil war's dark,
The break-up of Churchill-designed Iraq.
Liberty's slavery to voted law,
Freedom means occupation, peace means war.

The Heroes of the West shielded their trust
From Soviet missiles and aggressive thrust.
Now all's reversed, and the Syndicate great
Urge leaders to assault each oil-rich state
And summon, with dissemblings and lies, all
Who cheered when Berlin fell, and Berlin's Wall.
I, who can't cheer more "peaceful" *Shock and Awes*,
Summoned by truth, truth-tell: "peace" means more wars.
March–May 2003; revised November, December 2004; January 2005
Follies and vices theme: mendacity.

13
from *Classical Odes* (1994–2005)

At Beckingham Palace: Talent of a Meritocracy

I

How can we look at the flamboyant past
And not present fashion as its broadcast?
We live in a time when merit is queen,
The media's ruled by those whose skill is seen.
Models, pop-stars, footballers – all present
Physical prowess, beauty and talent.
I watch England's soccer team like a fan;
Their send-off to the World Cup in Japan
Held in Beckingham Palace's green grounds
For three hundred and fifty thousand pounds.
Fleets of limousines, people-carriers,
Sports cars, Mercedes and helicopters
Bring three hundred and fifty guests in white
Tie and diamonds, hair cropped or spiked, polite,
Through hundreds of bystanders who assess,
All holding signed photos of, the hostess.
The guests clutch invitations that are wrapped
In imported Japanese grass as they're clapped,
At a cost of ten thousand pounds, ingest
A hall that is an enchanted forest.
Each tree's a gymnast who suddenly waves.
A marquee, holding a gazebo, saves,
With black-out windows, the guests' privacy.
Before they drink *saké* and munch *sushi*
They're greeted by *geishas* in *kimonos*
Who pour Laurent Perrier champagne, which flows
(At a cost of seventy-five thousand pounds).
The host, in black with a red sash, confounds
As a samurai – he's in fancy dress.
His stubble and glittering diamonds impress.

A Japanese garden's been richly planned
With bamboo plants, grasses, sixty thousand
Specially imported orchids from the East
And a half-mile-long flower-bed with at least
Twenty-five thousand daffodils. (Chinese?)
Oriental lanterns hang in four marquees.
Orange-robed Buddhist monks with shaven heads
Intermingle with sportsmen with huge treads.
The menu's Japanese: asparagus,
Shitake-mushrooms, green-tea noodles, plus
Thai salmon salad topped with seaweed, set
By skewered chicken lemon-grass brochette,
Sashimi, platters of beef satay, nice
Monkfish, stir-fried vegetables, jasmine rice,
Crispy roast duck (a Chinese touch), blackened
Cod and luscious strawberries and cream to end
While an opera singer's arias flow
(Twenty thousand for ten-minute solo).
Now there's an auction, two pairs of Beck's boots
Go for twenty-nine thousand each, salutes
That also say money measures success.
Eight thousand – champagne signed by the hostess.
A million's raised for children's charity.
Stars of film, pop, entertainment, TV,
Chefs, presenters and DJs are all drawn
Though England's soccer prospects look forlorn.
There's a no-fly zone overhead, defence
Against a terror strike at such immense
Targets, such dazzling guests, ravishing blondes
(Or a heist to strip them of their diamonds).
Fifty private guards, sixty off-duty
Police with Rottweilers patrol – quietly –
The seven-foot fence, all having signed intense
Confidentiality agreements.
All picture rights have been bought by *Hello*
And *OK?* magazines for a (too low)

Hundred and fifty thousand pounds, and all
Television rights were bought for a small
Six-figure sum by ITV. Black-out
Is only till the colour photos shout.
Now dancing starts to Radio-One DJs.
This unique gathering elicits praise.
Three hundred and fifty thousand pounds gone
In one day, while outside a May sun shone.

                    II
O Pope, author of *Epistle to Boyle*
About noble landscaping, you would spoil
The response of all the celebrities
If you were with us now, stay away please.
We don't want to hear you describe Beck's day
As the ultimate in naffness, or say
One sixth of mankind goes to bed hungry,
A half earns less than twelve dollars weekly.
This was the glitziest party of the year
Thrown by a showbiz couple that's sincere –
By the best paid footballer in the world
(On seventy-eight thousand pounds a week curled,
Like a free kick, with twenty more for rights
To his image, for which a model fights);
And by the would-be best-paid, best-selling
Singer of songs that glitter like a ring.
How unfair to say they're ostentatious.
It's just the carping of the envious.
Affluence should be displayed for all to scan.
What's a peacock's tail for if not to fan?
The gathering took weeks to organize,
Gave employment to teams of private eyes,
Gardeners, caterers, the local laundry.
We now live in an Age of the Body
Where beauty's held to be the outer form.
Designer clothes and jewellery are the norm.

Diamonds stud ears, rosary beads to waist,
Decked out in gold and bling, we're chavs, we've taste.
What does it matter if young men, women
Who move so lithely cannot wield a pen,
Who have such beautiful surfaces, thigh
Muscles that ripple, nipples that are high
And curves from waist to bust that are a wish,
Don't excel in speaking the Queen's English,
Which is outdated, from a past century
And does not reflect the Thames estuary?
They are paid to move with skill, not to speak.
Their merit's in footwork, handwork that's sleek.
What's money for if it's not to be spent
On having a good time, drunk in a tent
With one's friends in hilarity or mirth
While showing off what one is really worth,
Measuring it in diamonds of good taste,
Dripping in them from ear-lobes down to waist
With some in nostrils and belly button?
One in a lip or nipple helps the con.
What matter if there is nothing to say?
How should a man be measured when at play
If not by what he wears, his taste in dress,
Pop and hair-style which help a girl to guess,
While making fun of Japanese culture,
Posing as a *samurai* or *geisha*
To help the tee-heeing over green tea,
Raw fish, rice wine, seaweed – mad mystery?
Who wants to know the real Japan, that hole?
Who wants boring stuff about Zen, the soul?
Understanding chrysanthemum and sword?
Get lost! They are expeditiously bored.
They are cut-outs hung with Japanese robes
In a Far-Eastern fairy tale – the globe's,
To project their fantasy on TV,
Its surface is seen each place men may be.

We live in an Age of Surfaces now.
We don't want to delve below skin and brow.
Externals is what we live by these days:
Rude, *risqué*, the more frank the bigger praise.
There are no taboos any more, nothing
Is sacred any longer – not living:
Peak-time soaps feature a Lesbian kiss,
Rape, child abuse, prostitution, drugs – this
In the name of what we viewers all know,
What we see as we bustle to and fro.
Britain's gone sleazy: adverts show nude breasts,
Two dozen Sky channels send unasked guests,
Bare ladies who caress, writhe rear and knee.
The *Sun* shows naked models on Page Three.
It's natural massage parlours attract whores.
It's sad if Aids is spread within their doors.
An Age of Body's acts have no meaning:
Body fluid's release is like peeing.
All should be glamour, what's superficial.
It's harmless to daydream, be fanciful.
We all have families but we can dream,
We fantasize that things aren't what they seem:
The million-dollar reception and look,
The image (we have rights to), telly-hook.
Not for us an office before a screen,
On the phone all day, what does that life mean?
We'd rather create our own fantasy,
One we can share, that gives publicity.
We live for pleasure, hedonism's great.
Gratification's best with a playmate.
The Age of the Body has its priesthood.
We are its high priests and don't live by "should".
Stay away, Pope, we don't want your mournful
View of our good time when we're on the pull.
We all live in our body, not our head;
We're fit athletes, and are a long time dead!

13 May 2002; revised 13–14 May 2002; 11 April, 27 May 2003
Follies and vices theme: ostentation, chaviness, blinginess, flaunting.

14
from *Sighs of the Muses* (2005)

Groans of the Muses

At first the Muses could only be found
Round Mount Helicon, the Pierian ground
Of their birthplace north of Olympus, crags
Where the daughters of Zeus roamed wild like hags.
To see them meant stumbling across its steep
Slopes as Hesiod did, pasturing his sheep.
In the grove of the Muses near the green
Spring on Helicon called the Hippocrene
(Which burst from Pegasus' hoofprint) the nine
Daughters of Mnemosyne guard divine
Elevated knowledge of sacred kinds,
Deify poets who're out of their minds.
Plato held that the philosophers know
"What is" whereas poets present false show –
Speak of war but know nothing of war's art;
Of medicine, don't know what doctors impart.
They're all appearances, just imitate,
Enchant, mimic and pretend, though lightweight.
But in fact poets wear Truth that comes down,
As a chain from the Muses, like a crown.
Philosophers scowled at what poets see
In Plato's mind, not in reality.
The Muses truth-tell. They told Hesiod:
"We know how to speak many false things" – God! –
"As though they were true; but we know when we
Will, to utter true things." It seems to me
On Helicon Muses lied to convey

Truth.... Then over the years they moved away
And appeared to poets in their abodes,
Inspiring them with lyrics, epics, odes.

And so it was I sat in my window
And cried out for a breeze to waft and blow
From beyond into my head and inspire
My glowing thoughts like embers in a fire:
"O Muses of Pierian Olympus
And Helicon, goddesses who helped us,
Who yearn for high standards but do not shrink
To destroy all mortals who dare to drink
At your spring, usurp your place, who inspire
But are contemptuous of mortals' lyre
As befits consciousness that is divine –
I toil to keep the standards up, and shine
In full knowledge that our time's not concerned
With Truth or Light: 'when dead you're burned and urned'.
So is it me and my use of language?
Or does the Age I show lack true knowledge?
O tell what you think of our present time;
Do literature and learning thrive in rhyme?
In our Age whose advances would amaze
Our grandparents – all walks of life draw praise –
We have sped feet with car wheels and plane wings
Faster than speed of sound, our hurtlings
Can girdle the earth in a mere two hours.
We've reached beyond this earth, the moon is ours;
Fired machines burn through the solar system.
We've preserved memory: tape, film and album
Can rerun in the present a past fled,
Relive what's gone, and scrutinise the dead
Who, in graves, move on cellulose, have speech.
One click through a cursor and we can reach
The other side of the world in a trice
Via a screen and some chips as small as lice.

We can tune in or phone all round the globe;
Listen, view, speak, send anywhere live, probe.
We've vanquished Nature by speed, wire and chip;
We hurtle on land, by sea, air, spaceship.
Satellites span distance. We, like a crow,
Alight in flashpoints like back gardens, go.
We are absolute, almost gods like you.
What do you think of our art? What's your view
Of our literature shops sell and we buy?
Is it of the right standard, or am I?"
So, in solitude at the land's edge, I
Lobbed my cry at the dark sea and night sky.

I sat in my window. Outside, the sea
Plashed and a fitful wind blew round the quay
Like laboured breathings of a man dying,
And as I listened I heard a sobbing.
I looked out and saw a maiden, half-bent,
Clad in white, who beckoned me down. I went
Outside, in cloudless dark I asked, "Can I
Help you?" She turned and pointed with a sigh
Down to the beach. I peered over the wall
Through dark at the moonflecked sea, heard a call;
In pale moonlight I saw an eerie group
Huddled round a flickering fire, all a-droop,
And heard a lamentation, quiet keening,
Above the gentle wind, each wave rolling.
Without a word she led me down a flight
Of steps onto stones in the moonlit night
And through the breakwater's gap to the rocks
Where eight maidens sobbed under long dark locks,
Young, nubile, with faces that were timeless,
Perhaps thirtyish, in white Grecian dress.
"What's the matter?" I asked. Could I ignore
These damsels in distress on a sea-shore?
They composed themselves, the one by my side,

Their dark-haired leader, spoke, husky, doe-eyed:
"You summoned us with your invoking air,
You conjured us with your vocative prayer."

"You ask what we think of your present time.
Your cultural desert's lies, there's no sublime.
We run the Elysian Club where all the great,
The six hundred finest spirits, debate;
The greatest artists we've inspired. I, still
Calliope, sit with Homer, Virgil,
Dante, Milton – we couldn't let in Pound,
His *Cantos* weren't epic; Eliot's profound.
Erato sits with Horace and Ovid,
Shakespeare and Shelley, who were both gifted.
In Spenser's day she wept. Then Shakespeare came.
We couldn't let in Hughes – it's not the name,
He was too raw, too bodied and raucous.
We Apollonians scorn Dionysus.
Terpsichore sits with Donne, Dryden, Pope,
Wordsworth and Tennyson – there's been no hope
For any since Yeats – they're not polished, though
We looked at Larkin, but he did not know
The spirit lasts for ever. What a weed!
Clio sits with Thucydides and Bede,
And Gibbon. We looked at Toynbee, but he
Distorted history, he wanted to see
A new world order flatten nationhood.
That's what Zeus wants, we think nations are good.
We're with Sidney and Byron, and Churchill,
Though his history pleads for his deeds and skill.
We agree he wasn't bad, though he took
Rothschilds' shilling to get off his debts' hook.
Melpomene sits with great Sophocles,
Aeschylus, Shakespeare and Euripides.
None today's as tragic as those of old.
We've looked at Miller but he's brass, not gold.

Thalia sits with sharp Aristophanes,
Plautus and popular Shakespeare when he's
Available. But today's pathetic.
The only hope for vision – a maverick!
Ficino, Botticelli and Dante:
Literature, art one with philosophy
Just as Plato and Pheidias both shared
What the Eleusinian Mysteries declared.
Sublime vision, Truth-bearing odes engage;
The artist sees what's real and shows the Age.
Unseen power, the invisible world, moans.
Our tears and sighs have long since become groans.

"It's all moved on since we were found near springs.
We look after all who've glimpsed highest things.
The six hundred heroes who strove and showed
The universe and what's real in an ode,
And, above all, the Truth – through what's untrue,
Imagined, never happened, lies that grew,
Yet nearer to the Truth than any shop,
As a monastery on a mountain top
Is closer to Heaven than a village fête.
Much of our time we converse with the great
But, like football clubs' talent scouts, we make
Forays to earth to spot those who may wake
Vision, some day join our immortal throng.
We appear in many guises – dance, song.
Alas, it's all become secular, none
Now reflects the metaphysical One
In the arts any more – excepting you.
We know you are obscure, but in this new
Time of false material values that's spread
We would not expect ones we have spotted
To be anything except little-known.
We're here to support you for you have shown
History's civilisations are inspired

By Light, and that philosophy expired
When it lost contact with the Light; and in
Literature, your journey to Light in skin
And through to mankind's unity – and more,
The mirror you've held up to show the war
Between Darkness and Light in your epic,
Your showing that Europe's culture's not sick,
Rest assured, we've noticed despite the Age!
You have a ticket to our Club, o sage,
For your vision's values, not for units
Sold, bought. Millions have been sold by misfits
Whose works are worthless but have deceived youth,
Don't carry an audience to the Truth.
We Muses bear Truth, and we recognise
You as one of our own, you're deep and wise.
You've borne our Truth but blind mankind's not grasped
A human's more than what his reason's clasped,
More than his senses, that he's also soul,
That his spirit endures within a Whole
That's both down here and up there with us nine.
But you're aware that you've opposed malign
Powerful interests who would suppress your work,
Who've blocked publicity, who do not shirk
Walling you round, 'death by silence' – their words.
To them you're a dissident, as with birds
They don't want your droppings, your free-speech stones.
That dismays us, intensifies our groans.
We salute you, so we've taken, in gown,
The unusual step of calling you down
From your window high above the sea's moan
To let you know, though you work on your own
Without support from an ignorant time
That thinks it knows but knows nothing, and climb,
You're not alone, we're watching over you
For you do our work when you hold your view.
I, Calliope, speak for all epic.

Nothing today's much good, much of it's sick
But at least you tried to present the war
As a metaphysical epic, more
Than merely Eisenhower chasing Hitler,
Two scoundrels we despise like that butcher
Stalin – not to mention Mao. We're weeping
At the decay of writing and learning.
I honour you, proud to give you your due."

Then Clio stood up. "I too honour you,"
She said, "at least you've tried to see the globe
As one whole with one story in your probe.
You've seen why civilisations rise, fall."
Then Erato stood and said, "Today all
Poets fail, none see the One, show learning's knot.
They write of memories – we ask 'So what?'
They describe the sense world, don't see the tide.
The standard's terrible. At least you tried
To show the world is more than material.
Sceptical poets are simply feeble.
Nothing can be salvaged from lines that miss,
That don't see Being behind the surface.
Art shows the universe and life are whole,
About the progress of the human soul
From this life into the next one. We nine
Encourage verse that looks beyond this life.
If we find none we weep like any wife
Neglected by her lord, spurned, rejected.
We are wedded to works of gold, not lead."
I said, "I am humbled, thank you my nine
Sisters, you've certainly made me feel fine!
I am honoured to be in your presence,
That you've come down to me, in my defence."

Clio lamented in the beach's dark:
"Everything's terrible today, it's stark.

Children know no history, and cannot quill
Who Nelson, Wellington were, or Churchill.
They're in rootless deserts, they've no green hills.
Epic's reduced to surface, *frisson* thrills.
It does not reflect ancient Greece – what cost!
Philosophy's about language, it's lost
The view of the universe Plato knew,
The One that gives meaning to all that's true.
Music's debased, tuneless, a strumming sound,
It brings the soul down to the body's ground,
It does not lift soul to a higher world.
Your soaps are slice-of-life blatantly hurled.
No one's fit to join our Elysian Club.
Polyhymnia, sitting with Bach, will blub
At modern squawks. Beethoven, Tchaikovsky,
Dvorak, Elgar console her – tearfully!
All look for harmony but there's no art:
A debased beat like blood pumping round heart,
All talent gone, just thud, thud, thud – a cage,
A mindless music for a mindless Age.
Euterpe sits with instrumentalists,
We let none, they're show-offs, rhapsodists.
They want to cut a figure, be admired,
More than interpret music we inspired
That whispers how the spheres move to an Age
That's sceptical and blank. I'm filled with rage."
"And I, Urania, sit with Ptolemy
And Newton. We've let Einstein in, gladly –
He's able but where has the vision gone?
Immaterial astronomy once shone.
I sit with Plotinus and Grosseteste.
The One behind the universe can't err.
Now your physicists seek a TOE
(Theory of Everything) and cannot see
Unity esemplastically – by flight.
Take out the One and they're seeking by night."

As Melpomene spoke their faces shone:
"There's no tragedy as values have gone,
There's nothing tragic, nothing can be shared
That stirs pity and terror in those spared.
"Comedy's terrible, in all who live,"
Sweet Thalia groaned, "everything's relative,
Values have gone, it's don't-care piffle, rot
That's trivial and pointless – we ask 'So what?'"
"Lyric poetry's all doodles, with no rules,"
Terpsichore complained. "I blame the schools.
It's dispiriting for us Muses, who
Resemble teachers who've trained in what's true
But find it can't be taught, the subject gone,
Like offering Latin when the world's moved on.
We stand for standards no one will explore,
So no one's inspired by us any more,
Only by BBC bureaucrats who
Dumb down all subjects, praise tin ears and spew
That deals with nothing, from the mouth of fools;
Permit rulelessness when the time needs rules."
"Alas," moaned Clio, "the Peace we strive in
Is being threatened by explosive sin:
Terror in New York, Madrid and London,
Blasts that turn men's minds from books in tubes on
To each other, as, looking warily
About them, alert to danger, they see
And no longer lose themselves in their books
But study faces, look for furtive looks."

Then Calliope spoke: "In this country,
Europe, the world, it's the same old story.
There's nothing. It suits Zeus who levels down
So all are equal under his great frown,
To inspire one world. We wish he would send
A flood to bring world culture to an end.
We come down to look, find little will last.

We're pathetic really, live in the past
With our six hundred greats, scorn the present.
We're the Tears of the World, which is torment.
We've come tonight to speak to you. O please
Make war on this dreadful culture and ease.
Critics no longer see what's truly good.
Can't Ricks speak for the One, expose falsehood?
Art's an unmade bed in the Tate, gone pop.
Music's an awful row, we have to stop
Our ears so we don't hear to keep our sense
Of beauty intact, reserve's self-defence.
Live Aid was a demonic din, quite sick.
We hated it, yet some said 'Great music'.
It numbed the five senses' environment.
Please be even more of a dissident,
Attack your Age and its revolting ways,
Salvage beauty from ugliness's daze.
In all you write in your Age's dark night
Continue to stand for Being's One Light
Even if it's no longer understood.
Most publishers are lost in a Dark Wood
Except for a few rebels we admire
Who would improve the Age, expose the dire
Lies leaders tell, for there's a Muse of Truth.
Shakespeare invoked a tenth Muse – for all youth.
We've told him he was seriously wrong.
The tenth Muse we honour's the Truth. That's strong.
You embody Truth, so we bow to you.
Zeus wants a levelling down so he can view
All men equal in a world government.
He's glad quality's gone, he is content.
Mediocrity, the average, is his joy.
Zeus is cross with us, we know we annoy.
All socialists want all to be the same,
Have no time for those who would make a name.
As backbenchers rebel against a Whip

We toe the line, but occasionally slip.
We have integrity and say again
We admire your stand for Truth and the strain
You've had to bear in this shallowest Age.
We Muses are rebels, and we engage."

"Alas," groaned Calliope, "who will sing
The epic vision now, while displaying
The rose of Dante in peerless blank verse?"
"Alas," groaned Terpsichore, "who, though terse,
Will shine out odes and lyrics that are new
And deft as a spider's web hung with dew?"
"Alas," groaned Erato, "who will now spin
The soul's quest in erotic symbols, in
The language of the body, outer sleeve?"
"Alas," groaned pale Clio, "who will now weave
History into rainbows, show patterned scenes
Of leaders choosing stages and routines?"
"Alas," groaned Melpomene, "who will show
Pity and terror, tragic awe we know
And *catharsis* in a great-sounding theme?"
"Alas," groaned pert Thalia, "who will now dream,
With light-hearted wit, of a comic fate
And convey Truth despite the pomp of State?"
"Alas," groaned Urania, "who will fix sun,
Stars in verse, mix astronomy, the One
And the universe, winds and tides that spread?"
Euterpe played a plaintive flute and shed
Hot tears as Polymnia sang plaintively,
A dirge on how the poet is a bee
Who leaves his hive and flies round many flowers,
Sips pollen, gathers nectar which in hours
He turns to honeycomb's honey – some shift.
The power that comes from Muses is a gift
Of honey from the divine gardens, sniffed
By the poet who gathers it, designs,

Transports, transmutes it into honeyed lines.
All nine Muses groaned, "Alas, when the Light
Has passed from verse, poetry will be a night.
Who will sing of Truth then? Alas! the last
Lone voice of a long line has nearly passed.
We who shed tears in Spenser's honeyed day
At literature's and learning's sad decay
Have seen a massive decline since those moans;
We've gone through sighs and now are full of groans."

They stopped and the waves plashed, and on that beach
I looked up at the moon; looking at each,
I said, "I will do everything you ask.
Dry your tears, I'll embody Truth – some task.
Your groans will become sighs, and then pleased coos.
You Olympians will rejoice at good news."
And there was a sigh like a gentle wave,
Of relief, satisfied at what I gave.
Calliope said, "Thank you so much. Soon
We'll remember this talk beneath that moon."
I looked up at the moon, which was quite raw,
Its face slightly awry; peering, I saw
Its eyes and smile, it was smiling at me.
And when I looked back I could no more see
Them, grasped they'd gone, and there was I before
The sea, near rocks on a quiet moonlit shore,
Convinced our Age is rotten, much decayed,
Resolved to rise above it, undismayed,
And transmit honeyed lines gifted me by
The nine Muses as their Tenth Muse, Truth. I
Now saw our Age may seem to have been lost
Under material coating like thick frost,
But beneath its decay, like winter lawn,
Underlying growth awaits a new dawn
When sun will melt all frost and grass show through;
So Light can thaw a culture that's untrue.

Behind the cold veneer the Muses shun
Souls grow, enmeshed in growth within the One.
28 May, 26–30 July 2005; revised 5 September 2005
Follies and vices theme: shallowness (of false secular art). Set in Charlestown,
Cornwall.

Authorship Question in a Dumbed-Down Time
(A Dramatic Monologue)

"Say, who do you believe wrote Hagger's works?
It can't have been this Loughton man who smirks.
How could a busy Principal of schools
Gather such knowledge, break so many rules?
Produce four massive tomes and yet not be
'On platforms', known to all humanity?
'Shy, loath to appear on stage' – when the rest
Of his fellow poets had all digressed
From the main issues? It doesn't make sense.
I don't buy the 'shy' story – it's pretence.
How could such vastness be unknown when fools
Found fame on gameshows, breaking all the rules?
How could the public not eat his heaped plate
When his fellow poets were snacks, lightweight?
How could the poet of so much sharp rhyme
Be content to be unknown in his time?
Write of 'the great secret that I exist'
As if obscurity is like a mist,
Beyond the control of the poetry world?
It couldn't have happened, a *poet* hurled
Aside with scorn, ignored and patronised
Because his verses scan and rhyme – *despised*!
What a reflection on the Establishment
If they'd looked away or sought to prevent
His works reaching a public, to contain.
Or if ignorant, they'd looked with disdain.

It's as if he'd been a dissident or spy.
He can't have been suppressed and walled round by
Silence, stifled with lack of attention
By a hostile State that knew how it's done.
He wasn't disqualified from 'platforms',
He put us off the scent with his 'shy' 'norms'.
How could a busy Principal of schools
Find time to gush words that filled such vast pools?
The author's brain leaked like a fractured pipe.
Essex men dump, fly-tip; fill lakes with tripe.
He's more verses to his name than Wordsworth
And Tennyson – and look at their works' girth!
More weight on scales than they had, more matter
Weighed with an ease that many now prefer.
He knew his history, politics and war,
And classics and was *au fait* with the law.
He had the depth of a philosopher –
He was a disillusioned courtier!
It was so in Elizabethan times:
Shakespeare, Marlowe, Greene, Nashe committed crimes
Of false pretences, fraud – conned the reader
Like Lyly, Chapman, Jonson and Spenser.
Who Shakespeare fronted for can make one ill:
Oxford, Bacon, now Neville – who you will.
Yet they were all fronts for courtier writers.
Spenser savagely satirised rulers –
The Cecils – in his 'Mother Hubberd's Tale'.
How could a clothman's son, brought up on ale,
Who lived in Ireland, write *The Faerie Queene*?
Hagger lived far from court, was never seen
Hobnobbing with royals, bobbing his bows.
He might as well have lived with Irish cows!
He fought no wars and yet wrote *Overlord*.
The author was a soldier sent abroad
Who travelled the length and breadth of Europe,
A classicist who toured where temples drop.

He owned a Hall – was an aristocrat;
Surely a courtier and diplomat
Who had access to all the Establishment
And used a front to mask secret dissent.
Perhaps he was UN Ambassador –
Sir John Weston, *alumnus* of Worcester?
Or a bitter Minister who, sacked, sulked –
Mandelson plotting through a front who skulked?
Perhaps 'he' was the Queen, who had opposed
The government and Syndicate who'd closed
England's thousand-year royal history
Since *Magna Carta*, cancelled sovereignty.
Hagger, like all front men, was literate,
A secretary whose patron would dictate
Words that he passed off blithely as his own
Like a market-man selling precious stone.
Hagger was a front man, a clueless cue
For a Prince? Minister? General? Spy? who: knew
Both Churchill and Montgomery, though born
Too late to claim credit for plans they'd drawn;
Was not behind Larkin, who owned no Hall;
Nor Pinter, who misunderstood the All;
Nor Colin Wilson, who despised the One;
Nor Eliot, for whom the Church was fun;
Nor Pound, whose *Cantos* broke all metric rules,
Who did not nurture children's souls in schools;
Nor Hughes, who did not care for politics.
Nor was Hagger a front for courtier Ricks!
Who had the knowledge and access to be
His patron, and be tidal like the sea,
Creep in and cover the beach, then go out
Leaving a wave's whisper a seaweed shout –
But who preferred Reflection to Shadow
And saw the dissident as a weirdo.
The authorship's a mystery that's still here.
Hagger's a front for someone – that's quite clear.

Don't be deceived by what's self-evident,
Hagger lambasts to put us off the scent.
Augustus banished Ovid – may not he
Have authored Ovid's *Tristia ex Ponti*?
Think 'Zeus's ass', then turn it on its head.
Satires on patrons distance, like the dead.
War, politics, Europe, Iraq, All, One,
World-government face that shines like the sun –
What bitter courtier wrote Hagger's works?
Why, Blair! He fits! And that's why Hagger smirks!"

All authorship debates are guaranteed
To fug the brain with madness, like hemp weed.
8 December 2005; revised 9–10, 12 December 2005; 29–30 January 2006
Follies and vices theme: gullibility, credulousness, fancifulness (of those
questioning Shakespeare's authorship). Set in Loughton and London.

15

from *Armageddon* (2008–2009)

[book 1, lines 1–30, invocation to Muse on Armageddon]

Tell, Muse, of terror and pre-emptive war;
Tell of world empire and of wild dissent,
Of *Pax Americana* that forbad
Nuclear proliferation, of *jihad*
To drive occupiers from Muslim lands;
Tell of crusaders and of Holy War
And of a nightmare: free America
Threatened with nuclear bombs in ten cities,
Simultaneous fiery Armageddon.
Tell of martyrs, planes turned into missiles,
Of America attacked and two wars,
Of the clash of two civilisations
(Or of extremist crusaders in each)

In fire and smoke and dread of rockets' roar
And of nuclear reprisal against might.
Tell of Bush the Second's transformations,
Of the obduracy of bin Laden
And how Satan – exiled towards the end
Of the Second World War, failed Overlord,
Intrigued the leaking of the atomic bomb
Which brought fifty years' peace and did God's will –
Deceived both sides, brought the world to the brink
Of the Apocalypse and Judgement Day,
And in the ensuing War on Terror
And tribulation of the final time
Brought in a New World Order in which West
And East were partners, did God's will again
And though the triumph of Light was assured
Brought universal order to the Earth,
The second phase of God's Millennial plan.
Follies and vices theme: systemic killing, mass destruction.

[book 1, lines 1000–1029, fall of World Trade Center's south tower]

In New York the Twin Towers, the skyscrapers
Of the World Trade Center gleamed in early
Morning sunlight against a clear blue sky
As, in unhurried, straight trajectory,
A sedate ninety-two-passenger plane
With ten thousand gallons of fuel in tanks,
A Boeing 767 piloted by
Mohammed Atta (who'd sat in 8D),
Flying from Boston to Los Angeles,
American Airlines Flight 11, smashed
Into the north tower at 8.46
Between floors ninety-four and ninety-eight.
The hijackers had stabbed and killed at least
One passenger and two flight attendants
According to phone calls by cabin crew.

Then United Airlines Flight 175
With sixty-five passengers, the same fuel,
A Boeing 767 piloted by
Marwan Alshehhi after the hijack,
Flying from Boston to Los Angeles,
Hit the south tower at 9.02 between
Floors seventy-eight and eighty-four. The planes
Did not explode like bombs. After impact
Fireballs consuming jet fuel expanded
And burning fuel poured through the Towers where heat
Was conjectured to have risen to as
Much as two thousand degrees Fahrenheit.
Molten metal poured down the south tower's side
Through a fissure like red-hot lava from
A long-dormant, erupting volcano.

Follies and vices theme: ruthlessness, systemic killing. Set in New York.

[book 1, lines 1679–1728, 1741–1752
fall of World Trade Center's north tower]

All day television film showed a plane,
The second hijacked airliner, drifting
Towards the smoking north tower in blue sky,
Smoke black as night, idling at the south tower,
A hundred-and-ten-storey skyscraper,
And smashing into glass. A fireball whooshed
From the other side of the placid tower,
Cascading *débris* hundreds of feet down
To rain shrapnel and glass shards on strangers.
Back in the White House Bush watched in dismay.
It was as if the pilot had trained on
The Microsoft Flight Simulation game.
He saw doomed workers clambering out of glass
Onto ledges and jumping, hurtling down,
A couple holding hands, a man diving,
Another on his back as if bouncing

Up from a gymnasium's trampoline,
Preferring swift death to choking in smoke
Or burning in billowing, blazing fuel,
Plunging slowly into eternity.
More than three thousand trapped on sagging floors,
Fierce heat rising, melting struts, fizzing wires,
Then blasts and shuddering walls and opening cracks,
A scything gash across the fractured tower's
Tubular steel columns braced by girders.
Down in the street, a crowd running away
Beneath the pinnacles thirteen hundred
And sixty feet high, snapped in two, tilting,
Turn and see the south tower tip and smokestack
Down in a cloud of dust and billowing smoke,
Followed by a roar and, slowly toppling,
The north tower slid down as if explosives
Packed in corners had been detonated.
Film showed rubble within the Pentagon
And a pile of charred *débris* in a field.
In many shots sat or lay the wounded,
One with his leg amputated, some crushed.
The World Trade Center was like a war zone,
An abstract landscape with bits of girders
In which lay a lone severed aircraft wheel;
Dust, water, sunlight in the smoky air.
It looked as if an atomic bomb had
Gone off, and, not knowing the fires would burn
A hundred days, Bush wondered if the planes
Had each carried a nuclear-suitcase bomb
Of half a kiloton that had seared such
A devastating scene as firemen stood
Knee-deep in rubble in a dust-like mist.
Whence figures loomed like ghosts in smoky Hell,
Faces caked in dust and dried streams of tears....
More film showed Manhattan's devastation,
A post-apocalyptic landscape; steel

Columns jutting slanting angles, collapsed
Buildings, bent skeletons of lower floors,
A graveyard of hopes where self-assurance
Had died. It looked like the end of the world,
But an old world had died and a new world
Of terror and retaliatory war
Had replaced it as history lurched forward.
A new Age had been born from smoking earth
Bush recognised the world had indeed changed.
It was at a beginning, not an end.
Follies and vices theme: ruthlessness, systemic killing. Set in New York.

[book 1, lines 1879–1941, fall of WTC7]

At his evening intelligence briefing
At the White House, the CIA expert
Discussed with Bush the afternoon's collapse,
At 5.20 of WTC7,
Which Bush had heard about while in the air,
A third building quite near the other two,
The forty-seven-storey Salomon
Brothers Building in the Rockefeller-
Inspired, vast WTC complex.
"It held the CIA command centre,"
Bush said. The CIA expert agreed.
Bush wondered again how such giant towers
Could have slid down and gone in ten seconds
With the velocity of a free fall.
He asked, "What caused Building 7 to fall?
There was no impact. I don't understand."
The expert looked uncomfortable and said,
"We're saying *débris* fell from an impact."
Bush said, "But it's quite a distance away
From the Twin Towers, it could not have happened."
There was a silence. Then the expert said
Connivingly as if talking in code,

"If we'd wanted to destroy it to erase
Evidence that should not exist, conduct
A huge controlled demolition, thermite
Enhanced with sulphur could achieve just that.
It's aluminium and iron oxide mixed.
When it burns it generates temperatures
Of around two thousand four hundred C.
Steel melts at fifteen hundred degrees C.
Fire by itself does not devour structures
Uniformly or pulverise concrete,
Not in the Twin Towers or Building 7.
At a high temperature thermite mixed with
Sulphur fuses and cuts heavy steel bars.
Perhaps the *débris* acted like thermite
And sulphur. Who knows? The fact is, the tower
Collapsed as quickly as the other two."
Bush looked down. He had not expected such
A frank answer. He did not want to know
How WTC7 or the Twin Towers
Could have been brought down by straight sabotage.
He wanted to stick with planes hitting towers.
He changed the subject, but now thermite teased.

Later the CIA expert returned
And said, "I was on the right lines. It was
Nano-thermite that brought all the towers down.
Large quantities of nano-thermite chips,
Which are red-grey, have been found in the dust
Round the World Trade Center, and this suggests
That several tons of nano-thermite, which
Is a high-tech explosive, were set off
To ignite at four hundred and thirty
Degrees Centigrade, which is far below
The temperature produced on combustion
By igniting conventional thermite.
Super-thermite can be handled safely

As super-thermite electric matches.
No planes brought down the towers. They fell due to
Nano-thermite bombs, nano-chemistry.
I won't speculate as to who used it."
Again, Bush did not want to know such things.
He was sticking with planes hitting the towers.
Follies and vices theme: ruthlessness, deception, deceit.

[book 3, lines 1740–1815, bin Laden's escape from Tora Bora]

Eight days the bombardment shook the mountain,
Five hundred huge bombs that sapped all morale.
A third of all the US explosives
Dropped in Afghanistan wrecked that forest.
What we sow we reap. Bin Laden had sown
The wind on 9/11, now reaped whirlwind.
Bin Laden's voice was heard within a cave
Better defended than all the others,
A bunker in a complex of five caves,
Barking orders on a two-way radio,
By US special forces using high-
Tech radio equipment, very short-range
Radio, urging al-Qaeda to fight on.
And now, when al-Qaeda was weary from
Sleepless days and nights spent in trench and cave,
The final blow: an American plane
Dropped a huge fifteen-thousand-pound "daisy-
Cutter" bomb whose deafening thunderous blast
That shook the ground left little in its path,
A swathe with a six-hundred-yard radius
Of destruction in which everything was
Blackened and broken, utterly laid waste.
Coming, as it did, at the end of eight
Days of bombing equivalent to all
The explosives dropped at Dresden, it broke
Al-Qaeda's spirit. Like rats, fighters crawled

Through shattered cave holes, stunned at what they saw.
Tall trees were burnt and shrivelled, their branches
Reached like arms to the sky, but now reduced
To merest jagged stumps devoid of leaves
On a bare moonscape pocked by mouths of caves.
Bits of uniform hung from branches, bits
Of bodies specked the soil like clumps of flowers,
Heads on the ground, lumps of legs in the trees.
The stench of death stank in the mountain air
Amid shredded clothes, bloodied shoes, unspent
Ammunition, soiled toilet paper, scraps
Of food. As in trance they filed slowly up
The rocks to surrender – a thousand men,
Broken by the awesome power of the bomb
To destroy landscape and man, smash morale,
Many heading, though they were unawares,
For internment in Guantánamo Bay –
But not bin Laden. He'd been located.
The Pentagon said that he was trapped in
A cave by anti-Taliban forces,
All exits were under surveillance. He
Would be smoked out. The cave was bombarded.
There was a rumour he had been wounded
In a shoulder by shrapnel under fire
And had been hidden, given medical
Care and assisted. Now, facing defeat,
The al-Qaeda force agreed to a truce
To give them time to surrender weapons.
Some besiegers thought the truce was a ruse
To allow al-Qaeda leaders to flee.
Now fighting flared again as a rearguard
Of some two hundred Arabs and Chechens
Distracted attention while the main force
Slipped out of unguarded, concealed exits
High up, guarded by steel doors and fighters,
On to mule trails on which supplies were brought,

Which led up to the nearby border, and
Escaped through the White Mountains, a thousand
Al-Qaeda fighters streaming across snow,
Stumbling towards the Pakistan border.
At Wazir near Tora Bora local
People saw bin Laden riding a white
Horse towards the safe Pakistan border,
A rifle slung on his back like a bow,
A white sash round his forehead like a crown –
The dashing leader on a white charger
Helped by local tribesmen he paid with bribes,
The elusive pimpernel bronzed by glare
From snow heading away as the deadline
For al-Qaeda to surrender passed by.
Follies and vices theme: ruthlessness, systemic killing.

[book 4, lines 1198–1259, 1327–1578, 1759–1802, Bush visits Hell]

Bush followed Satan down the rocky path,
Stepping between boulders, to the first Hell
Where he left uneven rock for a long
Tunnel and peered in the nearest chamber
Where he heard loud sighs and lamentations.
Here Satan gave him an overview, not
Deigning to refer to the Light from which
He was excluded by being required
By God to embody and choose Darkness.
In gloom, below horseshoe and pipistrelle
Bats hanging from the roof, dwell the virtuous
Who never found the Light in any faith,
Whose pride restrained them from knowing the Light,
Humanists whose rational-social ideas
Swaggered through rooms and sneered at all who thought
Reality, and the One, can be known,
Called all metaphysicals "demented"
And despised mystics as "self-indulgent";

Heretics whose souls remained in shadow,
Atheists and sceptics whose inner dark
Misled their students and charges, who taught
A wrong path through the universe's fire;
Holy followers of Dionysius
The Areopagite who asserted
That God is Darkness, failed to teach the Light;
Literary doyens, actors, playwrights,
Scholars who knew footnotes but missed the Light,
Philosophers of logic and language
Who missed the universe but were blameless
Except for their own myopic blindness;
Scientists who reduced the universe
To mathematical symbols and signs –
Lucretius, Russell, Wittgenstein and Crick;
Worthy placemen who ran society,
Lawyers, doctors, teachers and all police
Who went to work and returned home blameless
But missed the Light while filling consciousness
With workplace procedures and trivia;
Attenders of churches who sang the hymns
And prayed without awareness of meaning
And did not open shadowy souls to Light,
Remained enclosed in their own ego's shell.
Here were a few so-called celebrities,
Some of whom had excelled in one honed skill,
Some merely famous for being famous,
Stars whose photos were in the newspapers
But whose souls were murky, opaque shadows,
Attention-seekers whose vanity saw
Their egos in all mirrors and windows,
Who had not delved within, opened their souls
To the Light which cleans out all sense of 'I'
And makes humble whereas pride sets apart.
Here all souls repeat their Earthly mistakes,
Hiss their scepticism and heresy

And, swollen with overweening conceit,
Preen aloofly with pride and vanity
Of intellect or looks or merely self,
And knowing it is wrong, feel a sadness,
Live in torment of perpetual pride
That, puffed up, simpers but is unfulfilled,
And learn to master their great vanity
And restrain it with new self-discipline....

Satan led Bush on down the rocky path
To the second Hell, where the gloom deepens,
And allowed Bush to peer in the first cave.
Once more, like a tour guide in the dungeons
Of an ancient and feared castle, Satan-
As-Christ gave Bush an overview of all
Inmates congregating on this level,
Again studiously avoiding mention
Of the Light that is the context of Hell.
Here dwell the lustful and the lecherous,
Egos that were attached to appetite
And sensual desires and never detached
Soul from body so soul opened to Light,
Philanderers, serial adulterers,
Rapists, nymphomaniacs and priapic
Satyriasists with permanent itch,
People who boasted thousands of partners,
Cruisers, doggers, clubbers looking for kicks
Who lived in body consciousness and like
The hungry starved for flesh and used others
As objects, Don Juans and whores who saw
Birds and toyboys instead of real people,
Cleopatra, Alexander the Sixth
(The Borgia Pope with many mistresses,
A byword for the debased papacy),
Fallen women and notorious spenders,
Living to gratify self, not to grow,

Those who lived for love and for nothing else,
Who failed to transcend body for the Light;
Billions of false lovers and mistresses
Whose secret liaisons were for their self
To gratify body, not each other,
Who did not love with grand passion but scratched
Their need with another's help, self-centred,
Who broke up marriages and hurt others,
And kept their souls within their ego's shells,
Kernels on which the Light could never shine;
Kings, Queens and Ministers, nobility,
Professional people who lived for one thing,
Workers who spent their wages in brothels,
All who lacked self-restraint and discipline
That controls and channels all appetites
And showed inordinate sexual desire,
Voluptuous charm that, demure, submits
Yet deviously manipulates all –
Lucrezia Borgia and Lola Montez.
Here they live in torment of perpetual
Itching, desire and appetite which they
Can never fulfil, until they master
Their tiresome cravings and throbbings which kept
Them from knowing the Light and which they do
Eventually get under control
And learn to restrain with self-discipline.

Bush followed Satan down the rocky path
To the third Hell, where in darkening gloom
He peered deep into the first cavern. Here
Again Satan gave him an overview
Of all the inmates on the third level,
Abstaining from all reference to the Light,
Unable to bring himself to utter
A word so associated with God. Here
Dwell the gluttonous who could not control

386

Their stomach's appetite and lived for food
And alcohol, binge-drinking until drunk
Amid loud sounds of merriment that gave
Them the illusion of togetherness,
Of not being alone, while imbibing;
Who were the slaves of the stomach's desires
And did not fast and discipline body,
Rise above appetite to know the Light;
Party-goers, smokers with strong cravings,
Drug-takers of all kinds with appetites
Satisfied by swallowing Ecstasy,
Smoking cannabis, sniffing substances,
Snorting cocaine, injecting heroin,
Who for the sake of bodily cravings
Polluted their soul's higher consciousness,
Lived in a fug or haze and missed the Light,
Gargantuan feasters and knockers-back –
Lucullus, Henry the Eighth, de Quincey.
Here they live in a torment of famine,
Famished for food and thirsting for a drink,
Forever parched and craving for a fix
And never able to abate or quench
Their hunger, thirst and craving as they learn
To master tiresome bodily cravings
Which they slowly bring under their control
And learn to restrain with self-discipline.

Satan beckoned and Bush continued down
To the fourth Hell, where in a darker murk
He looked inside the first dingy cavern
Of the central arched rocky tunnel. Here,
Satan as Christ explained, pointing at wraiths,
Dwell the avaricious and prodigal,
The hoarders and spendthrifts, and the greedy
Whose selfish appetite was for money,
Who looted it as did the past members

Of the Syndicate out of self-interest,
Not to benefit others. And though some
Set up allegedly philanthropic
Foundations that professed to help mankind,
They were in fact tax dodges to preserve
The majority of funds they amassed.
Here came the Rothschilds and Rockefellers,
Drawn to the foul murk by the murk within
Their souls which never opened to the Light
As locked safes hoard gold bars in deep darkness;
Here they contemplate oilfields and pipelines
And relive short-changing their fellow men.
Here were corrupt politicians who spoke
For their constituents but were far more
Interested in lining their own pockets.
Here were MPs who fiddled expenses,
Took taxpayers' money to clean their moats,
Buy duck houses and prune acres of trees,
Flip homes, pay phantom mortgages, employ
Relatives to do constituency work,
Accumulate property portfolios.
Here were businessmen whose lives were spent on
Increasing profits and computing tax
Multinational CEOs, directors
Of companies, partners of legal firms
And bankers who received big bonuses
For gambling deposits made by clients;
Property developers, stockbrokers,
Accountants, tax inspectors and salesmen
Of cars and computers, solicitors
Who held their clients' money interest-free
And looked for more fees and compensation,
And boasted of trophy acquisitions,
Said "Hello, I'm the owner" to impress;
All who were too busy earning for self
So their social egos could live amply

To open their ego-encrusted souls
To the Light which burns out greedy desires
And appetites so grasping's transcended
By higher consciousness and growth of soul.
Here are the envious and covetous
Who want others' riches for their own selves,
Politicians who want equality
And say it's fair to strip the rich of wealth
So the poor do not feel disadvantaged,
Whose socialism is an envious creed.
Here they live in a torment of wanting,
Yearning for property and bank accounts,
For stocks and shares, gold and assets, craving
To hoard or spend, and, unable to own,
Cannot gratify their hunger for more,
Their appetite for possessions and wealth,
Their cravings to borrow, to buy or lease,
To acquire new material assets,
Addicted to acquisitive mindsets
Which they slowly bring under their control
And learn to restrain with self-discipline.

Satan indicated they must descend
And Bush followed him down to the fifth Hell
Which was in even deeper darkness, where
He peeped into the first dark cavern. Here,
Satan said, speaking as if he addressed
A touring party that had gathered round,
Dwell the wrathful who've succumbed to anger,
Who have not controlled their temper, and in
Disputes have been heated, intemperate.
They are addicted to venting their wrath,
A selfish appetite of the ego,
And in lower consciousness missed the Light.
Here dwell querulous neighbours, arguers,
Complainers, moaners, all who have quarrelled

With officials about the State system,
Abused traffic wardens, berated banks,
Lambasted doctors for bad news on health;
Demonstrators, drunk yobs who shout in streets,
Rowdy attenders where crowds are amassed,
Revolutionaries whose anger boils over;
Great men defined by one angry outburst
Such as Henry the Second, who was rid
Of a turbulent priest through one tantrum;
All who're easily offended and did
Not open their ego-encrusted soul
To the Light which burns all anger away
And brings serenity, peace with the world.
Here they live in a torment of seething,
Yearning to dispute, argufy, abuse,
Shout at each other, squabble and complain
But cannot gratify the resentment
That boils tumultuously within them,
Their appetite to vent stoked-up anger,
And, addicted to abusive mindsets,
Attempt to bring them under their control,
Learn to restrain them with self-discipline.

Satan took Bush by his elbow and led
Him down the rocky path to an opening,
The tunnel of the sixth Hell, where the dark
Was now like night and, peering, Bush could just
Make out shapes moving in the first cavern.
Watchful as he hooked up with what he'd planned,
Satan, wary, gave him an overview,
Careful not to mention the hated Light.
Here dwell the violent who have asserted
Themselves at the expense of their neighbours,
Who cared only for themselves and attacked
Their neighbours, who secured what they wanted,
Violent burglars, robbers and murderers,

Sadists, highwaymen, serial killers,
Those who swindled their neighbours of savings,
Fraudulent bankers whose scams did violence
To their neighbours and rooked them, treating them
As objects to be fleeced, not real persons;
Swashbuckling warriors quick to take offence
Such as Andrew Jackson, armed criminals
Who ruled the East End such as the Kray Twins
(And Tom Hammond, still brandishing shotgun).
Embezzlers of public funds, petty thieves
Who did great injury to people's lives,
Violent abusers of women and men,
Those who were addicted to the ego's
Self-assertive violence against others,
Assaulted and injured their fellow men,
Envying and coveting goods of theirs,
Gave in to an appetite for harming
And in lower consciousness missed the Light.
Among these are dictators and tyrants
Who ordered thousands of executions –
Hitler, Stalin, Mao, Pol Pot, mass-killers
Who had the blood of millions on their hands.
Here also dwell those who were violent
Towards themselves, self-harmers, suicides,
Who, hating themselves, ended their own lives
In lower consciousness, missing the Light;
And all who have been violent towards God
In wars and crusades, self-proclaimed *jihad*
Which had not God's approval, and all who
Have done violence to God's creation by
Violating art and Nature, God's works,
Polluting the Earth, causing climate change,
Leaving their environment much worse off.
And here dwell terrorists, who were convinced
They were on a divine mission, who used
Bombs to further causes they thought were right

But which lacked Almighty God's approval;
All suicide bombers for murderous ends.
Here they live in a torment of violence,
Raging to lash out, wound or maim or kill,
To thrust a knife or squeeze a gun's trigger
Or use their fists on shadows in the gloom,
Knuckledust, gouge eyes, glass cheeks and break bones,
Their appetite to yield to their smouldering,
And, addicted to violent mindsets,
Attempt to bring them under their control,
Learn to restrain them with self-discipline.
This was where Satan wanted to linger
Without making Bush suspect his motives....

Now Satan, subtly avoiding ending
The tour with what he'd wanted Bush to see,
Moved on. He beckoned and Bush followed him
And descended down the rocky path, and
Came to the tunnel of the seventh Hell
Where in night dark Bush groped to the first cave.
Pleased at having prompted Bush to invade
Iraq and bring chaos to the region
As Iran wanted so the Hidden Imam
Would come again, confusion he, Satan,
Would turn to disorder, on which he thrived,
Satan expansively explained the site
Without being able to bring himself to
Mention the Lie, which was too near the truth.
Here dwell the spiritually slothful,
Those closest to the Lie, all deceivers,
Fraudsters who perverted reality,
Panders and seducers who twisted truth,
Flatterers who deceived to get their way,
Sorcerers who claimed to have magic powers,
Grafters and barrators who caused discord,
Councillors on planning committees who

Told whoppers to get applicants refused,
Hypocrites whose deeds did not match their words,
Thieves who stole and concealed what they had done,
False counsellors who gave evil advice,
Sowers of scandal, discord and dissent,
Counterfeiters and impersonators,
All traitors who betrayed country and friends,
Deceivers who authorised genocide
And hid their command behind a false smile,
Those closest to the Lie who did not yield
To appetites but perverted the truth,
Who in the ego's twisting of the facts
In their lower consciousness missed the Light.
Here they live in a torment of lying,
Of craving to be mendacious and spin
And, addicted to a lying mindset,
Attempt to bring it under their control,
Learn to restrain it with self-discipline.
Just as a woodpecker drills a tree trunk
With its sharp beak for grubs hidden in bark's
Gnarled crevices, primed to probe surfaces,
So these deceivers drilled their souls for truths.
Follies and vices theme: pride, lust, gluttony, greed, anger, violence and sloth.

[book 4, lines 1803–1902, Hell as place of self-improvement]

Satan, speaking as if Christ, spoke of what
Those in Hell perceive in their consciousness
And now he had achieved his objective
Of a meeting between Bush and Atta,
Confident he could admit where they were
Without Bush being alarmed, and confident
That knowing where they were would give credence
In Bush's mind to what Atta had said,
For the first time he let slip the word "Hell"
Which he had covered up with "Underworld":

"How you perceive Hell is not how they do.
To outside observers Hell is in gloom
And appears caverned as if natural caves.
To participants it seems quite different,
Far more modern, like the life they have left.
Their spirits perceive through their memories,
Through subjective, not objective vision.
They see a virtual reality.
Or is this all a construct in *your* mind?
Are you the one who sees a virtual
Reality?" He jested, showing Bush
A different angle on what he perceived
But with light-heartedness, not seriousness,
So Bush would know it was a point of view
Not to be taken seriously. "They
Interact with a simulated world.
Just as chips store data in noughts and ones,
Spirits store software memories which seem
Real but are retrieved and repetitive
And these caves here seem luxurious halls.
Some see themselves in houses and meadows,
Like seeing what's on screen, not in your room.
Or perhaps this *is* a meadow, and you
Are seeing it as caves because you've been
Culturally conditioned to associate
Hell with caves because of Dante? Perhaps
All this is open air and *you're* the one
Who's seeing in virtual reality?"
Satan-as-Christ now suggested this view
Should be taken seriously, for he
Was promoting the standing and image
Of Hell as a place of self-improvement,
And casting doubt on what mortals could see
With their own eyes in this benighted place.
"They are attracted by their own dense forms
Into groups or classes of their level,

So all their neighbours are of comparable
Development, and are self-improving
From a similar base. There are degrees
Of darkness in the spirit-bodies here,
And they are drawn to similarity
And do not find that they have neighbours who
Are wildly different from themselves. And so
Ordinary folk are not with murderers.
All spirit-bodies are shades of black-white.
There is a spectrum with a thousand shades
From extreme black to extreme white, and in
Between there are many gradations, shades
Of grey, that determine where each spirit-
Body is drawn at the end of its life.
It's really organised here like a school,
And Satan's a bit like a headmaster
Who makes sure all the pupils are in their
Right classes but does not personally teach.
If people on Earth realised it's like this
After they die, there would be much more self-
Improvement on Earth to make things easier
For themselves when they are drawn to this school."
Satan spoke truly for souls are organs
Of Earthly perception, and do not see
The inner qualities of other souls
And their cave-like rough-hewn environment
As they work through their memories and burn
Out their imperfections, de-crust their souls,
Cure themselves from attachment to loved ones
Who they can watch over with far vision,
Earthly perception, telepathically;
Tune in to a scene on Earth as viewers
Ogle freaks on reality TV,
And communicate with them through mediums
As they recuperate and get ready
To be born again into a new life.

Satan was also spinning his own role,
Dignifying it into a school head's.
Then Satan, speaking as if Christ, said more:
"The Underworld is a corrective place,
A hospital for putting right the soul,
Only each spirit sits before its screen,
Intent on its own life, oblivious
Of other spirits for much of the 'time'.
Great care goes into their supervision,
The system's impressive. Your internet's
Taken from here, I leaked it out on Earth.
This is what men should follow and worship
As this is where the work's done after death."
He spoke truly until he took credit.
Though speaking as Christ he could not resist
Boasting and typically dissembling.
He did not mention the lightness of soul
That draws grown spirits to another place.
Follies and vices theme: burning out imperfections (of pride, lust, gluttony,
greed, anger, violence and sloth).

[book 5, lines 1–95, invocations to Churchill and Kassem]

O Churchill, you who were my MP in
The war, whose constituency Hitler
Attacked with V-1s and V-2s, so I
Lay awake at night listening for the whine
Of doodlebugs, the silence and the crash
That obliterated houses like mine –
Hitler whose bombers blew out our windows;
You who I heard speak at the Loughton war
Memorial on your way to Potsdam
When you stood on the first step with your wife,
And who, entering the High School, in nineteen
Fifty-one stopped and signed my autograph
Album and beamed at me under your hat;

You who devised the new state of Iraq
Out of the Mesopotamia that
Was granted to the British as a League-
Of-Nations, Class-A mandate when at Sèvres
The Ottoman Empire was divided
To the great dismay of T.E. Lawrence
And, as Colonial Secretary at
The Cairo Conference of nineteen twenty-
One which you presided over, you drew
A new kingdom from the ex-Ottoman lands
And combined under one ruler Sunnis,
Shias and Kurds – and forty years later
I, your constituent, went to Baghdad
To continue the implementation
Of your vision, which was not folly but
Worked forty-eight years ago as in my
Classes at the University I
Welded all three groups together with jests,
Classroom plays and my personality,
And our group respect for Omar Khayyam
In Fitzgerald's verses, where freedom reigned
As I spoke out despite dictatorship,
The strong rule of Abdul Kareem Kassem,
Benevolent Brigadier-General, our
Honest and Faithful Leader, whom all feared;
O Churchill, come to my aid now I tell
Of a new Anglo-American war
In Iraq that again sent tanks rolling –
As when you sent tanks in during the war –
Through the desert to capture *my* Baghdad.

O Kassem, dictator of Iraq when
I taught in Baghdad, driven to work at dawn
Through palm trees filled with shafts of golden light
And returning in a passing *baz* or
Group taxi I hailed, estate car with room

For three Arabs each side at the back, knees
Up under chins under their *dishdashers,*
A sheep or goat between us as we drove
Honking down the loud road to Bab Sharge
Where I got out and walked through stinking streets,
Sewage in a central runnel as in
The medieval time, to the arcades
Of Rashid Street, beneath bulging Turkish
Balconies for crinolines, and got on
A single-decker 30 bus whose floor-
Plates moved so I could see the road speeding
Below my feet as the red bus sped. You
Ruled on the edge of civilisation,
The desert and barbarism were near.
It felt like being on the *limes* in
Roman times, this was a frontier. And yet
I came and went in safety, no one jarred
Except the begging women in black veils,
Abbayas, who held out cupped hands for *fils,*
Imploring with their eyes, plucking my sleeve
With gnarled hands, pleading through their blackened teeth.
O Kassem, you who stood beside me in
The sultry Turkish-Embassy garden
In battledress, bare head, at the salute
And fixed your eyes on mine through the anthem,
You I saw sometimes waving to a crowd
From an armoured car, wearing a flat cap,
You who lived simply and gave to the poor
And had just one and a quarter *dinars*
On you when you fought to the last round and
Were shot at the Ministry of Defence
And had your head cut off and waved about
On television after the Arif
Coup, you were good as dictators go, you
Kept order in the city. Help me now
I describe how one of your successors,

Saddam Hussein, was ousted as you were
After a rule of opulence that would
Have filled you with disgust. He sent abroad
Forty billion dollars – Prime Minister
Iyad Allawi maintained fifty-seven
Billion dollars – that rightfully belonged
To your Revolution. I helped you weld
The Sunni, Shiite and Kurdish factions
Into the homogenous whole you sought
Forty-eight years ago when I was young.
Help me describe what befell *your* Baghdad.
Follies and vices theme: bombings, dictatorship, opulence.

[book 5, lines 736–810, *Shock and Awe*]

Lights shimmered on the Tigris near dark palms.
At 9 p.m. B52s unleashed
Operation Shock and Awe on Baghdad,
Striking Saddam's palace complex and his
Intelligence headquarters. A first wave
Of three hundred and twenty cruise missiles
Fired from American warships – more than
Were fired in the whole Gulf War – now shattered
The illusion of Iraq's defences.
A relentless assault rained thunder on
The heart of Baghdad in a fierce *blitzkrieg*
That set leadership and military
Buildings ablaze and swiftly sent towering
Plumes of red, pink and brown smoke to the sky
That were pierced by arcs of red tracer fire
From anti-aircraft batteries, and that
Had been conceived to terrify Iraq's
Gung-ho leadership into submission.
Ambulances, fire-engines, police cars
Rushed through the otherwise deserted streets.
RAF Tornado bombers fired their

Air-launched anti-radiation missiles
(ALARM) to smash integrated radar
Defence systems so bombers could follow.
Wave after thunderous wave of explosions
Shook Baghdad amid showers of orange sparks
And the horizon turned a hellish red.
Shock waves reverberated through the air,
Knocking observers back from balconies.
The ceremonial palace was on fire
From bunker-busting bombs that smashed straight through
Windows and exploded deep inside walls
And as its rubble fell a new palace
Went up in flames, and the ferocity
Of the attack unleashed and acrid smoke
Were devastating. General Tommy Franks
Said, "This is a taste of what shock and awe
Means, and there's more tó come if the regime
Doesn't crumble." There were (wrong) reports that
Saddam's body was stretchered from rubble
In an oxygen mask – rumours that spread
Confusion among cowering regime troops
While a decree from Saddam offered cash
To Iraqis who killed the enemy –
Ten thousand pounds for enemy soldiers.
But this was bravado, for all that could
Be seen was smoke blowing from hundreds of
Gigantic blasts that rocked the capital
As Saddam's palaces and Government
Buildings were pounded relentlessly by
The Allies' deafening raids. A thousand
Missiles sent fireballs and mushroom clouds high
In the night sky above the dark Tigris
And outlines of palms, and the firestorm left
Parts of central Baghdad in flames. Orange
Smoke billowed up the calm river. It was
An attack of unprecedented might

That was designed to leave the world in awe
Of American superpower. Its code-
Name was taken from a study of Gulf-
War strategy by Harlan Ullman, which
Recommended intimidating war
Adversaries to crush their will to fight.
Intensive bombing was programmed to last
Eight days but was reduced to a few hours.
It created damage costed at five
Hundred billion dollars. Reconstruction
Contracts were awarded to companies
With Syndicate and Republican links.
A contract to blow out wellhead oil fires
Worth fifty million dollars was assigned
To Kellogg, Brown & Root, subsidiary
Of Halliburton, for whom Cheney was
CEO. In one night *Shock and Awe* blew
Up much of beautiful Baghdad I knew.
Follies and vices theme: ruthlessness, systemic killing, destruction.

[book 6, lines 1215–1321, Zarqawi beheads Berg]

And now I watch this cruel creature, this *thing*.
Nicholas Berg, a US businessman,
Had travelled to Iraq to seek work for
His company, rebuilding antennas.
He had disappeared in Baghdad, kidnapped
By Muntada al-Ansar, which had links
With Zarqawi, was held in Falluja.
On May the eighth he met a dreadful fate.
I scan a video on the internet
Titled 'Abu Musab al-Zarqawi
Slaughters an American'. Five men stand
Before a white wall, dressed in black, wearing
Ski masks and *shemagh*s. On the floor, knees up,
Sits Berg in an orange jumpsuit, quite still,

His wrists bound at his back. The central guard,
With eye-holes in his balaclava hood,
Legs astride, sinisterly masked and slouched,
Reads from two sheets in firm-voiced Arabic.
Berg listens without understanding, pale,
Face white, blinks once as rough Zarqawi says
That the killing is to retaliate
For US troops' abuse of prisoners at
Abu Ghraib prison. The paper rustles.
After nearly three minutes of reading
To camera, al-Zarqawi puts away
His statement, draws a long knife from his chest,
Bends behind Berg and thrusts him to the floor
So he is lying bound on his left side.
Then all converge and stoop. One in a white
Shemagh with slit for eyes pins down Berg's side
To the floor, while Zarqawi grabs his head
And energetically saws at his neck.
A dreadful scream escapes Berg's dying throat
As they all chant *"Allahu Akbar"*, "God
Is great." Zarqawi wrestles with the knife,
Cuts and hacks into Berg's neck as blood wells
Round his feet as if slaughtering a lamb,
Saws like a butcher ridding a carcass
Of its unwanted head. At last the white-
Scarfed terrorist holds up the severed head
By its hair, eyes closed and looking mournful,
Blood dripping from the jagged flesh beneath
The chin and ears, and shows it to camera
As the picture fades to black. I feel sick
At the barbarity of the attack
On a fellow human with a blunt knife.
Zarqawi who had learned all the *Koran*
Had seen Berg as a butcher sees raw meat
That must be hacked and hung upon a hook,
Head tossed aside. The hacked torso was dumped

On a frequented Baghdad overpass.
I go back to the start where Berg sits still
And hope he was drugged so his brain was numbed
And could not take in the bestial violence
He's about to endure. I watch it through
Once more, noting Zarqawi wields the knife
With his right hand, which he only used for
Eating and shaking hands, a room-mate said.
But it was him, a voice analysis
By the CIA concluded: the masked
Man who read the statement was Zarqawi
"With high probability". And I stare
In cold revulsion at a barbarian,
And more than that, at an evil-doer.
Such disregard for his hostage, such coarse
Manhandling as if Berg were butchers' joint,
Not spirit, such brutal intent to harm
Were of the worst murders, the Holocaust,
And outside civilised society.

Evil is not just the absence of Good –
Ordered being as it should be, kindness,
Moral excellence that's commendable –
But base antithesis, reverse of Good,
Moral depravity and turpitude.
Evil's a deliberate will to harm,
To inflict pain, by a disordered soul.
And Zarqawi could not plead that Allah,
The Islamic embodiment of Good,
Wanted this butchering, and that his end –
Spreading the new Caliphate through the world –
Justified his gruesome means, his terror:
Desinewing flesh, ripping with a knife.
I still feel sick in my stomach, crying
Out for a fellow human, cry within:
'If God's almighty and perfectly good,

Why does evil exist? Because He wants
To obliterate it and's unable,
In which case He is not almighty? Or,
Because He's able but does not want to,
In which case He's not perfectly good?'
And then I know the universe is filled
With *yin-yang* opposites, order-chaos,
That God created a dialectic
Between Good and Evil in which the Good
Slowly triumphs after a long struggle,
The triumph of universal order;
That God created conflict as a means
Of achieving an end that's good for souls.
Now Berg's spirit rose, floating up to Light,
Released from torment and its time of trial,
Triumphing over Hellish hacking pain,
Serene as it wafted to Paradise
Where it would lodge before being reborn
To a new life and combat with Evil,
Eternal Recurrence of soul-making.
God made both dark and light as opposites
That together make up One atmosphere.
Follies and vices theme: ruthlessness, murder.

[book 8, lines 549–646, 665–671, execution of Saddam Hussein]

At 3 a.m. Saddam took his last flight
In a helicopter that flew him from
Where the Americans had held him in
The Green Zone to Camp Justice in north-east
Baghdad's Kadhamiyah district. There he
Was handed over to the Iraqis
For execution within half an hour –
In haste for fear that he might be freed and
Continue to act as a focus for
The insurgency. Also because he

Was four months from his seventieth birthday,
An age when Iraq's death penalty ceased
To apply. There was another reason
For haste: Bush wanted him dead before he
Could tell the Iraqis that he had no
Wmds and had been regime-changed
Wrongly; that America funded his
War against Iran; and the truth behind
The rumour that he stopped the Gulf War by
Paying two billion dollars in cash filched
From the Iraqi people to the Bush
Family. The dictator, who had killed
Two million of his people to keep power
Through Stalin-like purges, sat in a small
Ante-room impassively, deaf to taunts,
Dressed in a black overcoat, sure he would
Be reprieved, sure Bush would bargain his life
In return for his influence in halting
The insurgency he'd followed in prison,
Which had been conducted on his orders
And funded from dollars he had purloined.
Certain he was being put through a kind
Of mental torture he wore a bold face
To strengthen his bargaining position
In what he saw as mere theatre. He asked
To be buried in Ramadi, then held
By Al-Qaeda. If he had had nothing
To do with Al-Qaeda, why did he want
To be with Al-Qaeda in death rather
Than in Tikrit with his two sons? Perhaps
Tikrit stood for his humble origin
And he wanted to be with the fighters
For *his* Iraq of the insurgency
Who happened to be Al-Qaeda. He was
Ambiguous to the last. Masked men came
With round eyes and lips cut in Shiite masks

As he, a Sunni, was given to Shiites
Who led him up steps to a gallery
At one end of a concrete-lined room where
Two thick yellow ropes were rested with slack.
Official witnesses waited below
At the far end of the concrete-lined room.
"*Allahu Akbar,*" he intoned in prayer.
"Allah is great." He repeated his prayer
But showed no fear of judgement for his crimes.
The masked men jeered and chanted, "Moqtada,
Moqtada," the name of his adversary,
Moqtada Sadr, the Shiite cleric.
Aware that he faced sectarian justice,
Saddam said scornfully, "Moqtada, do
You consider *this* bravery?" One said,
"Why did you oppress us and make us weak?"
Composed, Saddam retorted, "I saved you
From the Persians and made you strong." His word
For "Persians", "Safawi", Safavids, spat
Out, was a derogatory word Sunnis used
To imply that Iraqi Shias are
Iranian pawns; a scathing, contemptuous
Word that would be bound to irritate pro-
Iranian Shiites. Now he was led
To the trapdoor of the gallows and stood
Repeating firmly, "Allah is great," while
Two masked men deftly looped a rope over
His head and put a white scarf round his neck
And laid the rope on it, with a huge knot
Resting on his left shoulder just below
His left ear. "Allah is great," he shouted,
Spurning the black hood that they offered him,
Defiant to the last with bravado
As the chant "Moqtada, Moqtada" drowned
His prayer, sectarian Shiites scorning
Their Sunni dictator and oppressor

Who stood calm and massive in overcoat,
Boomed, "Down with Persians and Americans,"
Giving back as good as he got although
On the scaffold, "Palestine is Arab,"
Unflinching, very brave with one last shout,
Still expecting to be bargain-reprieved,
"*Allahu-*" cut short by the falling trap
And the crack of his neck as, falling, it
Snapped and he dangled, limp, pirouetting
Round and round as small masked men cheered and danced,
Chanting, and the besuited witnesses
Below stepped forward to confirm he'd died.
Grainy film from a mobile recorded
His fortitude during his last moments
And transformed him from despot to hero
Posthumously when TVs showed snippets....
Saddam had at last fallen to his death.
And his spirit looked down at his twirling
Feet and, heavy in its light-body, sank
From the great burden of two million sins
That seemed tied to his ankles like concrete
Lumps and he plunged down through oceans of light
To find his way to new life he had earned.
Follies and vices theme: ruthlessness, cruelty, systemic killing.

[book 9, lines 317–371, 383–388, 426–460, rabbis threaten Bush with doom]

On January the ninth Bush made his first
Visit to Israel since taking office
In 2001, at a time when his
Relations with Israel were under strain
Due to the shocking NIE report
Which seemed to take Iran's, not Israel's side
As if "Rockefellers" or Democrats
Had influenced both the slant and wording.
Bush met Olmert and went to the West Bank

To carry forward the Annapolis
Agreement of a two-state solution.
Before he'd even arrived, on the sixth,
Hard-line Jews "presented" him with a scroll:
'*Megillat* Bush' ('Bush Scroll'). In a video
Rabbi Chaim Richman of the Holy
Temple and Temple Mount movements explained
The "Jewish nation's" response to two states,
Saying that Israel's Government did not
Represent the Jewish nation's beliefs.
His scroll was co-signed by Rabbi Steinsaltz
Of the Sanhedrin and Dr Eshel
Of the New Jewish Congress. As if scribed
By an Old-Testament prophet, it spoke
"In the Name of the Lord Eternal God"
And addressed "Mr George W. Bush,
The chief prince of Meshech and Tubal", which
Invoked *Ezekiel*: "I am against thee,
O Gog, the chief prince of Meshech" (long thought
To be Georgia) "and Tubal," referring
To Bush as Gog of the land of Magog,
Leader of the northern coalition
That would make war from the north on Israel.
It said that on his arrival Bush could
Make a declaration, like Cyrus, King
Of Persia, who in 538 BC
"Returned the exiled nations to their lands
And recognised the right of the Jewish
People to re-establish their Holy
Temple, 'the house of prayer for all nations'.
And in the manner of Lord James Balfour
Of England, who in 1917,
Called upon the Jews to re-establish
A national homeland in land of Israel.
Thus if you truly desire peace we call
Upon you to declare to all the world:

'The land of Israel was bequeathed to the
Nation of Israel by the Creator
Of the world, which He gave to his people,
Israel. Neither could I, nor the Muslims,
Ever take away the slightest grain from
The Eternal's gift. Thus I call upon all
The nations to save themselves from certain
Doom, to return and recognise that this
Land is the exclusive inheritance
Of the people of Israel....'
Do you imagine you will be able
To save yourself if you now implement
A plan that intends to steal the land of
'The people that survived the sword', and to
Cut off those who survived the Holocaust,
Rob the land given them by the Creator?"...
Bush received the scroll at his hotel and,
Not knowing what it was, thinking it might
Be an accolade for his tireless work,
Skimmed through the threatening wording as if
He had been served a writ summonsing him
To be a defendant in a lawcourt.
He took the message, which was in effect:
"If you continue with the two-state plan,
If you do not do as we want, God will
Bring doom, you won't be saved and you will be
Ruined in this life and damned in the next."
Doom could come in many forms. He might fall,
Be toppled as President, lose the war
In Iraq or there could out of nothing
Be a massive financial crash. Such things
Would also happen if Iran weren't bombed.
He smiled ruefully. The Rabbis were sure
God would destroy America. The scroll
Said, "Give us the wars we want or we'll take
The world down piece by piece, beginning with

America." Bush knew that the "founding
Father" of "Rothschilds", Mayer Amschel, said
"Give me control of a nation's money
And I care not who makes the laws." He feared
American banks would begin to fall
Without warning as Jewish financiers
Withdrew funds, precipitating chaos.
Sharon had been cursed by Rabbis for his
Support for Bush's two-state policy.
The Pulsa diNura seemed to have worked
As the Angel of Death had put him on
A life-support machine with no prospect
Of coming off, alive as a symbol.
Before he went on to Capernaum
Bush shivered at the "doom" in store for him.
Follies and vices theme: blackmail.

[book 10, lines 475–546, 565–581, financial crisis]

An economic 9/11 struck,
Stunning in suddenness like 9/11
Itself. Into this banking turbulence
Came a deliberately sent killer blow.
Black Thursday, Bush called it. On September
The eleventh, the seventh anniversary
Of 9/11, soon after 9 a.m.,
Seven years after the five Israelis
Were arrested for cheering at the fall
Of the Twin Towers in the provoked US,
A drawdown on money-market accounts
In the US panicked the Treasury.
Just as a small gaggle of white geese stand
Beside each other, necks stretched and beaks up,
And cackle at approaching footsteps like
The sentinels that once saved Rome with honks
And warn the owner of their country farm

Of the approach of possible danger,
So Paulson and staff at the Treasury
Sounded the alarm at impending doom
And alerted the custodian Bush.
An electronic run on banks withdrew
Five hundred and fifty billion dollars,
By 11 (as was later described
In a video by Representative
Paul Kanjorski). The Treasury pumped in
A hundred and five billion – but in vain.
4.6 billion dollars per minute
Had haemorrhaged in the largest transfer
Of money in history in such short time.
At this rate by 2, the cumulative
Flow would cascade, and 5.5 trillion
Dollars would be withdrawn from the US
Money market, whose system would collapse,
Eliminating some ninety per cent
Of US liquidity and lifeblood.
The world economy would die within
Twenty-four hours. The Treasury now closed
The accounts and announced a guarantee –
Two hundred and fifty thousand dollars
Per account; staunched the haemorrhaging wound.
The Treasury, Federal Reserve and Bush
Agreed that the raid should be kept secret
To avoid panicking Americans
And that the hole left by the withdrawn funds –
Six hundred and fifty-five billion in
All, and a forty-five billion buffer –
Should be plugged as swiftly as possible.
On September the fifteenth, Treasury
Secretary Hank Paulson and Fed Chairman
Ben Shalom Bernanke, testifying
Before Congress, said the economies
Of the US and the world would surely

Have expired if there'd been no guarantee.
On September the twenty-first Paulson
Requested seven hundred billion dollars
To "buy toxic assets from many banks".
This would replace the funds that were withdrawn,
Five hundred and fifty billion dollars,
And the hundred and five billion pumped in
To no avail, which had to be replaced,
And give a forty-five billion buffer.
Someone with hundreds of billion dollars
Was responsible for frenzied attacks
On the US capitalist system,
For slashing its financial jugular:
A key-man trillionaire of supreme power,
Scion of a Syndicate family,
Who'd unleashed financial Armageddon.
And whereas 9/11 was symbolic,
This onslaught was both savage and lethal
And could have bankrupted the entire world....

Now Bush linked the raid to the Rabbis' "doom".
The scroll had warned him to drop the two-state
Plan, and besides manipulating votes
It was paying him back for persisting
With the two-state approach to Palestine.
Bush had no doubt that "Rothschilds", commercial
Multinational conglomerate that owned
The Central Bank of Israel and banks in
London, Paris, Frankfurt, Naples, Vienna,
And controlled a hundred and eighty-seven
Central banks in the hundred and ninety-
Two UN member states, and was also
The power behind the Bank of England
And the Federal Reserve, were behind
This tinkering with the US election
Just as, he suspected, they'd been behind

Mossad's discovery of 9/11
For which Israel's enemies would be blamed.
Follies and vices theme: ruthlessness, vindictiveness.

[Coda to be placed at the end of *Armageddon*, death of bin Laden]

A hot May night in an Abbottabad
Compound in Pakistan, safe from attack,
Snuggled at the end of a dirt track, walled,
Osama lay in bed in his burrow,
Clad in nightclothes between two of his wives.
As silent owls swoop and pounce on their prey
Before 1 a.m. two US Black Hawk
Helicopters, modified into Stealths,
Glided through the dark with two teams of SEALs,
Twenty-four US Navy commanders
In night-vision goggles, body armour.
Delta Force captured Saddam, but they sent
Team Six to kill Osama bin Laden.
One Black Hawk (that Matt Bissonnette was on)
Was caught in a strong vortex-ring airflow
That sent washing whipping on a clothes-line
And rubbish swirling among goats and cows
Thirty feet below in the dark compound,
And bucked from stable hover, gyrated
And wobbled so no rope could be dropped down,
Crashed nose-down in the compound and tilted
Against the wall at forty-five degrees.
The other landed outside the compound,
SEALs scaled the wall and packed explosive on
The metal double doors of the guest-house.
More charged up steps onto the guest-house roof.
Inside there was shooting and glass clattered.
A door opened, and a woman clutching
A baby slunk out with three small children:
The wife of Al-Kuwaiti, Osama's

Courier, who (she said) had been hit and killed.
SEALs found him with his feet outside a door
And shot his corpse several times to make sure.
More sprinted to bin Laden's duplex house –
Or house occupied by two families –
And stormed into the ground floor's long hallway.
The leading SEAL, point man, shot at a head
That peered out of the first room on the left
And Al-Kuwaiti's brother fell and writhed.
SEALs killed him – and his wife, who shielded him –
And blew up an iron gate that blocked access
To the two upper floors, stormed up the stairs
And on the landing shot Osama's son
Khalid, whose body lay splayed on its back.
SEALs ran on up the dark narrow spiral
Staircase, and five steps from the top landing,
On their right side, ten feet away from them,
Like a shrew sensing danger from the air
Osama peeped his head out of a door
On the third floor near the top of the steps,
Tall, and swiftly pulled back into the room
As the point man 'Tom' (with Matt close behind),
Fired and missed – or he may have injured him,
It was too dark to know – and then bundled
His two aghast wives from the bedroom doorway
To clear a passage into the bedroom.
Fearing they were rigged with suicide bombs.
Rob walked into his dark bedroom and saw
Through his night-vision goggles Osama
Two feet away, cowering in the dark,
Standing, holding his youngest wife Amal
By her shoulders, having quickly grabbed her
To manoeuvre her as a human shield,
He towering above her, six-foot-four,
Wearing a cap and panic in his eyes.
For a second the two men's eyes were locked.

In case he wore a suicide vest Rob
Shot twice, bap bap, aiming at his forehead.
His head jerked and he fell, hit in the face.
Rob fired again. His skull open, he lay
In a crumpled heap on the floor, twitching,
And exhaled his last breath as his soul fled,
His forehead split in the shape of a V,
Convulsing in a pool of blood, a hole
On his head's right side, gore and brains spilling
From his gaping skull. He wore a sleeveless
White T-shirt, tan trousers and tan tunic,
Kurta paijama. Amal rushed screaming.
If she was wearing an explosives vest....
Humane, Rob took a risk and restrained her,
He tied her to a bedpost as she wailed
Above his convulsing, unarmed body.
One more bap using EOTech red-dot
Holo sight, and one final reflex breath.
Two SEALs (Matt, Rob) trained lasers on his chest,
And fired several rounds. Bullets tore through flesh,
Slammed his body into the floor until
It moved no more and now lay motionless,
Tongue out in last defiant resistance.
His boy stood stunned the far side of the bed,
Sobbing. The point man gently picked him up
And carried him across to his mother.
Osama had been silenced. He could not
Tell his side of 9/11 in court,
State his surprise that the Twin Towers crashed down,
Berate the West from a public platform.
SEALs examined his face, which was mangled,
The right side of his skull collapsed in blood.
The seeping gore had not stopped widening.
Matt took pictures of his profile, pulling
His beard to left and right, and Walt dipped swabs
Into his blood and mouth for DNA

And tried to syringe marrow from his thigh.
(Two sets of photos and swabs were needed
In case one helicopter was shot down
On its way back home to Jalalabad.)
Matt found a box of Just For Men hair dye
With which Osama blackened his grey beard.
Two women were asked who he was. Both said,
"Osama bin Laden." Sure it was *him*,
They found nearby an AK-47
And Makarov pistol, both unloaded.
He asked followers to wear suicide
Vests and fly planes into immense buildings
But had not made plans to defend himself.
Now all the SEALs crowded in and some whooped
And fired more shots into his lifeless corpse
Which jerked and danced. A hundred bullets tore
And riddled his dead flesh, desecrated
His soul to pay it back for fallen Towers.
They seized computers, videos and notebooks,
Dragged his body by its legs down the stairs.
SEALs handcuffed his two wives and stuffed his corpse
Into a body bag and heaved it up
Onto the dark floor of the good Black Hawk.
One of the two reserve Chinooks had now
Landed nearby to take some SEALs back home.
SEALs herded women and children inside
The guesthouse and blew up the crashed Black Hawk
So Stealth parts would not fall into wrong hands.
The undamaged Black Hawk rose into the night.
Osama took up space meant for the SEALs.
As he lay on the floor (all 6 foot 4)
A SEAL sat on his stomach. The man who
Waged war upon mighty America
And provoked attacks on Afghanistan
Was now a cushion for a Yankee rear.
The helicopters rose into the night,

And headed for Jalalabad, where SEALs
Loaded the corpse into a truck and drove
To Bagram. Matt yanked and the bag flopped down
Onto a cement floor like a dead fish.
He unzipped the bag. The skin had gone grey.
Congealed blood stained the inside of the bag.
A 6-foot-4 SEAL lay down beside it
To confirm measurement, for his dark beard
And caved-in head looked unlike Osama.
The bag was flown on to the *Carl Vinson*.
Soon Osama would be buried at sea,
Washed, wrapped in a white sheet, in a weighted
Plastic bag, placed on a flat board that would
Tilt upwards and sideways so his clean corpse
Would slide into the North Arabian Sea.
The leader of al-Qaeda now received
His just deserts for bringing down the Towers:
A watery grave that no one could visit.
He sank into a deep cavernous place
To ponder on the crimes he committed
So barbarously, in the name of war.
Obama, who had aborted three raids
As too risky, dithered till Hillary
Clinton pushed him into backing this raid,
Basked in credit. And in his Texan house
Bush smiled wanly at mission accomplished:
Bin Laden dead, Khalid Sheikh Mohammed
In Guantanamo. Nuclear-suitcase bombs
In ten US cities had been thwarted
And Armageddon contained – for a while.
1 September 2012; revised 13 March 2013; 7, 9, 16 November 2014
Follies and vices theme: ruthlessness, systemic killing.

INDEX OF TITLES

BOOKS

O is a symbol of the world, of oneness and unity; this eye represents knowledge and insight. We publish titles on general spirituality and living a spiritual life. We aim to inform and help you on your own journey in this life.

Visit our website: http://www.o-books.com

Find us on Facebook:
https://www.facebook.com/OBooks

Follow us on Twitter: @obooks